Department of the Environment

Planning Research Programme

The Effectiveness of Green Belts

Report prepared by

Professor Martin Elson
Stephen Walker and Roderick Macdonald
School of Planning
Oxford Brookes University

in association with

Jeremy Edge
Weatherall Green and Smith

London: HMSO

1993

ACKNOWLEDGEMENTS

The study team wish to thank the case study local authorities, and the representatives of conservation and development interests interviewed, for their co-operation and considerable assistance during the project. In addition they would like to thank the invited experts on both urban fringe and transport issues who attended day seminars in Oxford. The local authorities who provided date for our case studies were also particularly helpful in responding to our queries and requests for subsidiary information.

In addition the study team would like to acknowledge the excellent support and advice of the Department's Steering Group during the project. In particular Richard Wakeford (Chairman of the Steering Group) and Des Coles (Nominated Officer) were unstinting in their contributions at every stage of the research.

It should be noted that the views expressed in this report are those of the Contractor and do not necessarily represent those of the Department.

Cover illustration: Historic Oxford in its Green Belt setting

Contents

Executive Summary

THE EFFECTIVENESS OF GREEN BELTS

EXECUTIVE SUMMARY

The aim of the research was to review the effectiveness of Green Belt policy and investigate how this might be improved. The study assessed systematically:

i)   the effectiveness of Green Belts in relation to their existing purposes;

ii)   the implications of possible new purposes;

iii) the roles of Green Belts in the management of sub-regional change;

iv)   the permanence of Green Belts, and the extent of provision for long term needs;

v)   their implications for transport and CO2 emissions;

vi)   urban fringe issues, including Community Forests, golf courses, agriculture, wildlife and other land use pressures and changes; and

vii) the impact of development control policy within Green Belts, including the re-use of redundant buildings, the interpretation of 'institutions in extensive grounds', and of appropriate rural uses and the treatment of existing inappropriate uses.

This summary gives the key findings, with references to where they are discussed in the text in square brackets. Recommendations are listed numerically at the end of each section of this summary.

The study covered Green Belt policy in England and Scotland. Twenty eight local authority policy case studies were complemented by detailed analysis of development control data and information on appeals. Interviews were conducted with a wide range of development and conservation interests, and two invitation seminars were held to obtain further expert views and opinion.

Existing Purposes of Green Belts

1.   *The first two purposes of Green Belts, checking unrestricted sprawl, and preventing towns from merging, are being achieved.*

We found no dissenters to the view that Green Belts are successfully being used to check unrestricted sprawl and prevent towns from merging. Alterations to boundaries in development plans had affected less than 0.3 per cent of Green Belts in the areas studied over the last eight years [2.10-2.14]. Most planning approvals are for small-scale changes which do not significantly affect the open rural appearance of Green Belts [2.15-2.20]. The appeal system strongly upholds Green Belt policy [2.21; 3.16].

2. *The third purpose, safeguarding the surrounding countryside from encroachment, has significantly overlapped the first two purposes.*

Green Belts have safeguarded the countryside from further encroachment. This purpose has however overlapped the first two purposes, not adding to the already very firm restraint on development offered by Green Belts. Safeguarding the surrounding countryside from encroachment was not a specific purpose for including land in Green Belt until 1988. Its inclusion appears not, in practice, to have added to the already very firm restraint offered by Green Belts in the 1955-88 period. In its present form this purpose does not provide a clear criterion for decision-makers. Current practice suggests this purpose is seen as complementing countryside policies by assisting in safeguarding the countryside from encroachment [2.23-2.25].

3. *The relationship between Green Belt restraint and increasing levels of economic activity, and their impacts on the cores of cities of special historic character, are unclear.*

Green Belt boundaries around historic towns are particularly tight, and future development requirements have been assessed conservatively. Green Belts have been used with little dispute to protect the settings of, and define the approaches to, such towns. These purposes should be stressed in guidance. It is less clear how far peripheral restraint is necessarily linked to the protection of their historic centres. Department comments suggest such towns may have limits to their growth. These issues should be further investigated by a comparative study of historic towns [2.26-2.34].

4. *The role of Green Belts in urban regeneration has been to focus development interest on sites in urban areas.*

For local authorities in urban regeneration areas Green Belt restraint has acted to encourage development within urban boundaries. At the same time, for some local authorities a major catalyst for urban regeneration is seen to be the freeing of prime industrial sites from the Green Belt. Local authorities in regeneration areas are concerned to have a portfolio of urban and greenfield sites readily available for new economic activity. In some areas larger-scale mixed-use developments have been proposed as parts of city-wide urban regeneration strategies. Denying a range of peripheral site development options will not secure the regeneration of under-used urban sites on its own. Policies to encourage the re-use of urban land will be of greater importance. There is a need for more detailed work on the relationship between Green Belt restraint and urban regeneration [2.35-2.43].

5.   *Most decisions on Green Belt boundaries in plans involve making assumptions about urban intensification.*

Throughout the case study areas planners, and the Department's Regional Offices, are making decisions about the balance between development by infill within urban areas, and peripheral expansion of various kinds. However, little is known on a systematic basis about land use changes in the suburbs and their effects on movement, open space, pollution and other quality of life indicators. In the future local authorities, particularly in the South, are likely to be presenting arguments on 'overheating' problems as a reason for altering Green Belts. There may be areas of green space in towns and cities which, if developed, would adversely affect living conditions for more people than if equivalent land of lower amenity and ecological quality in Green Belts was developed [2.22].

6.   *The time taken to approve Green Belt boundaries in local plans is too long.*

In a number of counties the Structure Plan has been altered or replaced before local plan boundaries based on the original plan have been agreed. This may be due to unresolved problems over the location of development following approval of the broad totals in the Structure Plan. The Department has advised Authorities who do not have agreed boundaries in local plans that they risk greater amounts of development in their areas. Slow progress also creates uncertainty, particularly at appeal, where it may be difficult to assess the status of land [2.11].

It is recommended that:

R.1   *Green Belts should be seen as a policy instrument for shaping patterns of urban development at sub-regional and regional scales. They help to ensure development occurs in locations decided upon in development plans, and they assist in protecting the countryside. Green Belt policies should also, by creating contained forms of new development, assist in moving towards more sustainable patterns of urban growth [2.23-2.25; 6.14-6.19].*

R.2   *The purposes for including specific areas of land in a Green Belt should be:*

   •   *to check the unrestricted sprawl of large built-up areas;*

   •   *to prevent neighbouring towns from merging into one another [2.10-2.22];*

   •   *to assist in safeguarding* the countryside from encroachment [2.23-2.25];

- to preserve the *setting and* special character of historic towns [2.26-2.34]; and

- to assist in urban regeneration [2.35-2.43].

R.3 Sites for large-scale employment in areas where urban regeneration is a priority should not be released from the green belt except as part of the regional guidance-development plan process [2.35-2.43].

R.4 The relationship between Green Belt restraint and increasing levels of economic activity, and the special character of historic cities should be investigated by a comparison of land use, traffic and other policies within a number of historic cities and their surrounding daily journey to work areas [2.29-2.34].

R.5 The need for up-to-date approved Green Belt boundaries, so as to avoid ambiguity and allow the proper consideration of future development options, should continue to be stressed [2.11].

Development Control

7. *The use of inset and washed over village policies varies across the country.*

In some of the northern case study areas insets can exclude clusters of 50 dwellings from Green Belt controls. In the Home Counties settlements of 500 dwellings are washed over. Circular 50/57 suggests that washed over villages should be divided into those where infill is allowed (their names being listed in the development plan) and those where it is not. The tendency is to allow infill in all of them. The major distinction emerging locally however is that within inset settlements, because they are not in Green Belt, there is leeway for new and expanding employment concerns to develop. The currency of paragraphs 6 and 7 of Circular 50/57 should be made clear, and reference could be made to the differences is treatment of employment uses implied where settlements are excluded from the Green Belt [3.2-3.7].

8. *Most local authorities have elaborated development control policies in greater detail than is specified in PPG 2.*

The scan of existing and new local plans suggested on average nine Green Belt development control policies were included. The development control study showed that three quarters of all applications were housing-related, focusing particularly on small-scale extensions [3.12-3.15]. The size and bulk of extensions, and the criteria for replacement dwellings, were also important.

iv

The policies most frequently included in plans related to dwelling extensions and alterations, replacement dwellings and leisure uses [3.17-3.20].

9. *There is confusion over policies on the re-use of buildings in Green Belts, linked to the different approaches in PPG 2 and PPG 7.*

This issue caused more comment than any other. PPG 2 states that *redundant* agricultural buildings may be suitable for conversion for small firms, tourist activities or individual residences. The Pehrsson ruling removes the need for the buildings to be, or have been, agricultural. Guidance in PPG 7 states that a wider range of uses are now acceptable in the countryside, and removes the redundancy criterion. Thus the main difference between Green Belt and the countryside beyond is now the redundancy test. Following consideration of the various options we consider policy in Green Belts should be brought into line with that in the wider countryside. We do not believe that diversification by farmers should be made more difficult in Green Belt. Accordingly we do not consider the continued use of the redundancy test is appropriate. Where agricultural buildings are being re-used for non-agricultural purposes we recommend that permitted development rights for future agricultural buildings on the holding should be removed [3.28-3.38].

10. *The category of institutions in extensive grounds is considered to be outdated, inappropriate to Green Belt, and subject to problems of definition.*

Wide-ranging views demonstrated difficulties with the concept. Allowing a new institution in Green Belt was seen as inappropriate as, in its effects, it could be little different to a B1 business use. There were also difficulties in defining an institution, for example how far it should be for a private as opposed to a public purpose. Much difficulty surrounded the issue of what comprise extensive grounds. Costly legal proceedings have not served to clarify the concept. We propose that institutions should no longer be regarded as an appropriate Green Belt use. The institutional re-use of existing buildings would fall within the terms of current building re-use policy generally [3.39-3.44].

11. *Special attention should be given to existing employment sites in Green Belts.*

In all Green Belts there are employment sites located in the open countryside or washed over settlements. Most local authorities wish to protect such sources of employment, and allow for reasonable expansion requirements. Employment uses are however regarded as inappropriate in the Green Belt. Any approvals must be justified by very special circumstances. Where local authorities have sought to include policies in district-wide local plans these have been rejected by the Department. A local authority wishing to allow for employment changes should consider the following; first, specification of the material considerations to be applied to any development approved in the Green Belt; second, providing an employment inset; or third, ensuring that any redevelopment of this sort should improve the visual amenities of the Green Belt, reduce traffic and make a positive contribution to the management of Green Belt land. Similar provisions occur in guidance in Scotland relating to Green Belt [3.46-3.49].

12. *The attitude to proposals for Park and Ride car parks should be clarified.*

There was a strong feeling that Green Belt guidance should take a view on the increasing number of Park and Ride proposals coming forward. There are different views. First, Park and Ride schemes could be regarded as clearly acceptable in Green Belt, as an ancillary to the normal road system, with the additional virtue of encouraging people to transfer from cars to public transport. Alternatively they could be seen as inappropriate due to their impact on openness, very special circumstances being required to be established. A third view, which was recommended as the preferred basic approach, was to identify such sites during local plan preparation, putting them forward as proposals in the plan [3.59-3.61].

13. *A number of authorities have sought to define and list the very special circumstances in which they would depart from Green Belt policy in plans.*

A policy clearly listing all appropriate Green Belt uses would be a benefit to decision-makers. PPG 2 advises against local authorities preparing policies for exceptional circumstances as these create a new round of difficulties in interpretation, and can raise false expectations among applicants. Although the Department itself has written guidance on very special circumstances for low cost housing and hospital sites this runs similar risks. Many local authorities, for example, dislike the advice on low cost housing because they consider it creates new ambiguities and room for dispute [3.9-3.11; 3.69].

It is recommended that:

R.6 *The basic distinction between inset and washed over settlements in Green Belts, referred to in Circular 50/57, should be retained [3.2-3.7].*

R.7 *Where infill is to be allowed in small washed over settlements 'infill boundaries' should be defined in plans. Such infill would therefore constitute appropriate development within the Green Belt [3.2; 3.7].*

R.8 *The difference of treatment of existing employment uses in washed over settlements and Green Belts insets should be made clear [3.7].*

R.9   Local authorities should normally be allowed to include specific policies on dwelling extensions and alterations, replacement dwellings, and outdoor sport and recreation (including golf courses, driving ranges and equestrian activities) in Green Belts in development plans [3.17-3.20; 3.68].

R.10   The PPG 3 policy relating to the special circumstances in which Green Belt sites may be released for housing for local needs should be monitored in terms of the amount and type of sites involved and conditions [3.24].

R.11   The redundancy test in respect of the re-use of existing buildings in Green Belts should be removed, but a policy should be introduced to make it normal for permitted development rights to be removed by condition in any approvals given where farm buildings are involved [3.28-3.38].

R.12   The PPG 7 safeguards relating to the re-use of buildings in the countryside generally should be re-affirmed for Green Belts [3.28-3.38].

R.13   The impact of approvals for the re-use of buildings under PPG 7 should be monitored in terms of how far they are compromising the openness and visual amenities of the Green Belt and the countryside beyond, and how far they are assisting the local economy [3.28-3.38].

R.14   Farm diversification proposals should be encouraged within the parameters of R.11 and R.12 [3.33-3.38].

R.15   Institutions standing in extensive grounds should be deleted as an appropriate land use in Green Belts. The institutional re-use of existing buildings would fall within recommendations R.11 and R.12. New institutional buildings would require to be justified in very special circumstances where a non-Green Belt site was unavailable [3.39-3.44].

R.16   Development plan policies should state that where development is approved in the Green Belt, including alterations to the size and appearance of existing buildings, the scheme will contain provisions to improve the landscape, enhance visual amenity and support the achievement of open land objectives [3.46-3.48].

R.17   Development plan policies should state that where proposals for the redevelopment of existing employment uses present the opportunity, development control should aim to reduce the visual impact, and off-site traffic flows, related to future use [3.46-3.48].

R.18 *Where employment areas and major sites are of national or regional importance consideration should be given to creating Green Belt insets [3.46-3.48].*

R.19 *Local authorities should identify sites for Park and Ride car parks in development plans, seeking alterations to Green Belt boundaries if necessary. Individual proposals in approved Green Belts would be treated as very special circumstances, applicants being required to show that no other suitable site outside the Green Belt was available [3.61].*

R.20 *Utilities should only be allowed in the Green Belt if there is no alternative location outside the Green Belt [3.63].*

R.21 *The phrase 'other uses appropriate to a rural area' in para 14 of PPG 2 should be replaced by the more appropriate phrase 'new buildings ancillary to open uses of land in the Green Belt' [3.64].*

R.22 *Development plans should not refer to specific very special circumstances in which development would be contemplated in Green Belts [3.9-3.11; 3.69].*

Urban Fringe and Open Land

14. *The functions performed by open land in Green Belts should be recognised in the guidance and should be listed as Green Belt objectives.*

We can expect to see a more multi-activity countryside near towns. The role of the Green Belt as a locale for outdoor sport and recreation is recognised and encouraged by local authorities. The Green Belt can also be a focus for environmental and greening strategies, aiming to restore damaged land, protect wildlife and attractive landscapes. Consistent support for agriculture, not least for its contribution to a healthy landscape, was also noted [4.22-4.27; 4.1-4.8].

15. *Problems of generating sufficient resources for the environmental improvement of damaged land in Green Belts have led to proposals for 'enabling' development.*

Green Belt policy reduces the scope for environmental improvement in conjunction with new development, except through the balancing process accompanying the establishment of very special circumstances at appeal. However suggestions that areas can exceptionally be defined in Green Belts where different 'enabling' policies should apply, would appear to confuse the Green Belt concept and reduce its effectiveness. Such land would better be excluded from Green Belts in development plans in the absence of sufficient non-private resources for their improvement [4.11-4.13].

16. *There is scope for using planning conditions to secure environmental objectives in Green Belts.*

Although development is severely limited in Green Belts, a wide range of land use changes are approved each year, as the development control scan illustrates. These can include proposals for the re-use of buildings for industrial and office purposes and a range of leisure-related schemes. In negotiations with applicants planners should address issues of enhancing the environment of the Green Belt as part of such schemes [4.20; 3.75].

17. *There is some scope for using planning obligations to secure environmental improvements in Green Belts.*

Where development affects a resource present on-site, authorities may negotiate equivalent off-site benefits. Where development is approved local authorities should seek to negotiate landscape and open land improvements. Acceptable development near to Green Belts may assist in funding Green Belt environmental improvements, but only if the need arises as a direct result of the proposed development [4.21].

It is recommended that:

R.23 *The following objectives of Green Belts should be listed in guidance:*

- *to promote the use of land for outdoor sport and recreation [4.7; 4.23-4.25];*

- *to retain and improve landscapes near to where people live [4.26];*

- *to enhance and improve damaged and derelict land in the urban fringe, and secure the nature conservation interest [4.27-4.28].*

R.24 *Significant development or redevelopment of land which occurs in the Green Belt should demonstrate benefits for the environment and landscape of the Green Belt. Such provisions should, in particular, apply to new consents for minerals, the tipping of waste, and road and other infrastructure developments or improvements [4.8; 4.20-4.21].*

R.25 *Community Forests in Green Belts should continue to work within Green Belt policies [4.14-4.19].*

R.26 *Use of the principle of enabling development to fund environmental improvements should not be allowed in approved Green Belts [4.12-4.13].*

R.27 *Where development occurs on sites adjoining Green Belts, either in suburban areas or by infilling and rounding off within settlements inset in the Green Belt, developers could contribute by agreement to environmental improvement or tree planting both on-site and on adjoining land. The need for such improvements would have to arise as a direct result of the proposed development [4.21].*

R.28 *The scale and types of environmental improvement which have been negotiated in association with planning permissions in the urban fringe and Green Belts should be further investigated [4.21].*

Permanence

18. *Exceptional circumstances for the alteration of approved Green Belts in structure plans have most often been substantiated for employment-related development.*

Some of the exceptions agreed in structure plans were already agreed in Regional Guidance; others were argued more locally. Most refer to high amenity, well-located sites, intended for high technology or other 'leading edge' firms. The Department has challenged the number, size and location of such sites where local authorities have interpreted the guidance over-generously. It would appear counterproductive for local authorities to specify what 'exceptional circumstances' might be in policies in structure plans. Local authorities should, however, set out to demonstrate exceptional circumstances if they wish to alter boundaries in a structure plan, and not merely argue that the normal process of review can allocate new supplies of land. Changes to Green Belt boundaries should be considered in relation to structure plan alteration and replacement, and not first at district plan level. General policies which allow almost continuous small-scale review of boundaries should also not be allowed as these devalue the concept [5.5-5.10].

19. *Structure plan policies allowing for the general small-scale alteration of Green Belt boundaries by districts, as part of the local plan process, are not acceptable.*

The argument advanced in favour of such policies is that there is a level of Green Belt boundary alteration which is not of structural importance. Whilst minor technical adjustments, to allow for appeal decisions and drafting errors are clearly acceptable, there is a risk, if such policies were accepted, that Green Belt policy would proceed entirely by continuous 'nibbling' at short-term policy reviews [5.8].

20. *Where exceptional circumstances have been demonstrated in altering a Green Belt boundary in a structure plan, it may be unnecessary to require districts to also prove exceptional circumstances for the release of land on a site by site basis.*

This argument surrounds what it is necessary to prove to secure the alteration of an agreed Green Belt boundary in a local plan. If the circumstance is a ruling on a district housing land total, which all parties at the EIP accept implies Green Belt changes, a general locational steer for the district in the structure plan may be appropriate. Also the district should only have to show that the sites chosen are better than other sites in the district (see para 9 of PPG 2) not that there are exceptional circumstances independent of those demonstrated in the structure plan. This situation may occur in future as boundaries in some district-wide plans require alteration [5.9].

21. *There is a need to set out the criteria to be satisfied for the establishment of new Green Belts, or major extensions to existing ones.*

Proposals for new Green Belts continue to be made. However Green Belts should be seen as a policy instrument to be used only exceptionally, when other development control policies have proved inadequate. They should fulfill Green Belt purposes. Authorities should assess how appropriate such a measure would be to the problems of the locality concerned, and how far circumstances had changed rendering an alteration to existing policy necessary. Clear evidence should be sought by the Department on these points [5.11-5.12].

22. *There is a strong case for making safeguarded land ('white land'), or its equivalent, a normal requirement in development plans.*

Only one half of the local authorities studied had white land or its equivalent in plans, although the number proposing to include white land in new district plans was higher. It is important in terms of sustainable development to have a long-term view on the direction of development in localities. This should also aid infrastructure provision and the negotiation of community benefits. A new emphasis on avoiding town cramming, put forward in advice in PPG 3, and a concern to protect urban greenspace, suggests development outside existing urban boundaries may be the most suitable option in some circumstances. The need to minimise travel also suggests that mixed use peripheral or corridor developments, well related to public transport routes, may provide the opportunity to minimise the growth of traffic and accompanying emissions. Where no white land had been included in plans local authorities regretted its absence. There would appear no advantage in placing a specific time period, in terms of years, on the phrase 'long term'. However, it would be most useful if the phrase referred to well beyond the plan period [5.13-5.25].

23.   *The issue of the extent of, and policies to be applied in, white land should be clarified.*

Circular 14/84 states that the normal processes of development control will apply in white land. Advice in Circular 50/57 suggests a model policy whereby the same land use prescription should be applied as in the Green Belt. However the Department does not now favour 'presumption against' policies outside the Green Belt. Some authorities prefer a development control policy which suggests no development should occur which would prejudice later comprehensive development. White land should be capable of development if needed in the medium term. Policies in the interim should protect valuable wildlife and landscape features and recreational access. Such land should be well related to infrastructure and existing and planned public transport facilities [5.23-5.24; 6.18].

It is recommended that:

R.29   *Where exceptional circumstances for the alteration of Green Belts have been substantiated in structure plans these should not need to be established again at site level [5.9].*

R.30   *Where new Green Belts are being proposed local authorities would need to demonstrate what major changes in circumstances had made the adoption of this exceptional measure necessary, and why normal development control or other policies would not be adequate [5.11-5.12].*

R.31   *Green Belt boundaries should be regarded as enduring well beyond the plan period. The provision of safeguarded land would be a normal requirement in development plans for Green Belts, unless local authorities could demonstrate where development would be located over the succeeding twenty years [5.19-5.25].*

R.32   *If a local authority is not proposing to provide white land in its plan it should justify the circumstances that have led to this decision [5.19-5.25].*

R.33   *Development control policy in white land should state that no development should occur which would prejudice later comprehensive development. Policies should, in particular, protect valuable wildlife and landscape features, and existing access for recreation [5.24].*

R.34   *White land should be well related to existing and planned infrastructure including public transport facilities [5.24].*

Transport and Vehicle Emissions

24. *Contained patterns of development can support policies which are designed to reduce the need to travel.*

The literature reviewed, and expert opinion, suggests containment policies can assist in creating more sustainable patterns of development. The influence of land use planning is likely to be long-term. Shorter term reductions in the growth of pollution are more likely through public transport enhancement, and such measures as the pricing of road and car parking space. Green Belts are important because they control costly private car-dependent sprawl, creating compact forms of development, thus minimizing the distances between activities [6.9-6.13].

25. *Green Belts allow issues of the relative concentration or dispersal of activities at the sub-regional level, and their transport implications, to be clearly addressed.*

Because most Green Belts cover a number of local authority areas they can implement decisions made on the balance between urban intensification, peripheral development and additions to small freestanding towns and villages at sub-regional level. Scottish Office advice makes this sub-regional role more explicit than advice in England, stating that in defining Green Belts authorities should relate the demand for all forms of development to a long-term settlement strategy for the plan area [6.14-6.16].

26. *Where there is a requirement for the development of greenfield sites, principles of sustainable development may conflict with policies for the retention of existing Green Belt boundaries.*

If Green Belt boundaries are too tight, in the absence of urban infill new development will be pushed beyond them. If Green Belts are too wide the distance between activities will be unnecessarily increased. The result will be wasteful extra journeys, often by private car. Given these problems, well-contained urban peripheral developments and, occasionally, free-standing settlements along public transport corridors within and beyond city fringes, may be the preferred 'models'. If principles of sustainability are to be given greater importance in the future then the re-drawing of the inner boundaries of some Green Belts may be necessary. These principles will need to extend to the definition of white land [6.14-6.17].

It is recommended that:

R.35 Local authorities should take account of the need to promote sustainable patterns of development when drawing up Green Belt boundaries in development plans [6.14-6.17].

R.36   *The boundaries of white land should also create the potential for compact forms of development well-related to public transport [6.14-6.18].*

R.37   *Green Belt boundaries should represent the outcome of a considered judgement on the sustainability attributes of development in urban areas, development beyond the Green Belt, or development by additions to towns and villages within it [6.14-6.16].*

R.38   *The possibility of freestanding new settlements located along very high quality public transport corridors in the Green Belt should be evaluated in deciding on settlement strategies [6.17].*

1. AIMS OF THE STUDY

Green Belts

1.1 Green Belts have been a cornerstone of planning policy for more than 35 years. Introduced around London in the late 1940s, they were adopted around a number of other towns and cities following the publication of the 1955 Green Belt Circular. Over the past 15 years the extent of fully approved Green Belts in England has doubled, to over 1,550,000 hectares (Figure 1.1). In Scotland approved Green Belts cover just under 200,000 hectares.

1.2 Perceived as successful in achieving their purposes, which include checking sprawl and safeguarding the countryside, Green Belts attract widespread support. The strength of feeling among the general public and local authorities is evidenced by recent pressures for new Green Belts in areas as diverse as South Hampshire, Humberside and the Central Belt of Scotland. Green Belt policy has also been firmly upheld by Ministers through support for development plans, as well as through individual decisions. Currently there is strong support for Green Belt policy in the White Paper *This Common Inheritance*, and in a range of planning guidance. In 1991 the then Secretary of State for the Environment, Michael Heseltine, announced his intention to assess the introduction of additional objectives for Green Belt. Two were proposed; to enhance and improve the natural beauty of the countryside adjoining cities, and to increase opportunities for its quiet enjoyment.

1.3 The main purpose of this research is to review the current effectiveness of Green Belt policy in England and Scotland, and to assess how this may be improved. The study aims are to assess:

- the effectiveness of Green Belts in relation to their existing purposes;

- the implications of possible new purposes;

- the roles of Green Belts in the management of sub-regional change;

- the permanence of Green Belts, and the extent of provision for long-term needs;

- their implications for transport and CO_2 emissions;

- urban fringe issues, including Community Forests, golf courses, agriculture, wildlife and other land use pressures and changes; and

- the impact of development control policy within Green Belts, including the re-use of redundant buildings, the interpretation of 'institutions in extensive grounds' and of appropriate rural uses, and the treatment of existing inappropriate uses.

1

The study does not set out to seek a replacement for Green Belt policy. Emphasis is placed on assessing the relevance of Green Belt to current policy priorities, in both urban and rural areas.

The Study Process

1.4   The study process involved six major tasks. These comprised a variety of methods, including interviews with a wide range of development and conservation interests, detailed case studies, desk research and the conduct of invitation seminars to obtain a variety of expert views and opinion.

Policy Case Studies

1.5   Studies of the operation of Green Belt policy were carried out in 28 selected local authority areas in England and Scotland. The areas selected covered a wide variety of economic conditions and policy responses at local level (Figure 2.1). The sample therefore included counties, districts and metropolitan boroughs where different Green Belt policy purposes have prominence, as follows:

- checking sprawl, preventing coalescence and safeguarding the countryside;

- urban regeneration; and

- preserving the special character of historic towns.

The work involved study of development plan documents, and interviews with local authority officers responsible for the policy. Attention was focused on issues of Green Belt policy, the definition of boundaries and permanence, and development control policies in plans.

Literature Search

1.6   Here a review of the major relevant material, published since the production of the most recent guidance in England in 1988, was undertaken. The review, found at Appendix B, includes a brief history of the development of the Green Belt concept, a discussion of the reported successes and perceived shortcomings of the policy. A brief analysis of urban fringe issues is found in Appendix G. A review of existing policy guidance, and regional guidance referring to Green Belt policy, is also included.

Interviews

1.7   Here a standard protocol covering the main research questions was developed, and used to guide some 25 semi-structured interviews. These covered four main groups of respondents, Government Departments, professional groups, land and business interests, and organisations with particular concerns for the environment and leisure. Conservation organisations were fully represented, including the Council for the Protection of Rural England, the London Green Belt Council, English Nature and the Countryside Commission. Although the interviews covered the full range of project topics views were especially sought on the appropriateness of existing Green Belt purposes, possible new purposes, and urban fringe issues.

Seminars

1.8 An invitation seminar was held to discuss urban fringe issues and their relationship to Green Belt policy. A second seminar discussed the implications for transport of the continued operation of Green Belt policy in the context of Government's expressed interest in minimising the growth of environmentally damaging, unnecessary travel. In each case a briefing paper was produced. This led to the development of a list of questions which were discussed by a small group of experts, operating under Chatham House rules. Rapporteurs also produced reports summarising the main points made. These seminars provided a forum for the *exchange* of views between experts in the relevant fields, a dimension not achievable by interviews alone.

Development Control Case Studies

1.9 These involved detailed studies of the outcomes of development control decisions in parts of four selected County areas in England. The detailed work covered six Districts spanning the South East, West Midlands, North West and Yorkshire and Humberside Standard Regions. The data obtained from local authorities related to numbers and types of planning applications made, approvals and refusals by land use, and the level of appeals and their outcomes. The data cover the four year period April 1988 to March 1992.

Generic Study of Development Control Issues

1.10 This part of the study involved an analyses of appeal decisions in all Green Belts in England made in the year April 1991 to March 1992. Some 21 categories of development were identified (for example categories such as farm workers dwellings, garden centres or golf courses), and a sample of at least 25 cases in each category were assessed. The aim was to isolate the relevant material considerations considered important by Inspectors or the Secretary of State (as appropriate) in aiming at the decisions on each type of development, and their implications for Green Belt policy.

Contextual Work

1.11 In addition to the above tasks, two further analyses form inputs to this Report. First, a content analysis of 27 submitted local plans for Green Belts not covered in the policy case studies sample (see paragraph 1.5) was carried out. At least one local plan in each Green Belt was, in this way, analysed for the study. This assisted in confirming the robustness of the conclusions and

3

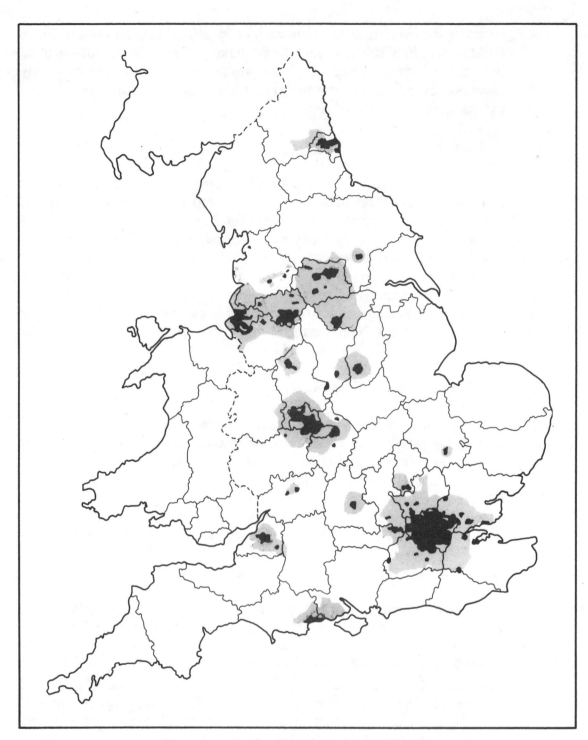

Figure 1.1 : Green Belts in England.

recommendations. Second, all Regional Offices of the Department of the Environment, and the Scottish Office Environment Department, were interviewed to ascertain their views on the full range of topics in the project brief.

1.12   The Report which follows is structured around the seven major aims of the research, and contains detailed arguments to support the recommendations made. Fuller material is included in the appendices at the rear of the volume.

2. THE EXISTING PURPOSES OF GREEN BELTS

Introduction

2.1 Green Belts are an instrument for managing urban growth and shaping patterns of urban development. The five purposes of Green Belts in England are:

- to check the unrestricted sprawl of large built-up areas;

- to safeguard the surrounding countryside from further encroachment;

- to prevent neighbouring towns from merging into one another;

- to preserve the special character of historic towns; and

- to assist in urban regeneration.[1]*

This Chapter assesses these purposes through study of development plans, development control, and appeal decisions.

2.2 The purposes of Green Belts have evolved through time in response to changing priorities within the planning system. In 1955, when the first guidance was introduced, Green Belts were seen as assisting policies of dispersal from larger cities. Part of a three-pronged policy, which also involved the use of New and Expanded Towns, the guidance stressed 'checking the further growth' of large built-up areas, and the prevention of coalescence.[2] In some areas the special character of towns was to be protected by the policy. Green Belts were not envisaged as stopping development, but were seen as guiding it to particular locations and shaping it into particular forms. A Government Booklet published in 1962 stated this well, noting Green Belts were '... a means of shaping the expansion of a city on a regional scale, and not just an attempt to combat the forces making for growth'.[3] Although the 1960s and 70s saw considerable pressures on Green Belts, from expanding leisure demands as well as urban development, the advice was not altered. Despite the popular appeal of the idea of Green Belts as a means of protecting landscape, and providing for recreation, these were not introduced as new purposes. Green Belts were retained and expanded in Structure Plans introduced following local government re-organisation in 1974.

2.3 In the late 1970s new priorities entered the scene. As people continued to leave the cities in large numbers their economies declined and inner city services deteriorated. In other areas economic restructuring was rapid leading to the loss of jobs in basic industries such as iron and steel, coal extraction and other manufacturing. In 1984 a fourth purpose 'to assist in urban regeneration' was included in the Green Belt advice.

* *References appear at the end of each Chapter.*

6

2.4   The guidance published in 1988 added a fifth purpose 'safeguarding the surrounding countryside from further encroachment'. This was the first reference to a rural objective for Green Belts, the previously accepted purposes being urban, and directed towards towns and cities. This in practice overlaps with the longstanding purposes of checking sprawl and preventing coalescence. The 1988 Guidance made a further amendment stating the aim of protecting the special character of towns was now to apply to *historic* towns. This may be seen as a clarification and limitation of the scope of the concept, and a response to some of the proposals to surround small freestanding towns with Green Belts, made in the early 1980s. By 1988 the original purpose of 'checking further growth' had been altered to that of 'checking unrestricted sprawl', thus avoiding the association of Green Belt with the notion of stopping growth.[4]

Green Belt Purposes in Development Plans

2.5   This analysis is based on case studies of the policies of five Counties and 17 Districts and Boroughs in England. The results of case studies in Scotland are presented in Chapter 7. The sample was chosen to represent areas of high, medium and low development pressure. Also areas where urban regeneration and the protection of the special character of historic towns was of importance, as well as the prevention of sprawl and coalescence, were selected. The areas are listed in Table 2.1.

2.6   In each of our case study areas Green Belt policy has developed differently. It has taken some time for the purposes listed in guidance to feed through to *approved* development plans. Where structure plan reviews and alterations are recent, as in Hertfordshire and Cheshire, the five purposes in PPG 2 have been listed in policy. In some cases local authorities are selective about which purposes are relevant. They also adapt the wording in the guidance in subtle ways. For example the approved Green Belt in the South East Dorset Structure Plan (1990) has the following purposes:

   '... •   to protect the separate physical identity of individual settlements in the area by maintaining wedges and corridors of open land between them; and

       •   to maintain an area of open land around the conurbation'.[5]

Protecting the physical identity of settlements is referred to in the Scottish Office advice, but not that for England. The West Midlands Structure Plan (1986) stresses urban regeneration, and protection of the special character of settlements:

   '... the purpose of the Green Belt is to support the regeneration of the Priority Areas by controlling the growth of the built up area. In addition, the Green Belt will prevent neighbouring settlements from merging and help to preserve their special character'.[6]

7

In this case special character may, or may not, refer to the *historic* character of the settlements involved.

2.7   In some areas *additional purposes* have been identified and approved for Green Belts. In Oxfordshire the Green Belt around the City of Oxford has long been approved, in order to:

'... • protect the special character of Oxford and its landscape setting;

   • check the growth of Oxford and prevent ribbon development and urban sprawl; and

   • prevent the coalescence of settlements'.[7]

The need to protect the landscape setting of Oxford has a lengthy planning history, dating back to the Thomas Sharp Plan in the 1940s. Green Belt was seen as the principal physical planning measure available with which to protect the special character of the City.

Table 2.1: Policy Case Study Areas

Green Belt Purpose	County Council	District/ Metro Borough
Sprawl and Coalescence	Dorset	East Dorset
		Purbeck
	Hertfordshire	Dacorum
		Broxbourne
	(Greater London)*	Enfield
All Purposes	Staffordshire	South Staffordshire
		Cannock
	(West Midlands)*	Walsall
		Wolverhampton
	Cheshire	Macclesfield
Urban Regeneration	(South Yorkshire)*	Sheffield
		Barnsley
	(West Yorkshire)*	Wakefield
		Leeds
Historic Towns	Oxfordshire	Cherwell
		City of Oxford
	Cheshire	City of Chester

*   Although these Councils have been abolished Green Belt policies in plans approved by them remain current

8

2.8   The other additional purposes listed in approved structure plans relate to recreation and access. For example, the structure plan for West Yorkshire (1980) does not stress the Green Belt principle of checking sprawl but aims:

'...   • to regulate the size and shape (of large built-up areas) in order to prevent uncontrolled growth;

       • to preserve areas of open land extending into the urban area from the countryside which have an existing or potential recreation or amenity value; and

       • to preserve easy access to open county and outdoor recreation in pleasant surroundings'.[8]

A number of draft local plans and unitary development plans (UDPs) have taken up the issue of recreation. For example the deposit draft of the Walsall UDP suggests an additional purpose of the Green Belt will be to provide for the outdoor recreation demands of the urban population which cannot be met in the built-up area. Similarly the draft Oxford Local Plan Review suggests an additional Green Belt purpose will be, '... to provide an area of amenity and recreational value for residents'.[9]

2.9   A number of approved local plans do not formally reiterate the purposes of the Green Belt in their area in policy. They may generally refer to the structure plan, or another source, before going on to discuss detailed development control issues. For example, the Dacorum District Plan of 1984 discusses the purposes of the Metropolitan Green Belt in an introductory paragraph in terms of '... limiting the Greater London built-up area and preventing its spread, as well as preserving green wedges, recreation and agriculture'.[10] It does not, however, specifically list the purposes of the policy in the District.

Checking Sprawl, Avoiding Coalescence and Safeguarding the Surrounding Countryside

2.10   A basic test of effectiveness must be to judge how far land approved as Green Belt has been kept open. Some changes to boundaries are to be expected as the guidance allows for Green Belts to be altered in exceptional circumstances. A second test is how far exceptional circumstances have been proven where alterations have been made through the development plan process. A third test is how far decision-making has been consistent between different agencies. An indicator here is the performance of the appeal system in upholding the policy. These are discussed, in turn, in this section.

2.11   Assessment of the achievement of the above purposes is complicated by the absence of fully-confirmed Green Belt boundaries in many cases. The process of incorporating detailed Green Belt boundaries into formally approved local plans has been slow. This is a longstanding problem reflected in exhortations

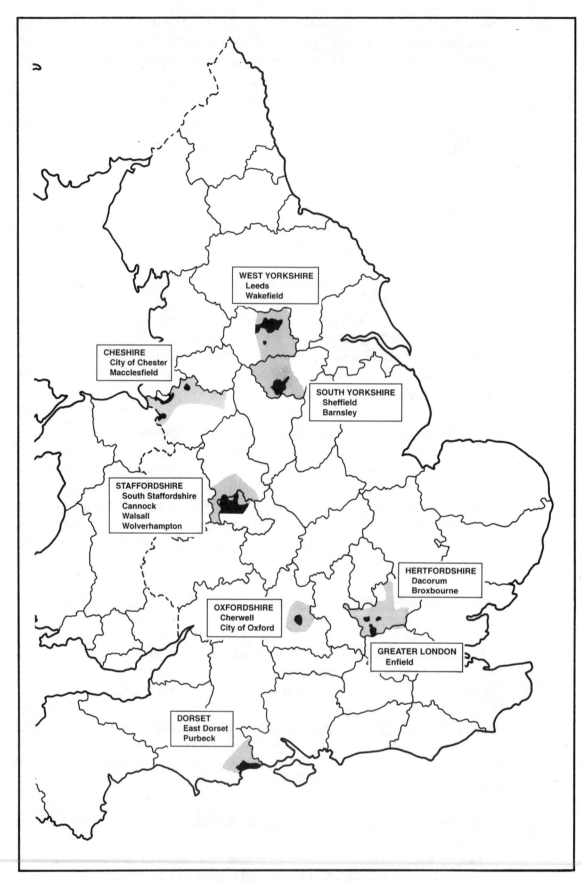

WEST YORKSHIRE
Leeds
Wakefield

CHESHIRE
City of Chester
Macclesfield

SOUTH YORKSHIRE
Sheffield
Barnsley

STAFFORDSHIRE
South Staffordshire
Cannock
Walsall
Wolverhampton

HERTFORDSHIRE
Dacorum
Broxbourne

OXFORDSHIRE
Cherwell
City of Oxford

GREATER LONDON
Enfield

DORSET
East Dorset
Purbeck

Figure 2.1 : Policy Case Study Areas.

by the Department to local authorities to speed up definition, contained in PPG 12.[11] In Dorset only one third of the boundaries of the Green Belt approved in 1980 had been formally approved in local plans by the first alteration of the Structure Plan in 1990. In the West Midlands local government reorganisation led to the cessation of the final stages of approval of the County-wide Green Belt Subject Plan in 1986. In formal terms boundaries now date back to a Ministry approved map in 1975, and earlier Town Maps. In Oxford virtually all of the Green Belt boundary has never formally been approved within the City, a distinction shared with other historic Cities such as York and Cambridge.

2.12   The interviews revealed no dissenters to the view that Green Belts are successfully being used to check unrestricted sprawl, prevent towns from merging, and safeguard the countryside from further encroachment. Apart from our interviews three sources of information support this view:

   •   evidence of changes made to Green Belts in approved development plans (see Appendix C);

   •   analyses of development control data at the strategic monitoring and district levels (Appendix F); and

   •   evidence from appeal decisions (Appendix H).

2.13   The extent of changes made to Green Belts over the last eight years in the development plans studied is small. In most cases interim or draft boundaries have been in the process of receiving formal approval in local plans, sometimes with boundary alterations. The case study areas contained 385,000 hectares of Green Belt, yet the changes recently approved and in proposals amounted to no more than 1,500 hectares. In Purbeck and East Dorset small-scale changes to town insets are being made to accommodate Structure Plan requirements. In each case the boundaries of the insets were of interim status. On the southern edge of Oxford some 100 hectares of land are under development for housing and high technology business use. These also previously had interim Green Belt status. The Leeds UDP proposes the development of around 100 hectares of Green Belt, parts of which are in the Otley area and only have interim status. All of the developments noted in the case studies would, if implemented, constitute contained peripheral additions to towns and cities.

2.14   The case study Counties where changes have been made to fully-approved Green Belts are Hertfordshire, Cheshire and Staffordshire. Exceptional circumstances were accepted by the Department in respect of an area of derelict glasshouses in the West Cheshunt area of Broxbourne. The 1988 Hertfordshire Structure Plan approval stated the land should be developed for around 1,000 dwellings.[12] In Stevenage the lack of land for long-term needs was the justification for setting back the approved Green Belt boundary. In Cheshire the approval of the Structure Plan in 1992 recognised that not all of the predicted requirement of 7,600 dwellings to 2001 could be accommodated in the existing urban areas of Macclesfield District. National Park constraints to the east, and coalescence problems to the north, suggested an allocation on the southern edge of the town of Macclesfield.[13] In the case of South Staffordshire it was similarly accepted that the housing requirements approved in the Structure Plan would require the development of some land in approved Green Belt.[14] The total land area involved in South Staffordshire and Macclesfield is likely to be under 200 hectares.

Development Control Evidence

2.15 Development control studies are capable of showing how firmly Green Belt policies have been upheld, and may also illuminate trends in land use pressures. However, in approaching any interpretation, it should be recognised that Green Belts already cover (wash over) existing areas of urban development. A survey of the London Green Belt in 1960 showed eight per cent of its land area in villages or groups of houses, or devoted to other urban development.[15] Indeed a range of developments may occur in conformity with policy. Many of these involve extensive areas of land. They include:

- the change of use, or construction, of institutions in extensive grounds;

- outdoor sport and recreation uses, including golf courses; and

- the redevelopment of redundant hospital sites, where the existing buildings are unsuitable for conversion.

In addition infill is allowed within areas of low density housing, pre-war ribbon development and small washed over villages. More recent policy initiatives allow the conversion of redundant buildings, including agricultural buildings, to other uses, and the provision of extra sites within some rural settlements for housing for local needs.

2.16 The West Midlands Green Belt covers 209,200 hectares, and forms an area of open countryside 8-10 miles wide around Birmingham and Coventry. Data for major applications, those for five dwellings or more, or 500 sq m of employment-related uses, show a small throughput over the last four years with strong adherence to Green Belt policy by the local authorities. Very few large applications were made in approved Green Belt. The rate of applications for residential use however remained similar for each year of the period, despite a decline nationally in the number of planning applications being made. (Table 2.2). The rate of approval of residential proposals has increased recently. More detailed analysis suggests a number of approvals in Staffordshire were for conversions of farm buildings to dwellings, often in the 5-10 units range (see Appendix E, Table 5).

Table 2.2: Planning Decisions in the West Midlands Green Belt: 1988-92

| | 1988-90 | | 1990-92 | |
| | number | | number | |
use applied for	approved	refused	approved	refused
housing	33	87	51	54
business/office	11	2	17	11
manufacturing/warehousing	12	8	22	6
retial	1	6	6	4
leisure	na	na	42	28
other/mixed	12	26	24	27
total	69	129	162	130

na = not available
Source: West Midlands Joint Data Team

2.17   The number of proposals for large employment-related uses was small, at around 15 per year. A number of the approvals relate to the business use of large country houses, or buildings previously used as institutions in extensive grounds. Some approvals replace existing employment uses. The level of leisure approvals, for uses such as golf courses, driving ranges and country park-style developments, now forms a significant part of the picture. Data from the West Midlands Joint Data Team show the highest pressures south and west and north west of the conurbation reflecting the physical attractiveness of areas in Warwickshire and Lichfield District, and their level of accessibility in relation to Motorways. Large scale applications also cluster in areas where Green Belt boundaries are not fully confirmed, or where changes are presaged in regional guidance or structure plans (See Appendix E, Tables 1-5).

2.18   Data on development control in the London Green Belt, collected by SERPLAN for the year to April 1992, suggest just over 300 hectares in approvals for what are termed 'unacceptable' developments (Table 2.3). These include approvals on redundant hospital sites, and for some business and commercial uses approved in 'very special circumstances'. The 1,400 hectares of approvals in 'acceptable' uses are dominated by golf courses, which appear to comprise over 90 per cent of the total.[16]

Table 2.3: Development Approvals in the London Green Belt: 1991-92**

                                        hectares

authorities	'unacceptable'	'acceptable'	area of green belt
Shire Counties*	254	1,343	480,000
London	60	100	39,000
Total	314	1,443	519,000

*   excludes Hampshire, but includes Oxfordshire
** See Table E1 for full details.

Source: SERPLAN, 1991.

2.19   The detailed development control studies in South Staffordshire, Chester, Macclesfield and Wakefield implied virtually no new land-take for housing within Green Belts over the 1988-92 period. Table 2.4 suggests that between 10 and 30 per cent of applications were within the Green Belt in these areas. However the approval rate in the Green Belt is, on average, 10 per cent lower than for urban areas. The Green Belt has a strong deterrent effect greatly reducing the proportion of medium and large scale applications as a proportion of the total made. On average 75 per cent of applications in Green Belts relate to some aspect of housing, by far the majority relating to extensions or alterations to existing dwellings. Approval rates did not vary greatly between the case study Authorities, with the possible exception of Macclesfield, where a particularly firm stance is in evidence.

Table 2.4: Development Control in the Case Study Areas: 1988-92

	Chester	Macclesfield	South Staffs *	Wakefield
area of Green Belt **	14,339	39,413	32,702	23,333
per cent of District	32	75***	80	70
ave. applications per year	1,550	2,450	1,300	2,600
per cent of applications				
- in Green Belt	15	30	30	11
- approved in Green Belt	83	71	74	77
- approved in urban areas and insets	89	82	85	90

*   average for two years
**   estimated (hectares)
***   excluding Peak District National Park

Source: Green Belt Project Survey

2.20   Further analysis of the numerically-dominant residential applications was carried out to assess in more detail the impact on the Green Belt. Applications for one or more new dwellings in the Green Belt were a very small minority of residential applications in the Districts studied, around 10-20 per cent (see Table 2.5). The level of approval of these varied from 35 per cent in South Staffordshire to nearly 50 per cent in Chester. The absolute number of applications per year involved was however very small. Appendix F lists all of the approvals in the South Staffordshire Green Belt for the year to April 1992. The residential approvals comprised 105 new dwellings, 72 of which were on two sites subject to departure procedures as part of the release of land following the approval of the Staffordshire Structure Plan. In addition, there were 28 units in barn conversions, three approvals for farm workers' dwellings, and three for the removal of agricultural occupancy conditions. Overall the development listed in South Staffordshire appears to have had a marginal impact on the openness of the Green Belt.[17] The most significant areas in approvals were for uses generally acceptable in policy terms, 166 hectares relating to golf, and 30 hectares to cemeteries. Our other case studies suggested this pattern is repeated elsewhere.

Table 2.5: Approvals for One Permanent Dwelling or More in Green Belt

	Chester	South Staffs	Wakefield	Dacorum
average number of applications per year	15	18	28	34
per cent approved	48.8	35.6	42.9	48.4
proportion of total residential applications	12.4	11.9	19.2	n.a.

Source: Green Belt Project Survey

2.21   Green Belt policies are strongly supported by the decisions of the Planning Inspectorate and the Secretary of State at appeal. Of 1,201 appeals investigated, covering the year to the end of March 1992, only 22.6 per cent were upheld, a level one third lower than the national average of 33.7 per cent for all appeal decisions.[18] If residential extensions are omitted this figure reduces to 19.7 percent. Table 2.6 shows that for England only eight per cent of the 229 appeals for single new dwellings were approved, and some nine per cent of slightly larger (two to nine units) infill schemes. As expected the lowest figure relates to larger residential proposals. Only one appeal was upheld in the '10 + units' category out of the 19 made. This related to land whose removal from Green Belt had already been agreed in principle through the development plan process.

15

Table 2.6: Planning Appeals Upheld in the Green Belt: Residential Uses

use	number	per cent upheld
residential - extensions	245	34.3
residential - single units	229	7.9
residential - 2 to 9 units	65	9.2
residential - 10 + units	19	5.3

(See also Table 3.4 for a fuller analysis)

Source: Green Belt Project Survey

2.22 Thus although development continued in the outer parts of the towns and cities studied, virtually none was in approved Green Belt. The level of development permitted did not compromise the purposes of retaining openness, checking sprawl, and avoiding significant encroachment into the countryside. The local planners interviewed felt that policies designed to avoid coalescence by retaining relatively narrow 'gaps' between settlements had been particularly firmly upheld. Much of development permitted has involved the redevelopment of existing sites in urban areas, often with more intensive uses. This process of *urban intensification* had reached its highest levels in our Hertfordshire case study areas, but was also of significance in South Staffordshire and Macclesfield. As an indicator, in Broxbourne (Hertfordshire) the contribution of windfall sites to total new housing sites was found to be significantly reducing. In Dacorum, also in Hertfordshire, open space has been built on, and intensification in some residential areas has harmed their character. In Sheffield, where the Green Belt was approved in 1983, pressures are now reported on green areas in the City. However, in South East Dorset it is expected that virtually all new development will go into the Bournemouth-Poole built up area in the form of intensification, with only a small proportion comprising new greenfield development. Little is known on a systematic basis about land use changes in suburban areas and their effects on movement, open space, pollution and other quality of life indicators. In the future local authorities, particularly in the South, but also in the outer areas of other conurbations, are likely to develop policies to protect suburban residential environments. There may, for example, be areas of green space in towns and cities which, if developed, would adversely affect living conditions for more people than if equivalent land of lower amenity and ecological quality in Green Belts was developed. PPG 17 gives stronger support than hitherto to the protection of urban open space.

Safeguarding the Countryside

2.23 These three Green Belt purposes are important because they are used directly as criteria to justify the retention of individual sites and small areas in the development control process. By its location and position land can be seen as falling within these purposes. Checking sprawl and avoiding coalescence have proved clear purposes in this respect, passing the test of repeated application at appeal without successful challenge. Safeguarding the surrounding countryside from further encroachment duplicates the logic of much of that protected under the first two purposes. It is however a more general concept which can be applied to any non-urban land. Taken literally the phrase could be used to deny the development of any greenfield site. In terms of the location and position of the land involved it confuses the traditional purposes of Green Belt as an urban shaping device with countryside protection *per se*, which can be regarded as a general outcome of the policy.

2.24   Safeguarding the countryside from encroachment was only referred to in the preamble to Circular 14/84 and was not a specific purpose for placing land in Green Belt until 1988. In practice its inclusion has not added to the effectiveness by which they have been maintained. The development control evidence from High Wycombe and Stratford-on-Avon in Appendix E, and the results of Elson's National Study, referred to in Appendix B (para B.12) suggest that Green Belts had effectively been kept open and free from development before 1988.

2.25   Some of our consultees wanted this purpose removed in its present form as it provided a poor criterion for decision-makers. Two alternative formulations were mentioned to us. Firstly, that guidance should more closely reflect what currently occurs in practice. 'Safeguarding the countryside from *unnecessary* encroachment, in the context of other policies in the development plan' would be more realistic. For example, where there is an adequate supply of development land allocated for the plan period, and sufficient white land, and where urban intensification is not judged as too damaging, then there will be no necessity for encroachment onto surrounding countryside. If these circumstances do not obtain then some further greenfield development may be necessary. The test would be how far other policy objectives should override existing Green Belt policy, given that the latter should only be altered in exceptional circumstances. A second approach saw this purpose as *complementing* existing policies for protection of the countryside. It is clear from PPG 7 that there are a wide range of policies which exist to protect the countryside for the sake of its beauty, the diversity of its landscape, and the range of its natural resources.[19] There are policies to protect the most versatile agricultural land, and control building in the open countryside away from existing settlements, in addition to statutory and non-statutory landscape and wildlife designations. It is not the primary purpose of Green Belt to secure these objectives. Green Belt policy should, however, be seen as complementing countryside policies by assisting in safeguarding the countryside from encroachment.

2.26   This purpose has always been more sparingly deployed. In the late 1950s York, Chester, Oxford and Cambridge, a group of compact small cities with special character subject to high development pressures, instigated Green Belt policies. In 1988 the guidance added 'historic' to the purpose, thus making clear that new proposals around smaller settlements generally were not welcomed. Currently Norwich is seeking a new Green Belt using the special character argument and, in the last 15 years, coverage has been extended in areas such as Harrogate and Lancaster.

2.27   An analysis of policies relating to historic towns suggests that Green Belt has had various rationales. It has been used in different situations to:

- protect the *green and open fabric* of such cities, keeping open extensive belts of land which form important parts of the setting of town centres, neighbourhoods or groups of buildings;

- protect *gateways*, by keeping open approaches to a city, and providing a clear *definition* of town and country;

- protect the wider *setting* of a city. This may comprise, as in the case of Oxford, keeping open areas of higher ground which provide a green background to the City, and help give it a distinctive character; and

- seek control over the size of a city, with a view to influencing the *level of activity* which requires to be accommodated in its historic core, thus protecting the character.

2.28   In Oxford the special character arguments have been combined with the other two classic purposes of Green Belt set out in Circular 42/55. The Explanatory Memorandum to the 1987 Structure Plan gives the rationale well:

> '... the special character of Oxford ... means not just the University heritage areas and the views of the 'dreaming spires' from outside the City, but a much broader concept including the countryside around the City, the Cherwell and Thames floodplains and the relationship of adjoining settlements to the City. Character also includes a concept of the overall scale of activity in the City, since any considerable growth of the City will generate more activity, more traffic and pressures for further development which are all likely to threaten the nature, character and setting of the City'.[20]

This presents the interpretation that the Green Belt instrument can directly affect the overall scale of activity in the City. In the case of York the City Council sees the protection of the green wedges which run into the heart of the City as the critical element in preserving its historic character. The boundary in these areas should be inalienable in contrast to some parts of the outer edges of the built-up area where policy is more a matter of managing urban form. The firmness of boundaries in these outer areas would depend on long-term needs.

Green Belts and Environmental Capacity

2.29   The question of how far the policy should be used to limit the size of cities according to a notion of environmental capacity has gained importance recently. In comments on the Oxfordshire Structure Plan the Department suggested Oxford 'may have reached its limits', and that there was only very limited scope for further growth. This has been reiterated in the case of Chester where the Cheshire Replacement Structure Plan approval letter states '... Chester may, if its historic character is to be maintained, be reaching the limits of its growth'.[21]

2.30   The approval process of the Cheshire Structure Plan gave an opportunity for a number of these issues to be debated. The County and District proposed the alteration of the Green Belt on the southern and northern edges of Chester to develop 320 hectares for industry, offices and housing. Table 2.7 summarises the various proposals.

Table 2.7: The Chester Proposals

	Structure Plan	EIP Panel	Department Approved
new employment land	210 ha	150 ha	100 ha
dwellings	7,800	7,100	6,100
land from green belt	320 ha	100 ha	none

Source: EIP Panel Report and Structure Plan approval letter

2.31   The Examination in Public Panel summarised the issues in their report. Those proposing the highest rate of growth saw the City as having an international profile. Marketing the City as an attractive place to live and work had brought increased prosperity and economic activity. There was a need for a greater number of jobs in the North West Region. A continuation of this process, it was argued, would also provide for local needs by diversifying the employment base. Although such a strategy would have consequences for the Green Belt the resulting demands would be manageable. The extra infrastructure provided with the new development, notably a new section of ring road, would avoid unacceptable traffic demands on the historic core of the City. A more buoyant growth situation would help sustain conservation of the historic core by providing greater resources. The counter arguments suggested that development would increase the level of activity in the City and do irretrievable harm to its historic core. Extra increases in traffic, and redevelopment activity in the centre could result. A 'precautionary approach' should be taken by the local authorities if the effects of extra growth could not be predicted with certainty.

2.32   The Examination in Public Panel felt it was inappropriate for Chester to assume what amounted to a Regional role in growth promotion. They concluded that the proposals in the Structure Plan were not compatible with preserving the historic character of Chester, and therefore proposed a continuation of development at broadly past rates (see Table 2.7). This would have involved the release of three non-strategic, Green Belt sites. In the final approval letter, however, the Department took a more restrictive view suggesting that, with present information, it was doubtful whether releasing more land could be accomplished without damaging the historic centre, or harming the character of the City as a whole. Table 2.8 lists the way the Department interprets Green Belt purposes in the Chester area.

Table 2.8: Roles of the Green Belt Around Chester

1.   'The Green Belt of North Cheshire and the Wirral has played an important role in supporting urban regeneration in Greater Manchester and Merseyside'.

2.   'Chester's Green Belt has an important role in maintaining the separation of settlements' ... especially between Chester and Ellesmere Port.

3.   '... and of preventing the spread of development into open countryside'

4.   'The Chester Green Belt has an additional function of safeguarding the historic City, both its setting as a whole and its special character, particularly that of its central core'.

Source: Department of the Environment approval letter.[22]

2.33   The basic problem is that many of the links in the arguments being made were not conclusively supported by evidence. It proved difficult to make irrefutable links between the scale and rate of peripheral development proposed, and its impact on the historic core of the City. How far the concept of 'environmental capacity', introduced by the Council for the Protection of Rural England and English Heritage, could be translated into an operable decision-making structure, was also unclear.[23] The likely impact of traffic management measures proposed by the local authorities was not sufficient to convince those vetting the Plan that the precautionary principle should not prevail. Further work on what constitutes the special character of the City, and its ability to absorb growth, was recommended by the Panel.

2.34 The role of the Green Belt in protecting the character and identify of historic towns, by maintaining important green wedges and open land providing clear definition between town and country, has a well-established pedigree. Green Belt boundaries around historic cities are particularly tight, and future development requirements have been assessed conservatively. It is less clear how far peripheral restraint is necessarily linked to the more effective conservation of their historic core areas. In the case of Oxford, for example, despite more than firm Green Belt restraints there has been considerable growth in retail and office floorspace over the past fifteen years. The level of vehicle penetration to the historic core has however remained similar for twenty years despite more than a 30 per cent increase in car ownership nationally. This has been achieved by a traffic restraint policy and the introduction of a Park and Ride system. Peripheral restraint has acted as a backcloth to these more interventionist transport measures.

Assisting Urban Regeneration

2.35 Assisting urban regeneration was introduced as a purpose of Green Belts following the House of Commons Environment Select Committee inquiry in 1984. MPs at that time agreed with the Greater Manchester Council that '... Green Belt, originally conceived as a way of containing growth, has now become essential to dealing with the problems of decline...'.[24] Green Belts would have particular justification where derelict land in urban areas continued to be created and not effectively re-used. However it was never intended that Green Belts would 'deliver' urban regeneration on their own. Other complementary policies, going well beyond the denial of some land and sites on urban peripheries, would be required.

2.36 In this situation the term 'urban regeneration' has assumed a variety of meanings dependent on the local authority involved. In some cases it may be the intention of focusing on some form of economic priority area in the *inner city*. For others it may involve securing the redevelopment of brown land in urban areas generally, before greenfield sites are utilized. It may also imply that by denying some choices on the urban periphery developers will restrict their attention to land allocated in plans, or to more actively seeking out redevelopment and re-use possibilities within urban areas. In practice the attraction of jobs may be regarded by local authorities as more important than any land development objective *per se*. No studies have been carried out to test the hypothesis that firm containment has specific effects in assisting regeneration, although in the West Midlands it is accepted as a requirement for effective monitoring of the Regional Strategy.

2.37 The geography and administrative complexity of city regions also make any analysis of the outcomes of this aspect of policy difficult. The denial of development opportunities at the urban fringe is more likely to lead to the development of sites with similar attributes in other parts of the outer city. This may involve leap-frogging beyond the Green Belt, or development by intensification of uses in towns inset within it. The inner city, it has been

21

suggested, will rarely be a substitute location for uses seeking planning permission on the urban fringe. The housing market potential in the two locations is quite different (in terms of the size and price range of houses which may be marketed for example), and many of those developing other uses require the better accessibility (normally by private car) which a peripheral or outer city location affords. Where sites on the periphery and in the inner city are in the control of different Boroughs co-ordination of land release and restraint can be difficult. The peripheral Borough may wish to develop Green Belt land as a means of alleviating its own local economic problems, thus competing with the inner Borough.

2.38   In the policy case study areas, urban regeneration objectives were often thought to be enhanced by the *selective release of employment sites in the Green Belt*. There have been pressures for the release of land in particularly attractive parts of the North West such as Chester and in Trafford. In the West Midlands the Regional Guidance suggests a need to identify 330 hectares of land for high technology development to 2001.[25] A number of sites have subsequently been identified in the approved Green Belt. Policies for the regeneration of the Black Country are considered to warrant new sites in South Staffordshire and in the Green Belt west of the conurbation. Such sites are intended to be well-located in respect of motorways, and to have environments attractive to outside investors. The idea is to gradually release such sites in the Green Belt, from an agreed pool, to ensure a continued supply. Joint working among the local authorities has moved towards the identification of appropriate sites.[26]

2.39   In South Yorkshire the Regional Guidance suggests the process of preparation of UDPs provides the opportunity, exceptionally, to review existing boundaries where economic regeneration may be constrained by the lack of suitable sites.[27] As a result both Barnsley and Wakefield Districts have suggested the allocation of large sites adjacent to motorways for prime industrial use. In Wakefield, 29 hectares of land in the Green Belt were developed for incoming industry in 1989, and land for a new freight terminal was released in 1992. The intention of current policy is to provide a variety of sites in terms of size and location to meet the needs of potential users, with an emphasis on those that can be readily serviced.[28] Sites for employment-related development have also been released in Rotherham through departure procedures.

2.40   In Newcastle-on-Tyne the local authority see a clear contradiction between retaining existing Green Belt and future urban regeneration. The City suggest the success of a tight Green Belt in the past has led to the successful redevelopment of the inner city and blighted industrial areas. The ability of the City to retain a balanced population, and take advantage of improving economic prospects, is now harmed, it is claimed, by a lack of new land for development. The draft UDP proposes a general urban expansion into the Green Belt north and west of the City to provide for 5,000 new dwellings and 120 hectares of land for economic development to the year 2006. The development would take advantage of proximity to the Airport, and would be related to public transport infrastructure, including an extended Metro[29].

2.41 The urban regeneration philosophy has been taken farthest in Strathclyde Region in Scotland, where both housing and industrial land have been released from the Green Belt, as part of the regeneration strategy. Rather than work by a process of 'exceptional circumstances' the Strathclyde renewal strategy seeks to meet demands for new development by recycling redundant urban land, supported where necessary by the planned expansion of urban areas onto greenfield sites. The question is, at any one time, what the balance between the two forms of development is to be. Monitoring is fine grained, and biennial updates of the strategic plan are carried out. Most of the urban renewal sites require substantial investment in upgrading and preparation. Funds for this come from the development agencies such as the Scottish Development Agency and Scottish Enterprise. If urban sites do not come on stream fast enough, then further greenfield sites may be allocated. Over the 1979-89 period the Green Belt policy focused efforts on the development of preferred urban sites. Between 1980-90 a number of single user 'high amenity sites' were also released from the Green Belt. By 1990, with the easier brownfield sites developed, the Council specified some twenty Green Belt releases for housing. These have been accepted by the Scottish Office Environment Department in approval of the structure plan in 1992.

2.42 The roles of the Green Belt in the Strathclyde strategy are therefore:

- to relate future development of greenfield land to an identified need, whilst also achieving wider social benefits;

- to ensure speculative developments in the open countryside do not jeopardise the renewal process; and

- to ensure that action to upgrade the urban fringe environment can proceed with confidence.

This is a less absolutist view of Green Belt policy than in England, but the overall effect in terms of land release is rather similar. It is significant that the Regional Authority in Strathclyde has been able to progress a coherent strategy, with regular updating (see paras 7.29-7.37). The West Midlands situation appears more fragmented with the wide range of local authorities involved. Clearly pursuing urban regeneration objectives using Green Belts requires a conurbation-wide view, or at least a sub-regional view, for its effectiveness to be maximised.

2.43 The approach of PPG 2, suggesting that Green Belts can *assist* in urban regeneration, was broadly supported by local authorities and consultees. In practice local authorities are operating policies which aim to create a portfolio of sites of different sizes and environmental quality across their areas. This can imply that urban regeneration is also an argument for *taking land out of*

Green Belt. Lack of progress in the reclamation and improvement of urban sites places increased pressure on Green Belts. The new Urban Regeneration Agency will have a major role in maintaining the impetus of land recycling in cities, thus assisting with the maintenance of Green Belt. The use of Green Belts to assist in urban regeneration clearly requires a conurbation-wide view to be taken. As local authorities are frequently competing to attract new economic activities such co-ordination is not always possible. Regional Guidance, at least at the level of specificity of that for the West Midlands, may require to be developed in other regions. Greater speed is also needed in identifying specific sites after regional guidance has been agreed.

Main Findings and Recommendations

2.44 *The first two purposes of Green Belts, checking unrestricted sprawl, and preventing towns from merging, are being achieved.*

We found no dissenters to the view that Green Belts are successfully being used to check unrestricted sprawl and prevent towns from merging. Alterations to boundaries in development plans had affected less than 0.3 per cent of Green Belts in the areas studied over the last eight years [2.10-2.14]. Most planning approvals are for small-scale changes which do not significantly affect the open rural appearance of Green Belts [2.15-2.20]. The appeal system strongly upholds Green Belt policy [2.21;3.16].

2.45 The third purpose, *safeguarding the surrounding countryside from encroachment has significantly overlapped the first two purposes.*

Green Belts have safeguarded the countryside from further encroachment. This purpose has however overlapped the first two purposes, not adding to the already very firm restraint on development offered by Green Belts. Safeguarding the surrounding countryside from encroachment was not a specific purpose for including land in Green Belt until 1988. Its inclusion appears not, in practice, to have added to the already very firm restraint offered by Green Belts in the 1955-88 period. In its present form this purposes does not provide a clear criterion for decision-makers. Current practice suggests this purpose is seen as complementing countryside policies by assisting in safeguarding the countryside from encroachment [2.23-2.25].

2.46 *The relationship between Green Belt restraint and increasing levels of economic activity and their impacts on the cores of cities of special historic character, are unclear.*

Green Belt boundaries around historic towns are particularly tight, and future development requirements have been assessed conservatively. Green Belts have been used with little dispute to protect the settings of, and define the approaches to, such towns. These purposes should be stressed in guidance. It is less clear how far peripheral restraint is necessarily linked to the protection of their historic centres. Department comments suggest such towns may have limits to their growth. These issues should be further investigated by a comparative study of historic towns [2.26-2.34].

2.47   *The role of Green Belts in urban regeneration has been to focus development on sites in urban areas. Local authorities have also used Green Belt to create and maintain a balance between urban and greenfield development for economic growth.*

For local authorities in urban regeneration areas Green Belt restraint has acted to encourage development within urban boundaries. At the same time, for some local authorities a major catalyst for urban regeneration is seen to be the freeing of prime industrial sites from the Green Belt. Local authorities in regeneration areas are concerned to have a balanced portfolio of urban and greenfield sites readily available for new economic activity. In some areas larger-scale mixed-use developments have been proposed as parts of city-wide urban regeneration strategies. Denying a range of peripheral site development options will not secure the regeneration of under-used urban sites on its own. Policies for the re-use of urban land will be of greater importance. There is a need for more detailed work on the relationship between Green Belt restraint and urban regeneration [2.35-2.43].

2.48   *Most decisions on Green Belt boundaries in plans involve making assumptions about urban intensification.*

Throughout the case study areas planners, and the Department's Regional Offices, are making decisions about the balance between development by infill within urban areas, and peripheral expansion of various kinds. However, little is known on a systematic basis about land use changes in the suburbs and their effects on movement, open space, pollution and other quality of life indicators. In the future local authorities, particularly in the South, are likely to be presenting arguments on 'overheating' problems as a reason for altering Green Belts. There may be areas of green space in towns and cities which, if developed, would aversely affect living conditions for more people than if equivalent land of lower amenity and ecological quality in Green Belts was developed [2.22].

2.49   *The time taken to approve Green Belt boundaries in local plans is too long.*

In a number of Counties the Structure Plan has been altered or replaced before local plan boundaries based on the original plan have been agreed. This may be due to unresolved problems over the location of development following approval of the broad totals in the Structure Plan. The Department has advised Authorities who do not have agreed boundaries in local plans that they risk greater amounts of development in their areas. The slowness of progress also creates uncertainty, particularly at appeal where it may be difficult to assess the status of land [2.11].

It is recommended that:

R.1   *Green Belts should be seen as a policy instrument for shaping patterns of urban development at sub-regional and regional scales. They help to ensure development occurs in locations decided upon in development plans, and they assist in protecting the countryside. Green Belt policies should also, by creating contained forms of new development, assist in moving towards more sustainable patterns of urban growth [2.23-2.25; 6.14-6.19].*

R.2   *The purposes for including specific areas of land in a Green Belt should be:*

-    *to check the unrestricted sprawl of large built-up areas;*

-    *to prevent neighbouring towns from merging into one another [2.10-2.22];*

-    to assist in safeguarding *the countryside from encroachment [2.23-2.25];*

-    *to preserve the* setting and *special character of historic towns [2.26-2.34]; and*

-    *to assist in urban regeneration [2.35-2.43].*

R.3   *The importance of Green Belts in creating a balance between urban and greenfield development, where urban regeneration is a priority, should be stated. Large-scale employment sites should only be released as part of the regional guidance-development plan process [2.35-2.43].*

R.4   *The relationship between Green Belt restraint and increasing levels of economic activity, and the special character of historic cities should be investigated by a comparison of land use, traffic and other policies within a number of historic cities and their surrounding daily journey to work areas [2.29-2.34].*

R.5   *The need for up-to-date approved Green Belt boundaries, so as to avoid ambiguity and allow the proper consideration of future development options, should continue to be stressed [2.11].*

References

1. DOE (1988a) Green Belts, PPG 2, para 4.

2. MHLG (1955) Green Belts, Circular 42/55, London, HMSO.

3. HM Government (1988) The Green Belts, London, HMSO, p 26.

4. DOE (1988a) op. cit.

5. Dorset County Council (1990) South East Dorset Structure Plan, First Alteration, policy 1.2.

6. West Midlands County Council (1986) West Midlands County Structure Plan, First Alteration, policy ENV 12.

7. Oxfordshire County Council (1992) Structure Plan: Fourth Alteration, policy EN5.

8. West Yorkshire County Council (1980) West Yorkshire Structure Plan, policy N10.

9. Oxford City Council (1992) Oxford 2001 - Local Plan Review, Draft for Consultation, policy ENV1.

10. Dacorum District Council (1984) District Plan, para 2.3.

11. DOE (1992a) Development Plans and Regional Planning Guidance, PPG 12, Annex D.

12. DOE (1988b) Hertfordshire County Structure Plan 1986 Review, Approval Letter, paras 3.17-3.20.

13. Cheshire County Council (1992) Cheshire 2001 - Structure Plan, op. cit.

14. Staffordshire County Council (1991) County Structure Plan, Stafford, SCC.

15. Munton, R. J. C. (1984) London's Green Belt, Allen and Unwin, London.

16. SERPLAN (1991) A Regional Profile of the South East: 1991, RPC 2040, London, SERPLAN.

17. It should be realised that not all development approved may be implemented, as the evidence for High Wycombe, in Appendix E, demonstrates.

18. The Planning Inspectorate (1992) Chief Planning Inspector's Annual Report, London, HMSO, states the rate of appeals upheld as 33.7 per cent.

19.   DOE (1992b) <u>The Countryside and the Rural Economy</u>, PPG 7, para 1.9.

20.   Oxfordshire County Council (1987) <u>County Structure Plan</u>, Second Alteration, para 3.9.

21.   DOE (1992) <u>Cheshire Replacement Structure Plan</u>, Cheshire 2001, para 13.9.

22.   Op.cit., para 13.12.

23.   Council for the Protection of Rural England (1990) <u>Cheshire 2001: Comments by CPRE on the Cheshire County Structure Plan Review</u>, London, CPRE.

24.   House of Commons Environment Committee (1984) <u>Green Belt and Land for Housing</u>, HC 275-I, p xiii.

25.   DOE (1988) <u>Strategic Guidance for the West Midlands</u>, PPG 10, para 13.

26.   West Midlands Joint Data Team (1992) <u>Black Country Sector - Premium Employment Locations - First Monitoring Report</u>, WMJPT, Solihull.

27.   DOE (1989) <u>Strategic Guidance for South Yorkshire</u>, para 21.

28.   Wakefield District Council (1991) <u>Wakefield Unitary Development Plan</u>, Deposit Version, para 5.6.9.

29.   City of Newcastle-on-Tyne (1992) <u>Draft Unitary Development Plan</u>, Summary, pp 4-7.

3.   DEVELOPMENT CONTROL IN GREEN BELTS

Introduction

3.1   Pressures for development have always been considerable in Green Belts but recently issues of development control policy and its interpretation have assumed greater importance. A reduction in the profitability of agriculture has led to pressures for further diversification. This is most often manifested in applications for the re-use of farm buildings for other uses. Leisure demands, notably for golf courses and a variety of other active sports and passive recreation, have also increased. Infill and intensification in small villages within the Green Belt has continued for many years. Government policy is to sustain the process of diversification in the countryside generally and to accommodate change, while continuing to conserve the countryside for the enjoyment of residents and visitors. Policy also suggests the range of industries that can be successfully located in rural areas is expanding.[1] Within Green Belts however there continues to be a presumption against inappropriate development. Uses considered appropriate in Green Belts include new buildings or changes of use for agriculture and forestry, outdoor sport, cemeteries and institutions standing in extensive grounds. This Chapter discusses policies for rural settlements in Green Belts, before presenting findings relating to development control.

Existing Settlements

3.2   Policies for existing settlements are contained in Circular 50/57. They basically divide rural settlements into three categories:

- where *no new building* is the intention, the settlement should be 'washed over', that is included within the Green Belt;

- where *infilling only* is proposed, the settlement should be washed over, and listed in the relevant plan. Policies defining the scope of infill should also be included; and

- where *limited expansion* is proposed, the settlement should be inset, that is, removed from the Green Belt. Development control policies for such settlements should also be included in the plan.[2]

These policies are strict. Green Belt policy implies no new building, and this is reflected in the first policy category. The notation is likely to apply to small hamlets or pre-war ribbon development. The logic is to control urbanization where the hamlet or cluster of houses is basically loose-knit, and further development would harm the generally open rural appearance. Infilling in washed over small villages which have been listed in a plan (the second category) is therefore a slight relaxation of policy, particularly as such areas are within the Green Belt. In its strictest form infilling is regarded as closing a gap in an otherwise built-up road frontage by the construction of one new

29

dwelling. However, listing a settlement does not make clear the areas within it where infill is considered appropriate. This can lead to large numbers of time-consuming appeals. Nearly one fifth of all appeals in the Green Belt relate to new single dwellings (see Table 3.4 and Appendix H, para 5). In order to make policy more effective a number of authorities define infill boundaries within washed over settlements. For example, infill may be restricted in the central parts of Conservation Areas, or may be designed to keep open the fabric of parts of a village (for example orchards, paddocks, or gaps in the main street) in order to retain local character and variety. The third policy category implies that large-scale expansion of villages in Green Belt areas is not acceptable, by using the term 'limited expansion'. It would therefore appear to be a mis-use of the policy to have insets where no expansion is possible.

3.4   Insets have been used to consolidate areas of very low density or unconventional housing, some of which have poor infrastructure such as roads and drainage. In Macclesfield the Pickmere area, à location for holiday residences and chalets, is one example. The village was inset and the boundary drawn back to allow low density high quality development. In Broxbourne an area of 42 acres at St James Village is proposed for exclusion from the Green Belt. The area is one of fragmented ownerships with some derelict land, and a number of eyesores. Development of housing at four dwellings per acre is proposed to create a balance between the clearance of eyesores and derelict land, and the loss of an open rural feel in the area. In the case of the Grange Estate near Verwood, East Dorset, proposals to create an inset to help secure infrastructure improvements in conjunction with new development were not accepted.

3.5   There is considerable scope to influence the overall tightness of a Green Belt by such decisions on the number and form of insets. Green Belts in the northern half of England are looser than those in the south. In Dacorum (Hertfordshire) for example, a relatively buoyant area adjacent to the M25 with a significant concentration of high technology employment, only three rural settlements, all over 4,000 in population, are inset (Figure 3.1). All of the remaining rural development is washed over. In Chester District there are ten village insets in the Green Belt. The approved criteria for qualification as an inset village are:

- where infilling or rounding off is to be allowed and the village is suitable for accommodating small groups of houses, or

- where there are existing planning permissions for considerable amounts of new development;

- where there is spare capacity in public utilities that could be used economically; and

- where the village already possesses shops and a school.[3]

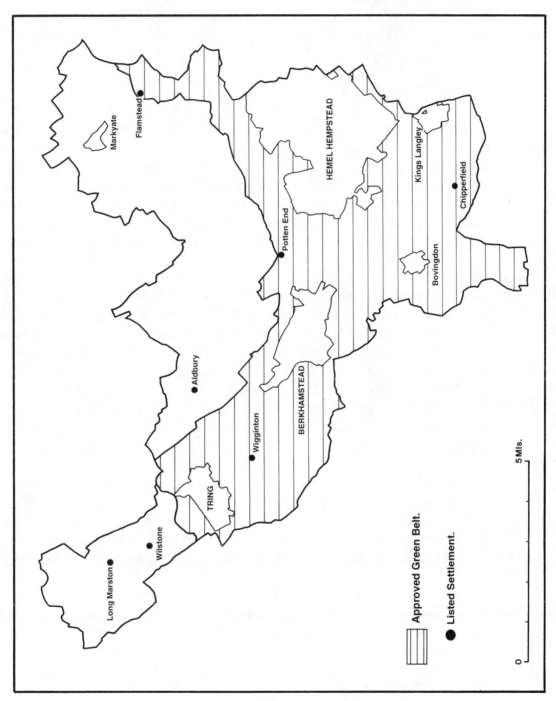

Figure 3.1: Dacorum District.

Markyate
Flamstead
HEMEL HEMPSTEAD
Kings Langley
Chipperfield
Bovingdon
Potten End
Aldbury
BERKHAMSTEAD
Wigginton
TRING
Wilstone
Long Marston

Approved Green Belt.

● Listed Settlement.

0

5 Mls.

In Leeds District the Wetherby and Garforth Local Plans contain over 25 Green Belt insets, and only five washed over villages. Relatively small groups of housing, with populations of less than 100, are inset (Figure 3.2).

3.6   Tightening the Green Belt can involve reducing the size and number of insets. In Enfield the draft UDP proposes the removal of two insets approved in the 1983 Borough Plan to reduce the level of infill. In the preparatory work for the Chester Rural Areas Local Plan it was decided that the former strategy of 'key villages' was less relevant for the countryside near the City. Accordingly more tightly-defined insets and infill boundaries in washed over settlements were approved in the 1983 Plan.

3.7   Where the requirement is for increased development then new insets can be created in very special circumstances. South of Macclesfield the requirement in the recently approved Structure Plan has led to proposals to create four new insets in the approved Cheshire Green Belt (see Figure 3.3). In Broxbourne, Hertfordshire, the need to release land in the derelict glasshouse area of West Cheshunt was established at Structure Plan level. This has led to proposals for three new insets for housing, and policies to secure developer contributions to improve the environment of the remainder of the derelict glasshouse area (Figure 3.4). In a number of case study areas the boundaries of insets have been drawn to stop any physical spread of the village concerned. The resulting infill policy sees residential applications treated similarly in inset and washed over settlements. One of the reasons that local authorities prefer to create insets is their intention to allow the retention of employment sites in villages. If located in washed over settlements they would be regarded as inappropriate development within the Green Belt. The proposition that existing industry should be allowed to expand in inset villages, subject to normal environmental safeguards, was supported by the Department in approving the 1985 Structure Plan alteration for Cheshire. Evidence from our interviews suggests the distinction between the following two situations is most important:

•   *the inset*; an area not subject to Green Belt presumptions, where small-scale growth is intended for housing and employment, and

•   *the washed over small village, hamlet or other low density development*; where infill will only be allowed within areas defined as 'infill boundaries'.

Current Guidance on Land Uses in the Green Belt

3.8   Current guidance, in PPG 2, makes clear that in contrast to other areas Green Belt carries a presumption against inappropriate development within it.[4] *Appropriate* uses, as defined in PPG 2, are the construction of new buildings or changes of use for:

•   agriculture and forestry;

•   outdoor sport;

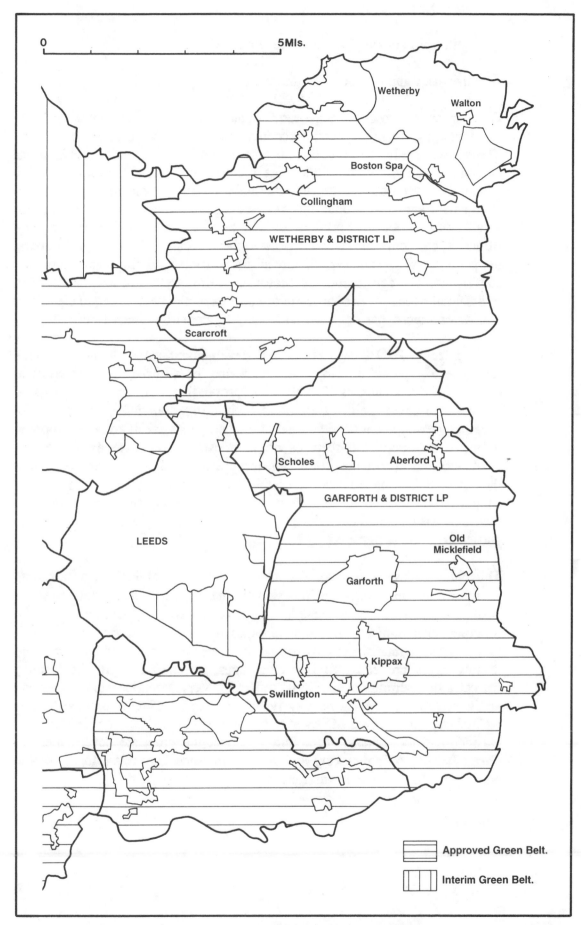

Figure 3.2: Green Belt East of Leeds.

- cemeteries;

- institutions standing in extensive grounds; and

- other uses appropriate to a rural area.

Outdoor sport provision may require the construction of small ancillary buildings, unobtrusive spectator accommodation or other essential facilities.[5] The re-use of redundant buildings is also regarded as acceptable; applications should not be refused unless there are specific and convincing reasons which cannot be overcome by attaching conditions to the planning permission. (Redundant agricultural buildings, it is stated, can provide accommodation for small firms or tourist activities, or can be used as individual residences). Minerals can only be worked where they occur. Accordingly mineral extraction may be allowed in Green Belts subject to high environmental standards.[6] The construction of Motorways, primary roads, and the location of essential public service infrastructure, for example that relating to electricity and water supply, has not been noticeably hindered by Green Belt policy.

3.9 The advice in PPG 2 also states that development plans should not make reference to types of development which may be allowed in Green Belts in exceptional circumstances. Development proposals should not harm the visual amenities of Green Belts by reason of their siting, materials or design.[7] If a proposed development is within one of the categories specified as appropriate in the Green Belt, and there is no demonstrable harm to an interest of acknowledged importance other than the protection of the Green Belt itself, then PPG 2 is a material consideration indicating that planning permission should be granted. If the proposed development is for an inappropriate use then permission should not be given except in very special circumstances particular to the application.

3.10 Thus where a use is seen as inappropriate by virtue of PPG 2, a balancing exercise must be undertaken in which the harm to the Green Belt, together with any other disadvantages, is weighed against the advantages of the proposed development. If the advantages outweigh the disadvantages then 'very special circumstances' will have been demonstrated. If the harm and disadvantages are equal to the advantages, or exceed them, then policy indicates that permission should be refused.[8] Very special circumstances can apply, *inter alia*, where a Motorway Service Area (MSA) is proposed. The lack of any other signed MSAs may be a material consideration justifying an exception to the general presumption against inappropriate development in Green Belts.[9] A further very special circumstance may relate to affordable housing for local needs in rural areas where it is suggested:

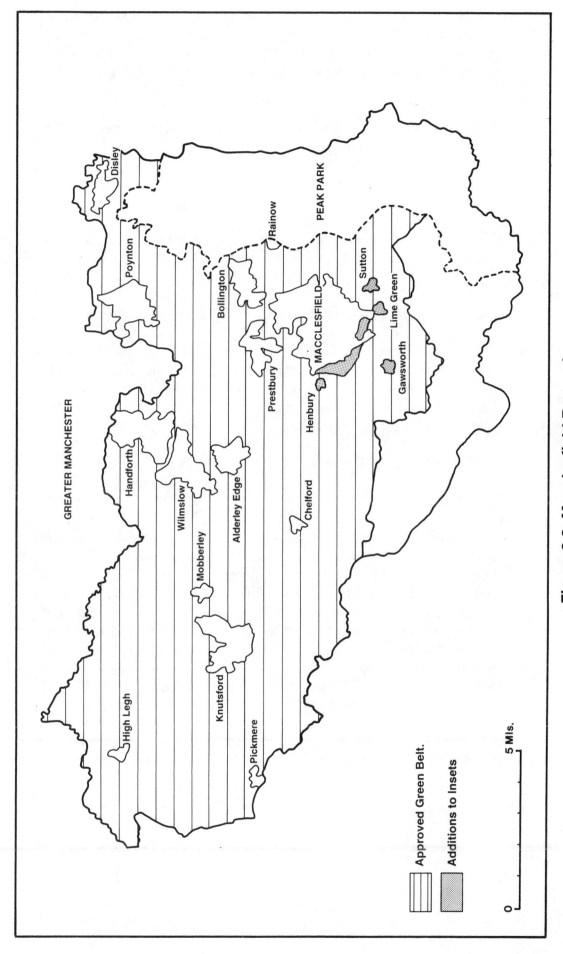

GREATER MANCHESTER

Disley

Poynton

Rainow

PEAK PARK

Bollington

Sutton

Lime Green

MACCLESFIELD

Prestbury

Henbury

Gawsworth

Handforth

Wilmslow

Chelford

Mobberley

Alderley Edge

High Legh

Knutsford

Pickmere

Approved Green Belt.

Additions to Insets

5 Mls.

0

Figure 3.3: Macclesfield Borough.

'... special circumstances may arise in some of the more extensive areas of Green Belt away from the urban fringe, particularly in areas where there are many small settlements and it may not be practicable or appropriate to define Green Belt boundaries around each one. Low cost housing development may:

- fall within the policies which allow very limited development within existing settlements, or

- exceptionally allow the release of other sites within settlements which would not normally be considered for development'.[10]

Very special circumstances may also exist in the case of redundant hospital sites where a change of use or replacement by new buildings is being considered.[11]

3.11   There has been a gradual accretion of guidance as Governments have responded to different pressures, whether for farm diversification, developments for tourism or sport, or housing for local needs. The guidance on redundant hospital sites, first introduced in 1987, and already revised, is detailed. Some of our local authority respondents were seeking advice with similar detail for other, more ubiquitous, uses such as employment sites, or redundant non-agricultural buildings in Green Belts.

Development Control Evidence

3.12   The detailed case studies relate to four districts; Chester and Macclesfield (Cheshire), and South Staffordshire and Wakefield (South Yorkshire). A broader scan, emphasising the area of land in major applications made, as well as the uses applied for, relates to Dacorum, Broxbourne and East Hertfordshire Districts (Hertfordshire). Green Belt development control involves dealing with large numbers of proposals for small-scale change. The main development applied for in our detailed case study areas, 65 per cent of the total, is residential change. This is mostly alterations and extensions to existing dwellings (see Table 3.1). As the majority of the small-scale residentially-related proposals are approved, the justification for the overall approval rate of around 75 per cent in Green Belts is clear (see Table 2.2). Employment-related uses, including industry and office, retail, warehousing and storage, total 13 per cent of applications. Applications relating to agriculture comprise less than seven per cent of the total. The 'other' category includes applications relating to education and community buildings.

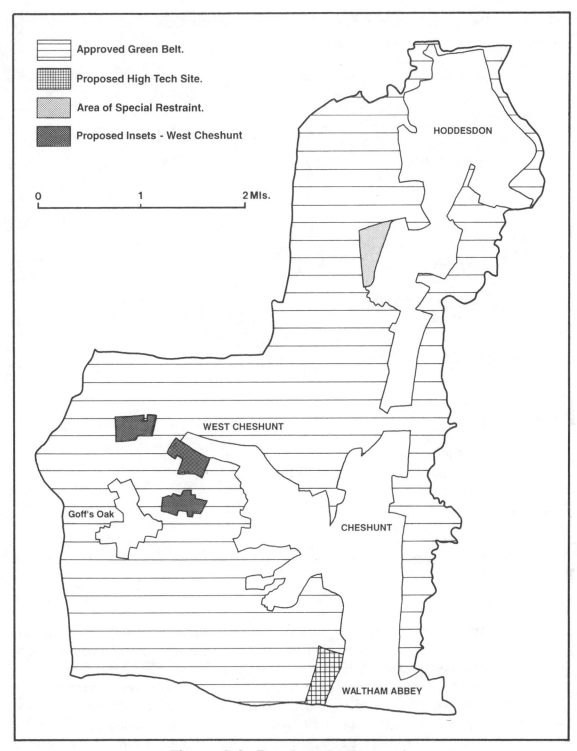

Figure 3.4: Broxbourne Borough.

Legend:

- Approved Green Belt.
- Proposed High Tech Site.
- Area of Special Restraint.
- Proposed Insets - West Cheshunt

Scale: 0 — 1 — 2 Mls.

Map labels: HODDESDON, WEST CHESHUNT, CHESHUNT, Goff's Oak, WALTHAM ABBEY

Table 3.1: Uses Applied for in Green Belt Case Study Areas 1988-92: Percentages

use applied for	Chester	Maccles-field	South Staffs*	Wakefield	Total
housing related	65.8	69.4	54.2	60.9	65.2
industry/office	2.0	5.1	5.8	3.8	4.5
retail	2.4	4.8	4.5	5.7	4.6
leisure	1.9	2.6	8.4	5.2	3.7
agriculture	8.0	5.9	9.7	6.3	6.8
warehousing/storage transport	3.0	4.5	4.7 ·	3.1	4.0
education/community/ other	16.9	7.7	12.8	14.9	11.2
applications per year	227	768	382	274	1651
ha of approved Green Belt per application per year	63.2	51.3	85.6	85.1	

* most recent two years only; the hectares per application figure for a four-year period is likely to be around 75.

3.13 Approval rates by policy area proved remarkably consistent across the four case study areas. Green Belt approval rates are around 10-15 per cent lower than those within urban areas and inset boundaries. The largest difference, 16 per cent, was found in South Staffordshire with the lowest, under seven per cent, in Chester District. The differences between approval rates in the Green Belt and the open countryside beyond were not as pronounced, although in each case the Green Belt approval rate was slightly lower. This reflects the views of a number of planners at interview that there was now little difference, except for the treatment of employment uses and redundant buildings, between the two policy areas (see Table 3.2).

Table 3.2: Application Approval Rates by Policy Area: Percentages

policy area	Chester	Macclesfield	South Staffs	Wakefield
green belt	82.5	70.9	73.8	77.1
open countryside	84.0	75.6	82.5	n.a
urban and insets	89.1	81.8	91.1	91.5

3.14   Table 3.3 represents the rate of approval by use applied for. Care must be exercised in its interpretation. The applications unlikely to succeed in the Green Belt are normally 'weeded out' through negotiation. Many of those that remain may be small in scale. In addition the absolute number of schemes approved may be low. For example Table 3.3 states that 88.2 per cent of leisure applications in the Chester Green Belt were approved over the four-year study period. This comprises some 15 applications, a rate of only four per year in an area of over 14,000 hectares. Despite these caveats, it is clear Macclesfield operate a tougher regime than Chester, with South Staffordshire and Wakefield in the middle of the range. Applications relating to agriculture, and industry/offices tend to have higher success rates than those for storage and transport, or retail uses.

Table 3.3: Approvals in Green Belts by Land Use: Percentages

land use	Chester	Macclesfield	South Staffs	Wakefield
housing related	78.4(122)	67.3(359)	69.6(145)	74.3(120)
industry/offices	76.4 (3)	75.7 (30)	81.8 (18)	82.9 (6)
retail	74.2 (6)	65.8 (26)	58.8 (10)	87.1 (13)
leisure	88.2 (4)	68.2 (15)	76.6 (25)	91.1 (13)
agriculture	86.3 (16)	84.0 (38)	89.2 (33)	73.9 (13)
w'housing/storage/ transport	77.7 (5)	66.6 (25)	69.4 (12)	77.7 (6)
other/education community	88.2 (34)	76.6 (45)	77.3 (37)	91.3 (29)
ha of approved Green Belt per approval per year	75.4	73.2	116.8	116.6
total	82.5	70.9	73.8	77.1

Note: The *average number of approvals per year* are given within the brackets.

3.15   Appeals, as for applications generally, were dominated by residentially - related schemes. Some 46 per cent of the 1,201 appeals studied related to these uses (Table 3.4). Around 10 per cent of the appeals involved the re-use of redundant buildings for residential or commercial uses. The proportion of appeals relating to leisure, sport, recreation and equestrian activities totalled five per cent. The proposals most frequently upheld at appeal related to the re-use of redundant buildings for commercial uses, office use, and the use of land by gypsies and travellers. Appendix H has a full commentary on this Table.

Table 3.4: Proportion of Appeals Upheld by Main Use Applied For

use	number	per cent of total	per cent upheld
residential - extensions	245	20.4	34.3
residential - single units	229	19.1	7.9
residential - 2 to 9 units	65	5.4	9.2
residential - 10+ units	19	1.6	5.3
agricultural occupancy	47	3.9	19.1
redundant buildings to residential	88	7.3	28.4
caravans, mobile homes	81	6.7	17.3
gypsies, travellers	29	2.4	44.8
nursing homes	27	2.3	29.6
hotels, pubs, conference	26	2.2	30.7
office	40	3.3	45.0
industrial	22	1.8	36.4
redundant buildings to commercial	37	3.1	45.9
retail	10	0.8	20.0
garden centres, nurseries	22	1.8	22.7
leisure, sport and recreation	29	2.4	34.5
equestrian, animal husbandry	31	2.6	35.5
agriculture-related (other)	25	2.2	36.0
transport, vehicles	61	5.1	6.6
storage	33	2.7	15.2
minerals, waste disposal	35	2.9	14.3
total	1201	100.0	22.6

Source: Green Belt Project Survey

Policies in Structure Plans

3.16   In the case study areas, policy statements on what constitute acceptable uses in the Green Belt have gradually been brought in line with PPG 2. The approved 1980 Dorset Structure Plan refers to holiday chalets, holiday caravans and tents as acceptable forms of non-intensive outdoor recreation, but this was removed in the 1990 plan. In Oxfordshire institutions in extensive grounds are not listed among appropriate uses in the Green Belt, thus making the policy slightly tougher than that operating nationally. A proposal in the 1992

Hertfordshire Structure Plan to allow waste transfer and recycling plants, and certain developments to enhance Community Forest objectives in Green Belt, was also rejected.[12] In a number of plans, notably those of Cheshire and Oxfordshire, the term 'outdoor recreation' is used as well as outdoor sport. Policy 70A of the approved Staffordshire Structure Plan (1991) refers to '... outdoor sport and recreation facilities where particular regard will be had to the scale of the related built development in order to retain the character of the Green Belt'.[13] Suggestions to list waste disposal sites and mineral extraction as normally acceptable were not agreed by the West Midlands Regional Office. This is related to the view that elaboration over and above the uses listed in PPG 2 should be resisted.

Policies in Local Plans

3.17   Two analyses were carried out of policies in approved, deposited and draft local plans. One referred to local plans in the case study areas, and the other to a sample of plans covering the remainder of Green Belts in England. The policies developed, and in use, reflect the day-to-day problems of development control experienced by local authorities. Many have evolved through time to ensure control over the retention of the open rural appearance of Green Belts, and the protection of amenity. The 1955 and 1957 guidance on Green Belts was developed at a time when the need to save every acre of agricultural land was paramount, and it was expected farming would, by itself produce a varied and attractive lowland landscape. Development control in Green Belts would stop development except that legitimately related to agriculture, defined in terms of husbandry of the land. The 1962 Booklet on Green Belts (re-issued in 1988) states the presumption against *any new building*, and the twin aims of keeping the *open character of the land*, and the *rural character* of such areas, in the following way:

> '... The object of including land in a Green Belt is to keep it permanently open. Consequently there is a clear presumption against any new building and against new employment which might create a demand for more building'.

> '... development which does not interfere with the open character of the land may be permissable'.

> '... it is the intention that a Green Belt shall have a rural character'.

It goes on to suggest the main difference between Green Belt and the rural areas beyond is that in the latter it may be necessary at some time to allocate areas for building which might be quite extensive.[14]

3.18   The criterion of relationship to agriculture is quite strict, using the definition in Section 336(1) of the Town and Country Planning Act 1990. This normally excludes business activities such as large commercial livery stables, contracting or landscape gardening activities which may form part of a modern diversified farm enterprise.[15] When proposals for such uses occur criteria of need are weighed against any damage likely to be done to the open rural appearance of the area. Thus in general terms the re-use of existing buildings is preferred, as is the creation of only small-scale extensions or new buildings, if they can be justified at all.

3.19 Policies in local plans also seek the retention and improvement of attractive landscapes. There are two principles here. First, the idea that *any* development permitted should be sited so as to blend into the landform and landscape as naturally as possible; and second, that new development should address the question of improving amenity and the visual appearance of the Green Belt by tree planting, shelter belts and the clearance of local eyesores. Thus we can see the need locally for a range of site-specific judgements to be made on the relationship between buildings and the countryside. The management of this small-scale change, a form of local environmental management, is vital to local public support for planning. As a result local authorities have interpreted the guidance in more detail for their own circumstances, and have put additional policies into plans. The 23 plans listed in Appendix D have, on average, nine policies each relating to detailed development matters covering Green Belts. A number also have landscape, amenity or siting policies which apply to all forms of development. Where newly-deposited district plans are compared with older approved local plans for the same area it is clear the number of such policies has grown over the last ten years. This is partly in response to the extra detail in guidance issued by the Department on matters such as the countryside, housing for local needs, and recreation and sport.

3.20 The policies most often included in local plans relate to:

- house extensions and alterations;

- replacement dwellings;

- agricultural workers' dwellings;

- redundant buildings;

- institutions standing in extensive grounds;

- employment activities;

- recreation and sport;

- tourist uses and caravans;

- garden centres;

- equestrian development; and

- agricultural buildings.

These reflect the development control case load illustrated in Tables 3.1 - 3.5. The policies elaborate the range of material considerations which will apply locally in making decisions. They sometimes attempt to define the limits of development which may be acceptable, for example, for a use such as outdoor sport, so that it does not impinge on the open rural character of the area. In some instances policies state a basic view about appropriateness, for example, in the case of garden centres. Some give the circumstances in which a different position might be taken locally to that implied in guidance. Appendix D gives examples of policies in use, and proposed, across the country.

Housing-Related Policies

3.21 These relate to the alteration, extension, and replacement of dwellings. Policies to control the size of extensions, and their character, were found in virtually all of the local plans studied. Most often policies limit extensions to 50 per cent, or sometimes 30 per cent, of the original size of buildings. Applications for frequent additions are particularly frowned upon. The two justifications for this policy are, to resist the creation of large houses of suburban appearance, out of character with the rural setting of the Green Belt, and to avoid reducing the supply of smaller houses in rural areas. One potential loophole, in the absence of greater definition, is the 'replacement' of dwellings. Most plans contain policies with a presumption against replacement, or they limit replacement to statutorily unfit dwellings, or those which have been destroyed. Policies usually state that replacements must be of similar size to the original dwelling.

3.22 The appeals relating to extensions upheld, one third of the total, were in circumstances where:

- the character and use of the existing building was respected;

- the appearance of the building was improved; and

- any increased bulk resulting was seen as not significantly eroding the openness of the Green Belt.

The schemes refused included extensions regarded as unduly prominent or bulky, or out of character with the existing dwelling. The cumulative effect of a variety of extensions of the same building over time was a reason for refusal. Personal circumstances were not accepted as a reason for approval.

3.23 The analysis of appeals found that isolated single dwellings in the countryside were invariably refused. Limited amounts of infilling, and a very few replacement dwellings, were found to be permissible. Infilling was typically approved in 'washed over' villages, with a high proportion occurring on existing residential plots. Replacement dwellings were only acceptable, other factors being equal, where the new dwelling would not constitute a radical increase in bulk over and above the former structure. In a number of appeals there was confusion and debate over what constitutes a 'settlement' for the purposes of infill policy.

Affordable Housing for Local Needs

3.24   This provision, introduced in early 1992 in PPG 3, specifies the very special circumstances in which the release of Green Belt sites may be appropriate.[16] The majority of Authorities interviewed saw the proposals as either irrelevant to their needs or causing extra problems for the effective implementation of Green Belt policy. The first argument was that local needs of the type specified did not exist within relatively prosperous Green Belt areas which, although away from the urban fringe, may nevertheless be within daily commuting distance of cities. Second, it was argued that such needs could be satisfied by negotiation with the developers of sites comprising infill and rounding-off within inset villages. Third, the need to decide what comprise 'more extensive areas of Green Belt away from the urban fringe' has already led to considerable debate. Finally, the possibility of allowing the release, exceptionally, of sites within settlements provides an opportunity for a number of marginal or over-intensive development proposals within villages to come forward with a prospect of success. Because affordable housing sites are regarded as exceptions (and the Department's Green Belt policy does not allow the specification of what constitute exceptional circumstances in plans) it is not possible for local authorities to 'allocate' such land in plans, so as to best protect local environments. As this policy has only recently been introduced, systematic evaluation of its effectiveness has not been possible.

Agricultural Workers' Dwellings

3.25   The policies relating to agricultural workers' dwellings have recently been elaborated in PPG 7, succeeding those in Circular 24/73.[17] To secure permission the applicant must demonstrate the dwelling meets a genuine operational need, and that it is essential for the proper functioning of the enterprise for the worker to be readily available at most times. Where this *functional* test is not conclusive a *financial* viability test may be applied to assess the genuineness of the erstwhile farmers' stated intentions. Many authorities also prefer to tie a dwelling approval to a particular holding through a Section 106 planning obligation.[18] Agricultural occupancy conditions are a standard feature of the controls applied. Policies relating to applications for the removal of occupancy conditions are stringently worded. Some state that the holding must no longer be in existence, in addition to the normal criterion of proof that there is no agricultural demand for the dwelling within the locality.

3.26   The appeal evidence covered 47 agricultural occupancy cases, some nine of which (19 per cent) were upheld. The dismissals occurred when the functional and financial tests could not be satisfied, and when environmental harm might be caused. Inspectors frequently distinguished between the needs of the farming enterprise, rather than the needs of the owner, or of relatives of the owner. Where viability is not established a temporary permission for a caravan may be allowed to give time for viability to be demonstrated. Security needs do not justify the erection of a dwelling, especially if other methods such as alarms can be used. Where removal of an agricultural condition is at issue proof of lack of need in the area must be given by showing the property has been marketed in the agricultural press over a considerable period of time.

Table 3.5 Agricultural Occupancy in the Green Belt: Appeal Outcomes

proposal	number upheld	number dismissed
dwelling for agricultural use	4	19
dwelling for horticultural use	2	6
dwelling for equestrian use	0	2
re-use of existing building for agriculture	0	7
removal of occupancy condition	3	4
total	9	38

Source: Green Belt Project Survey

3.27   A number of our case study authorities saw the advice on agricultural workers' dwellings in PPG 7 as too complex as well as too lenient. It was suggested that with depressed agricultural land prices the purchase of a relatively large area of land of, say 5-20 acres, was now more accessible to greater numbers of people. Dwelling permission was then sought. Where this was not forthcoming permission for the stationing of a temporary caravan was now more likely to be secured. Some saw the temporary caravan solution where viability had yet to be demonstrated as the 'thin end of the wedge', invariably leading to a new permanent dwelling.[19] This process, they felt, encouraged undesirable land ownership fragmentation. The Department has commissioned research into the effectiveness of the guidance on agricultural dwellings in PPG 7.

The Re-Use of Redundant Buildings

3.28   As interpreted by the Courts (in the 1990 *Pehrsson* case), national guidance is that the re-use of redundant buildings in Green Belts should not be refused unless there are specific and convincing planning reasons.[20] Very special circumstances are needed to justify the re-use of buildings which are *not*

45

redundant for purposes other than those referred to in paragraph 13 of PPG 2. In the countryside outside Green Belts redundancy is no longer normally an issue however, following PPG 7. The conversions of redundant buildings in Green Belts is subject to the general safeguards in PPG 7. The buildings should not be so derelict as to require reconstruction. Their form, bulk and general design should be in keeping with their surroundings. Proposals may be more acceptable if they reflect local building styles and materials. Conditions may be imposed to improve the external appearance of buildings in connection with structural changes. A cautious approach to residential conversions is advised.[21]

3.29   The re-use of redundant buildings caused more comment than any other issue we looked at. There is considerable confusion. Before the *Pehrsson* judgement, it was widely thought that policy in PPG 2 favouring the re-use of redundant buildings in Green Belts applied only to 'substantial and attractive agricultural buildings'.[22] Most local plans currently follow this interpretation. They require applicants to demonstrate that the buildings are substantial and attractive, which may exclude modern 'industrialised' farm buildings. They seek sympathetic conversion which retains as much as possible of the agricultural character of the buildings. Also they do not promote the conversion of redundant buildings generally, restricting policy only to those formerly in agricultural use.

3.30   The new policies of re-use have only recently been introduced in PPG 7. Despite the statement in paragraph 3.12 of PPG 7 that Green Belt policies prevail some local planners regard the most recent advice as most important. It is possible for farmers to erect agricultural buildings up to 465 sq m in the countryside under permitted development rights. Until recently the siting and appearance of such buildings was not generally controlled.

3.31   Three main issues bearing on future policy for the re-use of buildings in the Green Belt were raised during our study. They were appearance, redundancy and economic diversification.

3.32   A majority of the case study authorities considered that the suitability and character of the building and its site for re-use was more important than whether it was redundant (subject to stronger safeguards on permitted development rights (PDRs) - see paragraph 3.33). Many thought that only traditional buildings contributing to the character of the rural area should be converted, and only for small-scale activities. They were particularly concerned to avoid the conversion of larger groups of farm buildings, including modern barns, cattle storage units and intensive poultry rearing complexes, into 'mini-industrial estates'. They criticised as weak the advice in PPG 7 that building conversions *may be more acceptable* if they respect local building styles and materials. Agricultural interests on the other hand considered that the PPG 7 safeguards were adequate.

3.33   Some of our case study authorities wished to retain the redundancy criterion in the Green Belt to cut down the amount of re-use, particularly where small farm units led to the possibility of a dense pattern of building conversion within the landscape. They thought that new buildings would otherwise be erected in place of converted buildings which were *not* redundant. In particular farmers could use PDRs to erect a succession of new agricultural buildings for conversion to other uses. A number of authorities wished not only to retain the redundancy criterion for Green Belts but also to bring it back for the wider countryside. Farmers and landowners considered that PPG 2 should contain positive statements on the need to encourage diversification in Green Belts as much as in the open countryside generally. They should not be discriminated against because they happened to be situated in a Green Belt. Policy on the re-use of buildings should be the same in Green Belts as in the wider countryside.

3.34   Four options have emerged from our interviews:

- first, to revert to the policy of limiting re-use only to redundant agricultural buildings that are substantial and attractive;

- second, to retain the existing policy of a redundancy test combined with PPG 7 safeguards (para 3.20 above);

- third, to drop the redundancy test but limit conversions to small-scale buildings of traditional construction; and

- fourth, to remove the redundancy test in Green Belt, bringing policy into line with that which now applied in the countryside outside, but pay special attention to new buildings constructed under permitted development rights.

3.35   We see no justification for adopting the first option. There is no rational basis for treating buildings differently according to whether their last use was, or was not, agricultural. PPG 7 safeguards exclude buildings which are not substantial, in the sense of being derelict. Green Belts are not designated because of their attractiveness, and the appearance of buildings should not be considered differently there from in other areas of countryside.

3.36   We do not consider that a continued redundancy test (the first and second options in para 3.34) is merited. It is important to promote a healthy and diverse economy in Green Belt areas. Making diversification by farmers more difficult could damage the long-term future of land in the Green Belt.

3.37   There was widespread local authority support for the third option. Nevertheless, as with the first option, we do not see any justification for treating Green Belts differently to the wider countryside. Moreover, the logic of this position is that all redundant buildings which are not considered small in scale or of traditional construction would be left to decay. We believe however that, in view of the substantial concern expressed to us, the

Department should consider commissioning research on the current operation of policy on the re-use of buildings, both in Green Belts and in the wider countryside.

3.38   We consider that policy on the re-use of buildings in Green Belts should be brought into line with that in the wider countryside, but that special attention should be paid to new agricultural buildings constructed under permitted development rights (the fourth option). PPG 7 advises that, where there are sound planning reasons for wishing to control the replacement of old farm buildings by new ones, a local authority may consider withdrawing PDRs for new farm buildings when giving permission for the use of agricultural buildings for non-agricultural purposes. In view of the fundamental purpose of keeping Green Belts permanently open, and the particularly strong development pressures to which they are subject, we think that such a need may well arise in *most cases* when non-redundant farm buildings in Green Belts are converted to other uses.

Institutions Standing in Extensive Grounds

3.39   Appropriate categories of development in the Green Belt are defined on the basis that they will not interfere with the open character of the land.[23] Institutions standing in extensive grounds, either existing or new, were included in paragraph 13 of PPG 2 on the basis that they would not harm the overall impression of openness that is essential to the Green Belt.[24] Although the 1962 Booklet on Green Belts refers to '... hospitals and similar institutions standing in extensive grounds' there is no further definition of an institution, or what might constitute extensive grounds, in published guidance.[25] Those who devised the original prescription saw the institutions category as recognising a *pre-existing* land use in the countryside. Sanatoria and similar hospital buildings, often Victorian in origin, were seen as necessarily located in the countryside to avoid the spread of infectious diseases. The extensive grounds were also functionally related, being farmed to provide food for patients.

3.40   This category has come under various pressures through time:

- economic pressures on the owners of large country houses in Green Belts have led to applications for change of use to schools, nursing homes, and office and research use;

- the sale of surplus DHSS property has included many redundant hospitals and sanatoria in Green Belts. There has been a need to respond to demands for commercial and residential re-use of the redundant buildings;

- trends towards the privatisation of medical care have led to applications for new private hospitals and nursing homes on Green Belt sites of various sizes; and

48

- a number of highly contested applications have been made for new religious buildings (meeting houses and churches) on Green Belt sites. These have created confusion over interpretation of the policy. Auld, J. in a recent judgement on *Barnet Meeting Room Trust v The Secretary of State* (October 1992) suggested there was a need for the Secretary of State to give some precise guidance on how he intends to interpret the concept.[26]

3.41 Most local authorities interviewed had some criticism of the category. In summary the views were as follows:

- the category should be removed because it is outdated; and the concept has little meaning;

- allowing *new institutions* is illogical in the Green Belt, as many comprise major employment uses, with accompanying journey-to-work movements, and comprise large buildings having an impact on local amenities. In many of their impacts, institutions differ little from B1 office uses;

- allowing *new institutions* conflicts with the general idea in the 1962 Booklet that the Green Belt concept implies there is a presumption against any new building and new employment which might create a demand for more building;[27]

- there are difficulties in defining what constitutes an institution; in the absence of guidance inspectors at appeal make their own judgement based on the evidence of the particular case. The Oxford Dictionary gives a church, school, hospital, asylum, reformatory, mission or museum as examples of institutions. A recent decision of the Secretary of State approved a National Museum of Food and Farming in the West Midlands Green Belt. It is however unclear how far an institution must be for a public as opposed to a private object.

3.42 Local authorities have tended to take a firm view on institutions. In Oxfordshire the approved Structure Plan does not include them as an appropriate use.[28] In Hertfordshire institutional uses are restricted to the re-use of existing large country houses.[29] This appears common throughout the London Green Belt. In South Staffordshire institutional uses must show that a countryside location is essential, priority being given to the re-use of existing buildings, rather than new buildings.[30] In Leeds policy refers to institutions in *substantial* grounds. Proposals are required to demonstrate that the use must be in an open rather than a built-up area, that the substantial grounds are functionally-related, and that the grounds not the buildings are the dominant landscape feature.[31]

3.43 The appeals scan showed that issues of what constitute extensive grounds have caused most confusion and debate. A number of prominent cases have comprised new nursing homes in sites of one to ten hectares. Our analysis of appeals has shown no cases where inspectors accepted less than two hectares as comprising extensive grounds. Prominent cases nationally have related to church meeting houses in Watford, Northavon and Barnet. In the latter case the High Court has rejected two Secretary of State determinations. The following points of policy have emerged from the recent lengthy appeal case law:

- there is no need for the applicant to demonstrate a functional link between the institutional use and the use of the extensive grounds;

- a site of 3.2 acres (1.2 ha) does not comprise extensive grounds in terms of PPG 2 (the Watford decision);[32] and

- extensive grounds must be given a restrictive interpretation if an institutional use is not to threaten the overall impression of openness essential to Green Belt policy. An example of such an interpretation could be an educational institution standing in a large parkland setting with the buildings forming a small and unobtrusive part of the site.[33]

3.44   Allowing major new buildings under the guise of institutions in extensive grounds, can be akin to allowing new B1 uses in the Green Belt. Those who devised Green Belts saw the institutions category as recognising a pre-existing use in the countryside. The effectiveness of Green Belt policy is being harmed by extended debate over the concept of extensive grounds. A number of approvals have been given for institutions in relatively small grounds. It is doubtful whether such approvals are effective in retaining the open appearance of the Green Belt. It would be perverse to suggest that the founders of Green Belt intended major effort to be devoted to deciding whether new religious buildings are appropriate if sited in land parcels of one, two, four or ten hectares. We propose that the category of institutions standing in extensive grounds should be deleted as a category of land use in the guidance. New institutional building could still be justified in very special circumstances where a non-Green Belt site was unavailable. The institutional re-use of existing buildings would fall within comments made in para 3.38.

Redundant Hospital Sites

3.45   Local authorities appeared satisfied with the Guidance on redundant hospital sites in Green Belts in Circular 12/91. One or two felt that, if the redevelopment of hospital sites for a range of uses including housing and employment was allowable in very special circumstances, then other large 'problem' sites or uses should benefit from similar guidelines. Redundant schools, employment sites, power stations, railway sidings and a Home Office Corrective Centre were the main examples referred to. The sequence of steps in Circular 12/91, leading through the main choices for re-use, were seen as a valid way of treating other Green Belt problems. Principles of not allowing the new 'footprint' to have any greater impact on the Green Belt, and the idea of enhancing the amenity value of the site as a whole, were also seen as important.[34]

Existing Employment Uses

3.46   In all Green Belts there are employment sources located in the open countryside. These range from campus offices and converted country houses to isolated industrial estates and oil depots, and include land where uses were established before 1948. In Macclesfield for example there are over 8,000 jobs in the Green Belt in firms such as Ciba Geigy, ICI, Ilford and National Power. They pose a problem for Green Belt policy. As inappropriate uses they would need very special circumstances to justify granting permission when applications for rebuilding or extension are made. In all of our case study areas local authorities are seeking to protect existing sources of employment, and by far the majority also wish to provide for reasonable expansion requirements. In South Staffordshire the approved local plans suggest the expansion requirements of existing firms will be allowed if it is unrealistic to expect them to re-locate outside the Green Belt.[35]   Draft UDPs for Wigan and Trafford in Greater Manchester contain similar policies. The Department has entered objections to such policies as they do not accord with PPG 2, comprising the specification of exceptional circumstances, contrary to the advice in paragraph 14 which says that plans '...should make no reference to the possibility of allowing other development in exceptional circumstances'.[36] The appeals scan showed that replacing inappropriate existing uses with housing development was not normally considered justifiable (Appendix H, para 7).   Small-scale changes to existing inappropriate uses were often permitted if they caused no additional harm to the open rural appearance of the Green Belt.

3.47   In some districts the re-development of sites in existing industrial or commercial use is the main development opportunity in the plan period. Given the strictures in para 14 of PPG 2 local plans cannot address what are major development issues, in some areas, in a detailed way. It is unrealistic to expect such uses to be extinguished. In practice an increasing number of authorities are accepting the redevelopment and reasonable expansion requirements of large firms located in Green Belts for fear they would re-locate in other local authority areas. Our South and West Yorkshire case study authorities were particularly firm in this regard.

3.48   We recommend that the following measures be considered:

*   a general policy should be included in plans to the effect that any development approved in the Green Belt should preserve or improve the open nature and visual amenities of the area;

- where redevelopment proposals present the opportunity, reductions in the visual impact and off-site traffic related to existing sites (by reducing the bulk of buildings or the area they cover, for example) should be pursued;

- where employment areas and major sites are of national or regional importance consideration should be given to creating an inset; and

- site briefs and Supplementary Planning Guidance should be prepared where such opportunities form a major part of the land expected to be developed in a particular plan area.

Outdoor Sport and Recreation

3.49   Outdoor sport is, in principle, an acceptable Green Belt use. Informal countryside recreation is also, in practice, acceptable. Guidance published in 1991 in PPG 17 elaborated the position in respect of outdoor sport, suggesting:

- the suitable conversion of redundant buildings may be needed to ensure provision;

- the construction of small ancillary buildings, unobtrusive spectator accommodation, or other essential facilities may be required; and

- there may be opportunities for new outdoor sports provision in connection with the redevelopment of redundant hospital sites.[37]

The essential message of PPG 2 is that buildings for outdoor sport are appropriate in the Green Belt; they do not require to be justified in very special circumstances. Planning Policy Guidance Note 17 also makes it clear that such buildings must be *essential* for outdoor sport in order to qualify.[38]

3.50   The appeal scan suggested that 35 per cent of the 29 cases studied were approved. Inspectors judge whether the proposed activity is an outdoor sport or recreation, and is therefore in principle appropriate. If so a range of other issues came into play:

- how far the buildings proposed are ancillary (or necessary) to the successful operation of the sport activity;

- whether the impact on the environment and wildlife is likely to be acceptable; and

- whether traffic, and other matters such as floodlighting, will be intrusive.

The main difficulties arise with defining an appropriate scale of ancillary buildings for such facilities as club houses, pavilions and training space. Buildings which are over-sized, bulky or inappropriately located are normally refused. New outdoor leisure pursuits such as combat games are regarded as appropriate in Green Belt. However, particular attention has been given to sensitive environments such as ancient woodlands. Inspectors may require the preparation of management plans, specified by condition, in conjunction with such approvals.

3.51 A number of local authorities operate local plan policies designed to limit the scale of ancillary buildings, and to ensure that they are located unobtrusively. Buildings for indoor sports and stadia are not seen as acceptable, but the local needs of villages in the Green Belt (for example cricket or football pitches) and sport pitches generally are acceptable. Problems arise where a mix of indoor and outdoor activities are proposed (as in some tennis centres), where additional activities are the main source of revenue (for example restaurants, hotel-style accommodation, or fitness-sauna clubs), or where outdoor activities have elements which are seen as obtrusive (for example floodlighting, or noise and pollution from clay pigeon shooting). It has proved difficult to make policy rules for such a broad range of activities. Each scheme is unique, and the propensity for intensification outwith the planning regulations can be difficult to predict. Hertfordshire County Council have a policy which divides Green Belt into zones where medium intensity leisure activities are acceptable, in contrast to low intensity uses in other areas.[39] Authorities recounted examples of schemes where the original activity, for example a small-scale equestrian facility, had been considered acceptable, but it had proved subsequently difficult to control growth with the addition of a country club, bistro and other activities.

3.52 Because of the size of the structures involved major football stadia are not regarded as acceptable uses in the Green Belt. The guidance in PPG 17 suggests that very special circumstances are only likely to be substantiated where all other practicable options for location have been exhausted, especially those for development in urban areas. This process of alternative site search has recently been demonstrated in the approval, in very special circumstances, of a rugby league ground in the Green Belt near Dewsbury, West Yorkshire.

Golf Courses and Driving Ranges

3.53 Golf courses are in principle acceptable in Green Belts. The current guidance suggests they should be designed to ensure harmony with the surrounding countryside, and to conserve the natural environment. Special care, it is stated, should be taken over applications in Green Belt.[40] The main problems surround attempts by speculative developers to secure permission for hotels, restaurants or fairway housing to create a profitable element for schemes. The results of our development control case studies show the large scale of applications approved for golf courses in Green Belts. The SERPLAN data suggest 1,400 hectares in approvals for one year alone in the London Green Belt (see Table 2.3). Present funding difficulties have resulted in well over half of approvals not being implemented. In some cases schemes have been suspended due to bankruptcy during construction, with resulting adverse impacts on the landscape.

3.54 In the appeals studied Inspectors investigate questions of need, noting the Royal and Ancient Golf Club recommended target of one eighteen hole course per 25,000 population. Favourable consideration was given to 'pay-as-you-play' facilities, which enhance access to the sport. The conservation of the countryside is an interest of acknowledged importance in golf development, and schemes in AONBs and other areas of landscape importance have, on occasion, been refused permission. Club houses may be problematic and are likely to be dismissed if they stray above what is reasonably necessary for the successful operation of the golfing activity.

3.55 Some authorities feel that golf courses are not equally appropriate in all parts of the Green Belt. A number have prepared Supplementary Planning Guidance. The thrust of the policies proposed has been to:

- state a preference for 'natural' golf courses, those that fit into the pre-existing landscape without major engineering alterations, or the creation of a heavily-manicured landscape;

- avoid the location of golf courses on historic parkland;

- avoid the location of golf courses in areas of particularly attractive or fragile landscape; and

- state a preference for locations on the edges of urban areas, to form buffer uses, and to use such development as a way of improving damaged land and landscapes.

Some authorities have policies to control the cumulative impact of a proliferation of golf courses in the same vicinity. Over-concentration may harm the open appearance of the landscape, as well as introducing excessive traffic and activity generally.[41]

3.56 Golf driving ranges present particular problems. They can be intrusive, having an urban appearance with car parking, floodlights, large buildings (one or two storeys) and lengthy opening hours. As a result local authorities are particularly concerned about siting issues, and some seek to limit driving ranges to a few areas. Traffic generation, public safety and impacts on the amenity of nearby residents, are matters of greatest concern to local authorities. Although driving ranges are regarded as a legitimate ancillary activity to a golf course by many operators, local authorities are reluctant to accept new ones in Green Belt locations. The appeal decisions indicated that golf driving ranges were regarded in principle as appropriate in Green Belt, but all of the examples investigated were dismissed for reasons of visual intrusion, problems with floodlights, and the traffic generated.

Tourism Uses

3.57 New hotels and motels are not regarded as appropriate Green Belt uses. These views are reflected in PPG 21, relating to tourism.[42] One or two local authorities considered hotels would be an appropriate use to help maintain or improve country houses or other buildings of architectural interest in the Green Belt. In practice authorities accept tourism as an after-use for redundant farm buildings, following the advice in PPG 2.[43] A number also in practice accept small-scale and sympathetic extensions to existing hotels and public houses in Green Belts. Broxbourne District are seeking to include such a policy in their draft Local Plan. Static caravans are not normally permitted, being treated in the same way as housing, but touring caravan sites may be permitted where sympathetic siting can be assured by applicants.

3.58 The appeals scan showed that the majority of proposals for extensions to existing hotels were refused. Some six schemes in the 8-25 bedroom range were refused, for reasons such as visual encroachment, and inappropriate bulk and form. Three schemes of a similar size were however approved, being judged as having little impact on the visual amenities of the Green Belt. Where new hotels were proposed establishment of an unmet tourism demand in the area was not regarded as sufficient generally to override Green Belt policy. Other decisions suggested hotel development was not a recreational use appropriate to the Green Belt, or a means of assisting urban regeneration in a nearby town. We consider local authorities should take account of tourism development needs before proposing Green Belt boundaries in local plans.

Park and Ride

3.59 The treatment of Park and Ride car parks in Green Belts has varied across the country. In the Oxford Green Belt schemes have been allowed as exceptions to policy without intervention from the Department. In Bath a proposal has been refused, and in Chester a recent case was called-in and approved by the Department. The Draft Local Plan for Cambridge,[44] and the Draft York Green Belt Local Plan,[45] propose policies to allow Park and Ride schemes in their Green Belts in very special circumstances. The Bristol Draft Local Plan allocates Green Belt land for Park and Ride use.[46] In the York Draft Development Strategy it is suggested Park and Ride would be an acceptable Green Belt use because of its role in limiting car penetration to the core of the City.[47] The Oxford Draft Local Plan Review contains a policy to promote a new passenger rail service on existing railway lines through the City, including as part of the scheme a new parkway railway station and car park in the Green Belt.[48]

3.60 The number of Park and Ride proposals in Green Belts, near to non-historic and historic towns, is growing. In order to function effectively Park and Ride schemes need to be near main radial routes, so there is limited room for manoeuvre in their siting. Local authorities argue that if non-Green Belt sites cannot be found then the least obtrusive sites within the Green Belt should be used. Areas of permanent and extensive car parking would normally be regarded as inappropriate in the Green Belt, yet their purpose is to assist policies for a more sustainable pattern of development. Park and Ride schemes could be regarded in three ways:

- as part of the existing road system, including road improvements;

- acceptable as a contribution to patterns of sustainable development; or

- as inappropriate, requiring very special circumstances to be argued including, for example, demonstration of a lack of appropriate sites within the urban area.

The Inspector at the South Cambridgeshire Local Plan LPI favoured the first argument stating '... the locational constraints on ... (Park and Ride) car parks are considerable. In this they are no different from new roads or other transport infrastructure, and, although there may well be good reasons to reject particular sites because of their specific location in the Green Belt, I see no more reason to object in principle to Park and Ride car parks in the Green Belt than to road improvements or new roads there'.[49]

3.61 Park and Ride schemes would seem best treated as part of the road system, but subject to stringent siting criteria in respect of the landscape. Local authorities should be encouraged to identify sites in development plans, seeking alterations to Green Belt boundaries if necessary. Alternatively sites in Green Belt would be treated as very special circumstances, the applicant being required to show that no other suitable site outside the Green Belt was available.

Motorway Service Areas

3.62 For many years the control of motorway service areas (MSAs) has been at the discretion of the Department of Transport who utilised compulsory purchase powers to acquire sites. Service areas were generally spaced 30 miles apart. However the Government has now deregulated provision and is looking to developers to acquire and assemble their own sites and apply for planning permission. Government policy is that the minimum gap between any two MSAs should normally be 15 miles. MSAs should not include facilities which will make the site a destination in its own right, as opposed to one solely used by motorists. In terms of Green Belt policy MSAs are seen as inappropriate development, approval only being granted in very special circumstances. Such circumstances might include a lack of nearby MSA provision.[50] At appeal Inspectors will investigate how far any lack of provision may overcome the general presumption against inappropriate development. In September 1991 the Secretary of State granted permission to the Department of Transport for an MSA on the M40 at Barn Hill, Warwickshire. This was chosen as the best site from among five applications in the vicinity. A proposal for an MSA on the M40 at Booker, High Wycombe was refused on appeal in 1991. Reasons for refusal included the effect on the Green Belt and the Chilterns AONB, and safety risks posed by the existence of Booker Airfield (Wycombe Air Park) nearby.

Utilities

3.63   Green Belts, because of their location close to towns and cities, often provide convenient locations for public utilities. These relate to gas, water, electricity, telecommunications undertakings and waste recycling. As some of the relevant industries are privatised the regulations under which applications are dealt with have altered, now falling under normal planning controls. Such uses have not been listed as appropriate within Green Belts, as they can have significant impacts on the openness of the land. The principle established by approved local plan policies and development control practice is that utilities will only be allowed if there is no acceptable alternative location outside the Green Belt (see Appendix D).

Other Uses Appropriate to a Rural Area

3.64   The category of 'other uses appropriate to a rural area' in paragraph 13 of PPG 2 is now the subject of considerable debate. Intended to cover open rural uses not specified in the original 1955 policy, it has now been overtaken by events. Much time is now spent at appeals attempting to suggest that uses which would *prefer* to be in the countryside near towns, are *appropriately located* there. This is encouraged by the statement in PPG 7 that '... the countryside can accommodate many forms of development without detriment, if the location and design of development is handled with sensitivity'.[51] The objective of including land in a Green Belt is to keep it permanently open. There may be uses not specifically listed in PPG 2, but which would nevertheless retain the open character of the area. Various uses for nature conservation, or in conjunction with heritage interpretation, may be examples. Given the need to retain discretion to allow appropriate uses a phrase referring to 'new buildings ancillary to open uses of land' would better reflect the aims of policy.

Unauthorised Uses

3.65   Local authorities reported a very wide range of these. A number of authorities give priority to enforcement action, when other avenues of negotiation have not succeeded, in visually prominent areas of Green Belts and the urban fringe. The main uses reported to us at interview fall into six groupings:

- *transport-related business activity*, including car repairs and car breaking, scrap metal dealing, vehicle sales, skip hire and haulage;

- *tipping and extraction*, involving the deposit of waste, hardcore, and rubble on land, and the extraction of gravel;

57

- *storage*, including caravans, buses, mobile homes, lorries and containers;

- *car boot sales* and Sunday markets;

- *recreation activity*, including banger racing, karting, combat games and informal motorcycling; and

- *waste transfer* activities including skip depots and waste sorting facilities.

Many of these are 'bad neighbour' activities which are commonly found in urban fringe areas, others are essential urban services, which would be inappropriately located in residential areas.

3.66   The appeals scan showed that 16 per cent of all cases were enforcement proceedings. The major uses where enforcement appeals were significant are shown in Table 3.6. The unauthorised storage of vehicles, and the operation of transport businesses, often have considerable impacts in the landscape. These were the most prominent category. Similarly the unauthorised tipping of builders' rubble and other waste on farmland frequently causes planning authorities to intervene. In numerical terms, however, actions relating to caravans and mobile homes were the largest. The recreation activities referred to in the interviews do not achieve prominence among the appeals listing. Some 156 of the total of 192 enforcement cases were in the categories in Table 3.6.

Wider Policy Issues

3.67   Green Belts cover around 15 per cent of the countryside of England. Approximately two thirds of land in Green Belts is in agricultural use. Development control policies in the Green Belts and the wider countryside are becoming more similar. The 1988 Green Belt Booklet suggests that the major difference between the areas may be the occasional need, in the wider countryside, for some selected development to be approved. PPG 2 implies that extra controls apply in Green Belts stating '... the general policies controlling development in the countryside apply in Green Belts but there is, *in addition*, a general presumption against inappropriate development within them' (emphasis added). The results of our seven detailed development control case studies demonstrate the similarity of the operation of policy in the two areas (see Table 3.2 and Appendix F). Variations in policies for the re-use of buildings were one of the only clear differences noted. Indeed, if the relative proximity to the urban area is taken into account there may be an argument for allowing a greater intensity of use for outdoor sport and recreation in Green Belts than in the countryside generally.

Table 3.6: Major Uses Where Enforcement Appeals are Significant:
Green Belts

use	number		enforcements
	S78	S174*	per cent of total
transport, vehicles	24	37	61
waste disposal, minerals	16	19	35
caravans, mobile homes	40	41	81
storage	17	16	33
gypsies and travellers	19	10	29
office	30	10	40
residential - extensions	222	23	245

* Section 174 relates to enforcement procedures.

Source: Green Belt Project Survey

3.68   The second question arising from this analysis is how far the development control guidance issued centrally should be elaborated in local circumstances? Here local and central views diverge. The Department values consistency of application across the country based on a simple set of acceptable uses as a significant dimension of effectiveness. Local authorities feel the need, in the interests of reducing uncertainty and costly negotiations with applicants, to elaborate the material considerations used in development control. Most of these reflect current practice appearing through appeal decisions, as this Chapter demonstrates. At present the Department is entering objections to all policies which they judge elaborate the guidance unnecessarily. It would seem important, for the effective operation of policy, to allow policies for routine matters such as house alterations and extensions, replacement dwellings, and sport and equestrian facilities to be included in plans in the interests of informing applicants and owners of their position.

3.69   A similar set of arguments apply to the notions of very special circumstances. How far should local plans allude to them? Despite guidance to the contrary in PPG 2, a number of Authorities have attempted to include policies listing very special circumstances in the new district-wide plans. One or two existing approved local plans already contain policies of this kind. While it would be counterproductive to use local plans to list sets of very special circumstances, it would be useful if criteria which are intended to be applied to any potential development in the Green Belt could be given in plans. This has basically been the position in recent Department responses to draft local plans and UDPs.

3.70   A further question surrounds how far policies for land use should vary within
        Green Belts. One approach to this is that as long as the categories are equally
        or more strict than normal Green Belt controls they may be judged acceptable.
        There are two policy zones for holiday caravanning and camping in the South
        East Dorset Green Belt, and other local authorities operate policies (supported
        at appeal) which treat institutions in large grounds, leisure activities and horse
        grazing differently in parts of the same Green Belt. It should be possible for
        Authorities to propose tougher policies than those applying in the Green Belt
        generally where special amenity considerations make this necessary.

Main Findings and Recommendations

3.71   *The use of inset and washed over village policies varies across the country.*

        In some of the northern case study areas insets can exclude clusters of 50
        dwellings from Green Belt controls. In the Home Counties settlements of 500
        dwellings are washed over. Circular 50/57 suggests that washed over villages
        should be divided into those where infill is allowed (their names being listed
        in the development plan) and those where it is not. The tendency is to allow
        infill in all of them. The major distinction emerging locally however is that
        within inset settlements, because they are not in Green Belt, there is leeway
        for new and expanding employment concerns to develop. The currency of
        paragraphs 6 and 7 of Circular 50/57 should be made clear, and reference
        could be made to the differences is treatment of employment uses implied
        where settlements are excluded from the Green Belt [3.2-3.7].

3.72   *Most local authorities have elaborated development control policies in greater
        detail than is specified in PPG 2.*

        The scan of existing and new local plans suggested on average nine Green Belt
        development control policies were included. The development control scan
        showed that three quarters of all applications were housing-related, focusing
        particularly on small-scale extensions [3.12-3.15]. The size and bulk of
        extensions and the criteria for replacement dwellings were also important.
        Other policies most frequently elaborated related to dwelling extensions and
        alterations, replacement dwellings and leisure uses [3.17-3.20].

3.73   *There is confusion over policies on the re-use of buildings in Green Belts,
        linked to the different approaches in PPG 2 and PPG 7.*

        This issue caused more comment than any other. PPG 2 states that *redundant*
        agricultural buildings may be suitable for conversion for small firms, tourist
        activities or individual residences. The Pehrsson ruling removes the need for
        the buildings to be, or have been, agricultural. Guidance in PPG 7 states that
        a wider range of uses are now acceptable in the countryside, and removed the
        redundancy criterion. Thus the main difference between Green Belt and the
        countryside beyond is now the redundancy test. Following consideration of the
        various options we consider policy in Green Belts should be brought into line

with that in the wider countryside. We do not believe that diversification by farmers should be made more difficult in Green Belt. Accordingly we do not consider the continued use of the redundancy test is appropriate. Where agricultural buildings are being re-used for non-agricultural purposes we recommend that permitted development rights for future agricultural buildings on the holding should be removed [3.28-3.38].

3.74 *The category of institutions in extensive grounds was considered to be outdated, inappropriate to Green Belt, and subject to problems of definition.*

Wide-ranging views demonstrated difficulties with the concept. Allowing a new institution in Green Belt was seen as inappropriate as, in its effects, it would be little different to a B1 business use. There were also difficulties in defining an institution, for example how far it should be for a private as opposed to a public purpose. Much difficulty surrounded the issue of what comprise extensive grounds. Costly legal proceedings have not served to clarify the concept. We propose that institutions should no longer be regarded as an appropriate Green Belt use. The institutional re-use of existing buildings would fall within the terms of current re-use policy generally [3.39-3.44].

3.75 *Special attention should be given to existing employment sites in Green Belts.*

In all Green Belts there are employment sites located in the open countryside or washed over settlements. Most local authorities wish to protect such sources of employment, and allow for reasonable expansion requirements. Employment uses are however regarded as inappropriate in the Green Belt. Any approvals must be justified by very special circumstances. Where local authorities have sought to include policies in district-wide local plans these have been rejected by the Department. A local authority wishing to allow for employment changes should consider the following; first, specification of the material considerations to be applied to any development approved in the Green Belt; second, providing an employment inset; or third ensuring that any redevelopment of this sort should improve the visual amenities of the Green Belt, reduce traffic and make a positive contribution to the management of Green Belt land. Similar provisions occur in guidance in Scotland relating to Green Belt [3.46-3.49].

3.76 *The attitude to proposals for Park and Ride car parks should be clarified.*

There was a strong feeling that Green Belt guidance should take a view on the increasing number of Park and Ride proposals coming forward. Park and Ride schemes could be regarded as clearly acceptable in Green Belt, as with road improvements, particularly as they encourage people to transfer from cars to public transport. Alternatively they could be seen as inappropriate due to their impact on openness, very special circumstances being required to be argued for their acceptance. A third view, which was recommended as the correct basic approach, was to identify such sites during local plan preparation, putting them forward as proposals in the plan [3.59-3.61].

3.77 *A number of authorities have sought to define and list the very special circumstances in which they would depart from Green Belt policy in plans.*

A policy clearly listing all appropriate Green Belt uses would be a benefit to decision-makers. PPG 2 advises against local authorities preparing policies for exceptional circumstances as these create a new round of difficulties in interpretation, and can raise false expectations among applicants. Although the Department itself has written guidance on very special circumstances for low cost housing and hospital sites this runs similar risks. Many local authorities, for example, dislike the advice on low cost housing because they consider it creates new ambiguities and room for dispute [3.9-3.11; 3.69].

It is recommended that:

R.6 *The basic distinction between inset and washed over settlements in Green Belts, referred to in Circular 50/57, should be retained [3.2-3.7].*

R.7 *Where infill is to be allowed in small washed over settlements 'infill boundaries' should be defined in plans. Such infill would therefore constitute appropriate development within the Green Belt [3.2; 3.7].*

R.8 *The difference of treatment of existing employment uses in washed over settlements and Green Belts insets should be made clear [3.7].*

R.9 *Local authorities should normally be allowed to include specific policies on dwelling extensions and alterations, replacement dwellings, and outdoor sport and recreation (including golf courses, driving ranges and equestrian activities) in Green Belts in development plans [3.17-3.20; 3.68].*

R.10 *The PPG 3 policy relating to the special circumstances in which Green Belt site may be released for housing for local needs should be monitored in terms of the amount and type of sites involved and conditions [3.24].*

R.11 *The redundancy test in respect of the re-use of existing buildings in Green Belts should be removed, but a policy should be introduced to make it normal for permitted development rights to be removed by condition in any approvals given where farm buildings are involved [3.28-3.38].*

R.12 *The PPG 7 safeguards relating to the re-use of buildings in the countryside generally should be re-affirmed for Green Belts [3.28-3.38].*

R.13   The impact of approvals for the re-use of buildings under PPG 7 should be monitored in terms of how far they are compromising the openness and visual amenities of the Green Belt and the countryside beyond, and how far they are assisting the local economy [3.28-3.38].

R.14   Farm diversification proposals should be encouraged within the parameters of R.11 and R.12 [3.33-3.38].

R.15   Institutions standing in extensive grounds should be deleted as an appropriate land use in Green Belts. The institutional re-use of existing buildings would fall within recommendations R.11 and R.12. New institutional buildings would require to be justified in very special circumstances where a non-Green Belt site was unavailable [3.39-3.44].

R.16   Development plan policies should state that where development is approved in the Green Belt, including alterations to the size and appearance of existing buildings the scheme will contain provisions to improve the landscape, enhance visual amenity and support the achievement of open land objectives [3.46-3.48].

R.17   Development plan policies should state that where proposals for the redevelopment of existing employment uses present the opportunity, development control should aim to reduce the visual impact, and off-site traffic flows, related to future use [3.46-3.48].

R.18   Where employment areas and major sites are of national or regional importance consideration should be given to creating Green Belt insets [3.46-3.48].

R.19   Local authorities should identify sites for Park and Ride car parks in development plans, seeking alterations to Green Belt boundaries if necessary. Sites proposed in Green Belts would be treated as very special circumstances, applicants being required to show that no other suitable site outside the Green Belt was available [3.61].

R.20   Utilities should only be allowed in the Green Belt if there is no alternative location outside the Green Belt [3.63].

R.21   The phrase 'other uses appropriate to a rural area' should be replaced by the more appropriate phrase 'new buildings ancillary to open uses of land in the Green Belt' [3.64].

R.22   Development plans should not refer to specific very special circumstances in which development would be contemplated in Green Belts [3.9-3.11; 3.69].

References

1.   DOE (1992a) <u>The Countryside and the Rural Economy</u>, PPG 7, paras 1.6 and 2.12.

2.   MHLG (1957) <u>Green Belts</u>, Circular 50/57, paras 7 and 8.

3.   Cheshire County Council (1985) <u>Cheshire County Structure Plan Including the First Alteration, Explanatory Memorandum and Written Statement</u>, Chester, CCC, Section 9.

4.   DOE (1988a) <u>Green Belts, PPG 2</u>, London, HMSO, para 12.

5.   DOE (1991b) <u>Sport and Recreation</u>, PPG 17, London, HMSO, para 34.

6.   Ibid., para 13.

7.   Ibid.

8.   See 'Notes of Cases - Pehrsson v Secretary of State for the Environment and Royal Borough og Windsor and Maidenhead', in <u>Journal of Planning and Environmental Law</u>, October 1990, pp 764-775.

9.   DOE (1992c) <u>Motorway Service Areas</u>, Circular 23/92, para 10.

10. DOE (1992d) <u>Housing</u>, PPG 3, Annex A, paras 11-14.

11. DOE (1991a) <u>Redundant Hospital Sites in Green Belts - Planning Guidelines</u>, Circular 12/91, London, HMSO.

12. Hertfordshire County Council (1992) <u>Structure Plan Incorporating Approved Alterations</u>, Hertford, HCC.

13. Staffordshire County Council (1991) <u>Staffordshire County Structure Plan</u>, Stafford, SCC.

14. HM Government (1988b) <u>The Green Belts</u>, London, HMSO.

15. DOE (1992a) para 2.9 has the full definition.

16. DOE (1992b) op.cit.

17. DOE (1992a) op.cit., Annex E.

18. See for example Broxbourne Borough Council (1992) <u>Local Plan Review: Written Statement</u>, Cheshunt, BBC.

19. DOE (1992a) op.cit., Annex E, para 13.

20.   DOE (1988a) op.cit., para 16.

21.   DOE (1992a) op.cit., paras 2.15, 2.13 and Annex D.

22.   DOE (1988a) op.cit., para 16.

23.   DOE (1988b) op.cit., para 13.

24.   See Barnet Meeting Room Trust v Secretary of State for the Environment and Barnet London Borough Council, revised Judgement, October 1992, pp 28-9.

25.   DOE (1988b) op.cit., p 13.

26.   Barnet Meeting Room Trust, op.cit., p 38.

27.   DOE (1988b) op.cit.

28.   Oxfordshire County Council (1992) Oxfordshire Structure Plan, policy EN 5.

29.   Hertfordshire County Council (1992) Hertfordshire County Structure Plan Review, Hertford, HCC, policy 1.

30.   South Staffordshire District Council (1980) District Plan No 1, Codsall, SSDC, para 6.5.2.

31.   Leeds City Council (1990) The Control of Development in the Green Belt, Leeds, LCC, para 5.22.

32.   See Barnet Meeting Room Trust, op.cit., pp 29-30.

33.   Ibid., p 32.

34.   DOE (1991a) op.cit.

35.   South Staffordshire District Council (1980) op.cit., para 6.5.7.

36.   DOE (1988a) op.cit., para 14.

37.   DOE (1991a) op.cit.

38.   DOE (1991b) op.cit.

39.   Hertfordshire County Council (1992) op.cit., policy 16.

40.   DOE (1991b) op.cit.

41.   Surrey County Council (1992) Guidelines for the Development of New Golf Courses in Surrey, Kingston, SCC.

42. DOE (1992d) <u>Tourism</u>, PPG 21, London, HMSO.

43. DOE (1988a) op.cit., para 16.

44. Cambridge City Council (1992) <u>Cambridge Local Plan</u>, Draft Version, Cambridge, CCC.

45. North Yorkshire County Council (1991) <u>York Green Belt Local Plan</u>, Northallerton, NTCC, policy 7.

46. Bristol City Council (1992) <u>Draft Bristol Local Plan</u>, Bristol, BCC.

47. City of York (1992) <u>Development Strategy</u>, Consultation Draft, policy OS1, p 15.

48. Oxford City Council (1992) <u>Oxford 2001</u>, Oxford, OCC, policy TT29, p 220.

49. DOE (1992e) <u>South Cambridgeshire Local Plan</u>, Inspectors Report of LPI, para 4.32.

50. DOE (1992c) op.cit.

51. DOE (1992a) op.cit., para 1.10.

4. URBAN FRINGE AND OPEN LAND ISSUES

The Context

4.1   There is widespread agreement on the basic purposes of Green Belts. There is, however, greater concern over the future of open land uses, and landscapes within them. This theme was reflected in our interviews, and is demonstrated in recent reports by the Urban Fringe Special Advisory Group, the Royal Institution of Chartered Surveyors and the London Planning Advisory Committee.[1] Despite mention of urban fringe issues in the Environment White Paper, the 1992 Government statement *Action for the Countryside*, and in PPG 7, there is little detail in policy.[2] The general public, however, value Green Belts primarily for their environmental quality and accessibility as a *Which Magazine* survey has shown (see para B.10). Their continued support for the concept is likely to depend on how far an attractive working landscape can be retained in the long term. This requires effective land management policies which complement land use policies and development control.

4.2   A number of basic policy notions have traditionally been used in planning the countryside near towns. Firstly, the *urban fringe*, seen as the penumbra of the City, is an area of fragmented land ownerships and intruded farmland, adjacent to the urban area. In this definition the urban fringe is an area lesser in extent than the Green Belts.[3] Attention is placed on problems of urban intrusion, trespass and vandalism, and, in some areas, on the need for wider environmental improvement. Land uses are to be restricted to those 'appropriate to a rural area', such as agriculture and forestry. *Leisure and recreation* activity is also limited by policy to informal recreation and outdoor sport with few recreational buildings, designed to be fitted into the rural scene. Where conflicts occur between farmers and visitors, or where small-scale landscape improvements are required, day-to-day management is seen as important to solve local problems. The Department has traditionally held the view, however, that land management policies, unlike policies for land use, are not part of the normal content of development plans. This Chapter therefore focuses on the interface between policies for the environment of the countryside near towns, and what it is possible to achieve through policies in development plans and development control.

Existing Policy Guidance

4.3   The definition of Green Belts does not, by itself, actively promote new uses or countryside management. Current planning guidance, however, refers to wider themes and objectives in both Green Belt and urban fringe areas. Although the justifications for Green Belt are largely urban, PPG 2 refers to their positive role in providing access to open countryside for the urban population. Outdoor leisure pursuits, it is suggested, are likely to occupy an increasing proportion of the Green Belts.[4] Circular 14/84 encourages the environmental improvement of areas suffering from disuse and neglect, and suggests that local authorities can work with landowners and the voluntary sector to this end.[5] Guidance on *Sport and Recreation* in PPG 17 asks local authorities to encourage the provision of recreation facilities in the urban fringe, and to regard recreation as a buffer land use. There is also support for afforestation schemes, the enhancement of the rights of way network, and for nature conservation.[6] The guidance on the *Countryside and the Rural Economy* defines the urban fringe and puts forward a policy prescription:

> '... there are around some conurbations areas of 'urban fringe' where land use conflicts and environmental problems arise. Urban fringe is not a designation, though some urban fringe areas are found within Green Belts. The urban fringe often accommodates essential but unneighbourly functions such as waste disposal and sewage treatment, and contains areas of derelict land and damaged landscape and under-used land whose viability for agricultural use has been affected by urban pressures. It requires a positive approach to planning and management, aimed at securing environmental improvement and beneficial use of land, and increased public access, to provide an amenity for the residents of urban areas'.[7]

4.4   Michael Heseltine announced in March 1991 that he was considering extending the objectives of Green Belts. He stated:

> '... The value of Green Belts to our communities will not be fully realised if policies are applied in a purely negative sense of preventing inappropriate development ... I want us to consider extending the objectives of the Green Belts to give our policies a more positive thrust'[8]

The two new objectives put forward for investigation, following suggestions by the Countryside Commission, were:

- to increase opportunities for quiet enjoyment of the countryside, and

- to enhance and improve the natural beauty of the countryside adjoining towns and cities.

The 'greening' theme for Green Belt policy has been taken up in a number of Ministerial speeches in the last three years. In the White Paper *This Common Inheritance*, the Green Belt is listed under policies with a conservation theme, and PPG 12 on *Development Plans* sees Green Belt among policies with conservation and environment as their common flavour.

Problems and Conflicts

4.5   Our interviews, together with the review of relevant major literature, suggest wide agreement over broad land use objectives for open land in Green Belts.[9] At the same time there was more doubt about methods, resources and priorities. It was suggested that we can expect to see a more multi-activity countryside near towns in the future. Emphasis will be on the management of the interactions between different uses of open land, and the resolution of any resulting conflicts. The main themes which emerged from the interviews were:

- continued support for agriculture, particularly on better quality land;

- a wide role for sport and recreation, with greater attention to access issues;

- the need to enhance safeguards for nature conservation; and

- a wish to restore damaged landscapes and derelict land, and retain attractive landscapes.

4.6   However a number of current trends in the countryside near towns are likely to lead to problems in achieving these desirable objectives (see Appendix G). Among these are:

- reductions in the financial resources available to farmers to manage the landscape;

- conflicts between farm diversification objectives and the openness criterion contained in Green Belt policy;

- concerns about the impacts of increased sport and recreation activity in the countryside; and

- a lack of resources for major environmental improvement and countryside management.

There is a reduction in the primacy of agriculture, as a food production activity, in the urban fringe. But its importance as the most effective 'manager' of the rural landscape is likely to be enhanced. However farm incomes have declined sharply and are predicted to further reduce by over a quarter in real terms in the next four years. There will be a poor economic base from within agriculture for maintaining the landscape that many people want. Public sector support may also be thin on the ground. There is currently no specific targeting of landscape grants to Green Belt areas under the *Countryside Stewardship* scheme, for example. Farming interests contend that if new building for diversification is not made easier then the agricultural sector will not itself be able to improve the situation.[10]

4.7   Recreation demands and pressures, although predicted to increase, have remained rather the same over the last five years or so. One sector that has grown is active outdoor sport including motorised sports, and water-based activities.[11] Other relatively new activities, such as combat games, may affect areas of conservation value such as ancient woodlands. Increased footpath, by-way and bridleway use can also cause conflicts. Most of the problems posed by sport and recreation activity can be resolved by effective management. However the provision of such services is in its infancy, and far greater resources are required.

69

4.8   Parts of the urban fringe comprise derelict and damaged land left over after mineral extraction or tipping. Its poor appearance, and lack of management, reduce the effectiveness of Green Belts as open land for countryside recreation, and as an attractive setting for urban areas. Mineral operators are keen to minimize transport costs, and this places further pressure on the urban fringe. Demands for new landfill sites, incinerators and re-cycling plants are also occurring. Adoption of the proximity principle recommended in draft guidance on pollution and waste management could lead to a significant increase in the use of land for such purposes in the urban fringe.[12] Standards of restoration of mineral land remain a cause for concern, particularly where extraction pre-dates the planning system, or where permissions have not been re-negotiated. In the North and Midlands the derelict land grant (DLG) system has been used to tackle major dereliction, but long-term land management commitments remain. Revisions of the after-use priorities in 1991 led to a focus on 'soft' end uses, such as recreation and tree planting. These are replacing the need to restore land to agriculture as a priority in the programme. The Urban Regeneration Agency will take over responsibility for DLG in the future, and there is concern as to how much priority will be given to the urban fringe and the countryside and to 'soft' after-uses. Overall there is a lack of accurate data on what proportion of Green Belt by area suffers from damage and dereliction. Surveys conducted in the Community Forest areas, for example, show sites with very poor quality environments which require considerable sums of money for restoration and improvement before they can contribute effectively to Green Belt purposes. A lack of resources hinders the achievement of positive management improvements at the urban fringe. This is why LPAC and others have sought, without success, a specific Government urban fringe grant.[13]

Local Authority Priorities

4.9   The case study local authorities demonstrated a very wide variation in response to urban fringe and environmental problems in the countryside around towns. The County Councils had made most progress with structures, including the Countryside Management Service in Hertfordshire, land renewal project areas in Staffordshire and Dorset's *Green Link* scheme. One half of the Districts did not have area-based countryside management or ranger services. Two of the Districts had abandoned capital programmes of improvements due to budget problems. The following main conclusions were reached:

- much of the work on environmental management was not devoted to Green Belts *per se*, but to such areas as valuable heathland, wetland and water areas in the countryside near towns;

- local authorities had their *aims* well worked out; some had countryside management strategies (Purbeck), environmental strategies (Broxbourne) or green strategies (Leeds). In Walsall countryside area profiles had been developed for the inner parts of the Green Belt (these listed local environmental problems and those areas requiring treatment);

70

- shortages of resources of finance and labour, and frequently the lack of any sizeable capital budget to do any more than scratch the surface of problems, were significant;

- the presence of Green Belt acted as a major deterrent to solving resource problems by recourse to planning obligations, because of the strict restraints on acceptable development.

4.10   A number of local authorities, particularly in the Midlands, and Yorkshire and Humberside, were effectively re-cycling derelict and despoiled land. The main resources being used were Derelict Land Grants, EEC Rechar funds, Urban Programme and City Challenge money. In some areas Groundwork Trusts had been established with a view to operating with the private sector, to secure environmental improvements. However these were the exception rather than the norm. A number of authorities, for example Enfield Borough, had used planning conditions and agreements to secure environmental improvements to the Green Belt from developments which had been permitted.

What Can the Planning System Do?

4.11   Four possibilities are considered here. These are: enabling development; the creation of community forests; the use of planning conditions; and the negotiation of planning obligations.

Enabling Development

4.12   In a study of neglected sites in the London urban fringe it was concluded that restoration could not be financed due to limitations on permissible after-uses within the Green Belt.[14] The temptation, in this situation, is to release land for development as the only forseeable way of obtaining land improvements - 'enabling development'. The Urban Fringe Joint Special Advisory Group have recently suggested the designation of Urban Fringe Special Priority Areas (UFSPA). These would '... provide a context for striking a balance between the purely protective aspects of long established Green Belt policy and the positive management improvements that are essential to tackle urban fringe problems'. UFSPAs would be defined in development plans, in order to:

- establish or maintain open landscape;

- accommodate uses which need to be located on the edge of, but outside, urban areas;

- provide for and enhance nature conservation interests; and

- increase opportunities for public access and enjoyment.

In some cases, where costs are too high for conventional funding, it is suggested local authorities should consider allowing development exceptionally as part of a package guaranteeing land restoration, access and long term management through planning obligations. The Study *Planning in the Urban Fringe* suggests two alternative strategies:

- deleting the land to be built on from the Green Belt, to fund the environmental improvement, or

- dealing with such developments as exceptions to normal planning policy.

Given the primacy now attached to development plans, the Group feel that UFSPAs will need to be identified within the plan-making process, and exceptions identified in local plans or unitary development plans.[15]

4.13   This proposition was not generally supported by the case study authorities interviewed or, particularly, by the consultees. It was felt that to set up the basic objective of Green Belt as the retention of openness, and then approve development which compromised that openness, would be illogical. The definition of areas in the Green Belt where exceptions would be allowed is, in reality, creating a different form of designation. The objectives of UFSPAs would, if acceptable to all parties, best be treated by excluding such areas from the Green Belt. If and when the environment had been successfully restored then the land could be returned to the Green Belt at some later date. An example has already been given of creating a Green Belt inset to assist with local environmental problems, in Cheshire (see para 3.4). At present the exclusion of land at St James Village, Broxbourne, is being proposed to finance the removal of eyesores and other environmental improvements in the village and nearby in conjunction with new development. The policy in the deposit local plan suggests returning the area to the Green Belt five years after it is first excluded.[16]   If, however, the exclusion of land of poor environmental quality from the Green Belt, using this proposed system, were to become commonplace then landowners would be encouraged to run-down their land in order to secure planning permission. Similarly it would seem inappropriate to give a precise date for the return of land to Green Belt so far ahead. Circumstances by then may have changed, and the expected improvement may not have occurred, for example.

Community Forests

4.14   Community Forests are based on the concept that new multi-purpose woodlands in the countryside around towns will benefit the community at large by enhancing the landscape, providing new environments for recreation and wildlife, attracting development and helping to mitigate the greenhouse effect.[17]   The Forest areas are 20-40,000 hectares each, although it is expected that less than half of the land in the areas will eventually be planted. Forest project teams have been charged with preparing Forest Plans. Grant aid will be available to landowners and farmers for planting, including a special £950 per hectare community woodlands supplement. Our case study areas included three of the ten initial schemes: Watling Chase (Herts), the Forest of

Mercia (Staffordshire and Walsall), and the South Yorkshire Community Forest (Sheffield and Barnsley).

4.15 Early publicity for the schemes takes its lead from forests such as the Amsterdam Bos in Holland. The Continental European concept includes provisions for a variety of sports (for example football, athletics and watersports) among the woodland, and for informal recreation. In the Countryside Commission's 1989 statement developments such as dry-ski facilities, ice rinks and sports stadia are also mentioned. The vision is completed with discussion of holiday accommodation, craft workshops and riding centres.[18]

4.16 A number of these intended activities would conflict with current advice on acceptable Green Belt uses. The first drafts of the Forest Plans make it clear, however, that forest planners will work *within* existing Green Belt policies:

> '... the Forest of Mercia has a valuable role to play in reinforcing Green Belt designation. There is however a danger that the Forest is seen as an opportunity to promote development that otherwise might not be acceptable in the Green Belt. This is a notion that needs to be firmly rejected'.[19]

In Thames Chase the draft Plan is seen as a way of implementing the development plan policies of the five constituent authorities. It states:

> '... Some fear the community forests will open the doors to development in the Green Belt. But the local authorities are determined that only developments previously acceptable in the Green Belt would be favourably considered and that additional planting, landscaping or other features like public access will need to be incorporated'.[20]

The Forest is seen as *the* main framework for protecting and enhancing the Green Belt, and achieving local authority objectives within the defined area. The Plan sees the planning and environmental objectives of Thames Chase as:

- to regenerate the environment of the Green Belt and help to ensure that it is permanently green and open;

- to protect areas of high quality landscape, historical, archaeological or nature conservation interest;

- to improve the landscape, including the reclamation of derelict land; and

- to give the public and private sectors confidence in the long-term prospects for the area and provide a proper base for investment.[21]

4.17 However, issues of grant take-up and funding remain. The success of the Forests is heavily reliant on private interest. Participation is voluntary and large-scale changes in land ownership are not envisaged. As a result private sector take-up may be, at best, slow. A survey of landowners in three of the community forest areas indicated that less than ten per cent were considering woodland planting. The outcome has been suggestions to relax Green Belt policy to allow development which would fund tree planting and land restoration. In Hertfordshire, policy 15A of the submitted 1991 structure plan proposed the following:

'... Development which would not normally be permitted within the Green Belt may be allowed within the Community Forest, but only where:

- the development itself is acceptable in terms of the objectives of the Community Forest; and

- it is associated with significant proposals for tree planting, nature conservation or improved public access; and

- it involves re-use or redevelopment on a similar scale of existing redundant buildings or sites, or restoration of damaged land; and

- it does not lead to unacceptably high levels of traffic on the highway network; and

- it is designed, constructed and operated so as to minimise its environmental impact'.

An example given is the redevelopment, on a similar scale, of existing operational farm buildings for a hotel or equestrian centre, where the whole of the remainder of the farm unit would be given over to tree planting.[22]

4.18   The proposal was rejected by the Department as it constituted an attempt to create a policy specifying exceptional circumstances for development in the Green Belt. The policy was rather generally worded demonstrating the problem of specifying exceptional circumstances. A number of Districts in Hertfordshire saw it as inappropriate and likely to lead to a lack of control over new developments. The uncertainty created would also be an incentive to landowners to run-down their land and property.[23] However, if early action on the ground does not fit the ideals in the Forest plans there could be a re-opening of the enabling development argument.

4.19   Community Forest plans often involve detailed open land planning. Areas are defined for particular land uses such as recreational woodland, sport and recreation and conservation. In their consideration of planning applications local authorities are encouraged to have regard to the objectives of the Forest in deciding applications. For example a golf course on open farmland may, in normal circumstances, be approved in Green Belt. If the land is, however, shown as recreational woodland on the forest plan, this would be a material consideration. It would be preferable for local planning authorities to take Community Forest Plans into account in preparing their development plans,

74

and to include in them policies which are consistent with the Forest Plan.[24]

Planning Conditions

4.20 The use of planning conditions, and the negotiation of planning obligations, are potential ways of securing environmental benefits in conjunction with development which occurs in accord with Green Belt guidelines. The development control case studies have shown the scale of applications processed in Green Belts. Whilst many are for small-scale changes a number are large-scale and extensive in terms of their impact on the landscape. Golf courses, mineral extraction and waste disposal sites, and redeveloped hospital and industrial sites fall into this category. High quality landscaping, eyesore removal, and the reservation of wildlife areas can all be the subject of conditions. PPG 2 already refers to the need protect the visual amenities of the Green Belt in any development approved.[25] The Thames Chase Forest Plan suggests that all significant development approved in the Green Belt should demonstrate benefits for the general environment and landscape of the Green Belt and Community Forest.[26] Where new consents for minerals and the tipping of waste are granted the restoration should also make an effective contribution to the environment and landscape. These intentions should also be taken into account by Inspectors in any Green Belt case where they are considering upholding appeals in very special circumstances.

Planning Obligations

4.21 Provisions for planning obligations allow slightly more leeway than the use of planning conditions for local authorities to negotiate with applicants for local environmental benefits. For example where development compromises a resource on-site, an equivalent off-site gain may be negotiated.[27] Local authorities could specify that developers should contribute to an environmental fund which would carry out specific environment on-site improvement works listed in an approved development plan. It is open to applicants to propose works which would assist in preserving or improving visual amenities or access to the Green Belt, arguing that these comprise very special circumstances. An example of this process at work is the recent decision to allow the development of 'Prospect Park' Hillingdon in the London Green Belt as a corporate headquarters for British Airways. The Secretary of State agreed with the Inspector's conclusions that the business case was not on its own sufficient to demonstrate very special circumstances but the '... *combination* of the environmental benefits of the proposals (most importantly the removal of a potential risk from landfill gas and leachate and the positive use of urban fringe land for the general public good), together with the business case, did amount to very special circumstances'.[28] Through planning briefs and negotiation developers of suburban sites, and of land in village insets, could contribute to environmental improvement on adjoining land in Green Belts which is related to their development in that it forms part of its setting. This would, however, be beyond the current interpretation of the provisions of

Circular 16/91. In these ways a positive contribution, albeit often small in some cases, could be made to improving the environment of Green Belts.[29]

New Objectives for Open Land

4.22   The recreation and natural beauty (landscape) objectives referred to in the 1991 Ministerial speech have strong support from a wide spectrum of opinion. There is also strong support for the promotion of the nature conservation interest in the urban fringe and Green Belts.

Increasing Opportunities for Recreation

4.23   There was strong support among local authorities for the promotion of recreation as a valid Green Belt purpose. It was already a *de facto* purpose, and many authorities had policies to promote access. Recreation arguments have been used to help define the extent and shape of some Green Belts. Two purposes of the approved Green Belt in South Yorkshire are to preserve open land of existing or potential recreation or amenity value extending into the urban area, and to preserve easy access to open country and provide for outdoor recreation in pleasant surroundings.[30] In the Barnsley Urban Area Local Plan (1986) the Borough specifically included land with these characteristics in the Green Belt, and for these purposes. In interpreting the latter purpose, for example, they state 'areas of open land which lie between two built up areas and which provide access for persons on foot to open countryside beyond the urban area, were considered to be appropriate for inclusion in the Green Belt'.[31]

4.24   Greater concern was expressed over the particular notion of 'quiet enjoyment'. Whilst not promoting intrusive activities, many respondents felt policies to extend the area of quiet enjoyment might be exclusionary. These would squeeze out active recreation, or other activities sought by the urban population, such as sailing and motor boating, let alone the newer pastimes of combat games, microlighting or motor car trials and rallying. Some felt a Green Belt devoted to quiet enjoyment of the countryside might remove recreation altogether. Another implication might be greater restrictions on otherwise acceptable uses such as opencasting, quarrying or gravel extraction. It would be unfortunate if such attitudes reduced the number of acceptable uses, creating a new form of 'sanitized' countryside.

4.25   There was almost universal support for greater access to Green Belts, through increased footpath and bridleway use, and on small-scale informal recreation sites. Local resident interests were concerned about the side effects of a major growth in access, and were currently worried about excessive numbers of new golf courses with their intrusion in the landscape, and the extra movement generated. Others felt, however, that the land use planning system was now sophisticated enough to control significant externality effects. One cross-cutting factor here was seen as the potential for extra travel generated by major new leisure provisions in the countryside. The data for golf course approvals elsewhere in the study imply a potential for major transport growth, particularly if new schemes are located away from urban peripheries (see para 2.6). However Green Belt locations may be preferable, in travel terms, to locations in the deeper countryside. Overall there is a strong case for confirming the promotion of outdoor sport and recreation as an important objective of Green Belts.

Enhancing Natural Beauty

4.26 This was also a strongly supported objective of Green Belt. Respondents agreed that making the attractiveness of an area a criterion for the *definition* of Green Belt boundaries would however encourage landowners to run-down land to secure permission. As objectives for Green Belts once designated however the twin agenda of protecting the attractive landscapes that already exist, and improving damaged landscapes and derelict land, have universal support. Circular 14/84 encourages local authorities to work with farmers and other landowners to maintain and improve their land, and to develop and maintain a positive approach to land use management. However the main problems are priorities and resources. The study of local authorities (paras 4.9-4.10) shows that this aspect of policy tends to be marginal, work being carried out as and when funds are obtained, largely from outside sources. While Groundwork Trusts have a role to play as a catalyst, and Derelict Land Grants are significant in some areas in bringing land back into use, areas of lower priority are deteriorating slowly and are starved of funds. In the absence of a revival in agricultural fortunes, or a targeting and increase of Countryside Stewardship and other environmental improvement grants to the urban fringe, a continued decline in quality is predicted. However these objectives, including support for agriculture, should be supported in guidance so that they may be taken account of in framing local policies.

Nature Conservation

4.27 Urban residents place a high value, in terms of contribution to quality of life, on contact with nature and wildlife. Daily contact with nature was, in a survey in London, rated above that with sports facilities, libraries, leisure centres or theatres. The urban fringe is a valuable source of wildlife habitats. Greenspace penetrating towns, and linking towns and countryside, should be seen as a necessary part of urban form, to be protected and enhanced for its nature conservation value. Protecting the nature conservation interest involves:

* identifying the key semi-natural areas with nature conservation value;

* valuing natural areas both on biological and geological criteria, and as cultural resources for education and recreation;

* providing open corridors, or a network of areas, enabling key species to adapt to overall change such as global warming; and

77

- valuing wildlife quality as a factor in planning decisions.[32]

4.28   The implications of promoting nature conservation in the urban fringe include:

- the need to look across the rural-urban divide at nature conservation values and linkages;[33]

- the need to consider nature conservation as a valuable use of land set aside in the urban fringe; and

- the need to consider nature conservation benefits, though planning obligations, where development does take place in accord with Green Belt and other policies.[34]

Our relevant consultees felt that firm controls on development on Green Belt land of low nature conservation value could push development into non-Green Belt urban fringe areas. Because they were not always farmed the 'scruffy' parts of the fringe often had higher value for nature conservation.

Main Findings and Recommendations

4.29   *The functions performed by open land in Green Belts should be recognised in the guidance and should be listed as Green Belt objectives.*

We can expect to see a more multi-activity countryside near towns. The role of the Green Belt as a locale for outdoor sport and recreation is recognised and encouraged by local authorities. The Green Belt can also be a focus for environmental and greening strategies, aiming to restore damaged land, protect wildlife and attractive landscapes. Consistent support for agriculture, not least for its contribution to a healthy landscape, was also noted [4.22-4.27; 4.1-4.8].

4.30   *Generating sufficient resources for the environmental improvement of damaged land in Green Belts has led to proposals for 'enabling' development.*

Green Belt policy reduces the scope for environmental improvement in conjunction with new development, except through the balancing process accompanying the establishment of very special circumstances at appeal. However suggestions that areas can exceptionally be defined in Green Belts where different 'enabling' policies should apply, would appear to confuse the Green Belt concept and reduce its effectiveness. Such land would better be excluded from Green Belts in development plans in the absence of sufficient non-private resources for their improvement [4.11-4.13].

4.31   *There is scope for using planning conditions to secure environmental objectives in Green Belts.*

Although development is severely limited in Green Belts, a wide range of land use changes are approved each year, as the development control scan illustrates.   These can include proposals for the re-use of buildings for industrial and office purposes and a range of leisure-related schemes.   In negotiations with applicants planners should address issues of enhancing the environment of the Green Belt as part of such schemes [4.20; 3.75].

4.32   *There is some scope for using planning obligations to secure environmental improvements in Green Belts.*

Where development affects a resource present on-site, authorities may negotiate equivalent off-site benefits. Where development is approved local authorities should seek to negotiate landscape and open land improvements. Acceptable development near to Green Belts may assist in funding Green Belt environmental improvements, but only if the need arises as a direct result of the proposed development [4.21].

It is recommended that:

R.23   *The following objectives of Green Belts should be listed in guidance:*

-    *to promote the use of land for outdoor sport and recreation [4.7; 4.23-4.25];*

-    *to retain and improve landscapes near to where people live [4.26];*

-    *to enhance and improve damaged and derelict land in the urban fringe, and secure the nature conservation interest [4.27-4.28].*

R.24   *Significant development or redevelopment of land which occurs in the Green Belt should demonstrate benefits for the environment and landscape of the Green Belt. Such provisions should, in particular, apply to new consents for minerals, the tipping of waste, and road and other infrastructure developments or improvements [4.8; 4.20-4.21].*

R.25   *Community Forests in Green Belts should continue to work within Green Belt policies [4.14-4.19].*

R.26   *Use of the principle of enabling development to fund environmental improvements should not be allowed in approved Green Belts [4.12-4.13].*

R.27   Where development occurs on sites adjoining Green Belts, either in suburban areas or by infilling and rounding off within settlements inset in the Green Belt, developers could contribute by agreement to environmental improvement or tree planting both on-site and on adjoining land. The need for such improvements would have to arise as a direct result of the proposed development [4.21].

R.28   The scale and types of environmental improvement which have been negotiated in association with planning permissions in the urban fringe and Green Belts should be further investigated [4.21].

References

1. Urban Fringe Special Advisory Group (1992) <u>Planning in the Urban Fringe</u>, Final Report, Middlesborough, Cleveland County Council; Royal Institution of Chartered Surveyors (1992), 'Report of the RICS Green Belt Working Party', <u>Chartered Surveyor Weekly</u>, Planning and Development Bulletin, <u>1</u>, 7, pp 3-5; London Planning Advisory Committee (1990) <u>Damaged Land in the Urban Fringe</u>, Romford, LPAC.

2. DOE (1992a) <u>Action for the Countryside</u>, London, HMSO; DOE (1992b) <u>The Countryside and the Rural Economy</u>, PPG 7, London, HMSO.

3. DOE (1992b) ibid., para 3.13.

4. DOE (1988) <u>Green Belts</u>, PPG 2, para 5.

5. DOE (1984) <u>Green Belts</u>, Circular 14/84, para 6

6. DOE (1991a) <u>Sport and Recreation</u>, PPG 17, paras 32-4.

7. DOE (1992b) op.cit., para 3.13.

8. DOE Press Statement, 6 March 1991.

9. See, for example, Elson, M.J. (1991) <u>Green Belts for Wales - A Positive Role for Sport and Recreation</u>, Sports Study No 5, Cardiff, Sports Council for Wales, p 15; Staffordshire County Council et. alia (1992) <u>Forest of Mercia Plan</u>, Draft for Consultation, para 2.37.

10. McLaughlin, B. (1992) 'Agriculture and Rural Strategy: Diversification in the Farming Industry', <u>The Planner</u>, <u>78</u>, 21, pp 12-15; Ilbery, B. (1988) 'The Development of Farm Diversification in the UK: Evidence from Birmingham's Urban Fringe', <u>Journal of RASE</u>, pp 21-35.

11. Broom, G. (1991). 'Informal Countryside Recreation - The Context', <u>CRAAG Conference Proceedings</u>, Bristol, CRAAG.

12. DOE (1992c) <u>Planning and Pollution Controls</u>, draft PPG for consultation, London, DOE.

13. See LPAC (1990) op.cit; and Kirby, M. (1990) 'Environmental Protection in Areas of Development Pressure', <u>Town and Country Planning</u>, <u>59</u>, 9, pp 236-8.

14. LPAC (1990), op.cit, pp 51-9.

15. Urban Fringe Special Advisory Group (1992) op.cit., pp 6-10.

16. Broxbourne Borough Council (1992) Local Plan Review, Written Statement, policy WC3, p 143.

17. Bishop, K. (1992) 'Creating Community Forests: Problems and Opportunities', Tree News, summer, pp 14-16.

18. Countryside Commission (1989) Forests for the Community, CCP 270, Cheltenham, Countryside Commission.

19. Staffordshire County Council (1992) Forest of Mercia Draft Plan, p 55ff.

20. Essex County Council et. alia (1992) Thames Chase Plan: Draft for Consultation, Chelmsford, ECC, policy PE 2, p 25.

21. Ibid.

22. Hertfordshire County Council (1991) Hertfordshire Structure Plan Review: Proposed Alterations, policy 15A; Pitt, J. (1991) 'Community Forest Cities of Tomorrow', Town and Country Planning, June, pp 188-90.

23. DOE (1992d) Hertfordshire Structure Plan Review, approval letter, section 4.

24. See DOE (1992e) Development Plans and Regional Planning Guidance, PPG 12.

25. DOE (1988) op. cit., para 14.

26. Essex County Council et. alia (1992) op.cit., p 25.

27. See DOE (1991b) Planning Obligations, Circular 16/91, London, HMSO.

28. 'National Interest amounting to 'very special circumstances' for developing in the Green Belt', Journal of Planning and Environment Law (1993), March, pp 268-272.

29. See Elson, M. J. and D. Payne (1993) Planning Obligations for Sport and Recreation, London, The Sports Council, for some examples of the situations in which obligations have been secured.

30. South Yorkshire County Council (1980) South Yorkshire Structure Plan, Sheffield, SYCC.

31. Barnsley Borough Council (1986) Urban Area Local Plan, Written Statement.

32. Countryside Commission and English Nature (1991) Green Capital: Planning for London's Greenspace, CCP 344, Cheltenham, Countryside Commission.

33. See Elkin, T; McLaren, D. and M. Hillman (1991) <u>Reviving the City:
     Towards Sustainable Urban Development</u>, chapter 4 - 'greenspace and
     wildlife'.

34. DOE (1991b), op.cit.

5.   **THE PERMANENCE OF GREEN BELTS**

The Current Guidance

5.1   Questions of permanence, and the circumstances in which Green Belts may be adjusted, remain contentious. Much time is spent in negotiation between the Regional Offices of the Department and local authorities on issues such as how far safeguarded land, sometimes termed 'white land', should be provided between urban areas and the Green Belt for long-term needs. Some of our consultees saw the current Guidance as insufficiently clear or detailed to govern the process of accommodation between Government, local authorities and other groups, which arriving at an agreed Green Belt boundary involves.

5.2   The current wording of policy can be traced back to discussions in the House of Commons Environment Committee in 1984. Guidance in PPG 2 states:

'... the essential characteristic of Green Belts is their permanence and their protection must be maintained as far as can be seen ahead'.

Alterations to the general extent of a Green Belt, once approved, should only occur if 'exceptional circumstances' can be demonstrated by the local authority. Similarly, boundaries in approved local plans or earlier development plans should only be altered 'exceptionally'. No elaboration is given of what might comprise exceptional circumstances.

5.3   Green Belts are long-term. When drawing up new, or revised, development plans local authorities should ensure that Green Belt proposals:

'... should be related to a timescale which is longer that normally adopted for other aspects of the plan'.

The test of the long term nature of a Green Belt in a local plan is also put forward:

'... the local authority should be able to demonstrate that Green Belt boundaries will not necessarily need to be altered at the end of the plan period. In *some cases* this will mean safeguarding land between the urban area and the Green Belt which may be required to meet longer-term development needs' (Authors' emphasis).

Circular 14/84 says that such land should be protected by the normal processes of development control.[1]

5.4   The House of Commons Environment Committee inquiry in 1984 pointed to the potential confusion between the idea of permanence and the notion of a long-term policy extending an indefinite time beyond the end date of a plan. Green Belts were not seen, by any of those giving evidence, as literally permanent or immutable. They were regarded as a creating *a presumption against development for an indefinite period*. This implies that when a Green Belt is defined in a plan, it should endure as far ahead as can be foreseen, and that there should be no prospect of changing the designation. The security of a Green Belt would also be enhanced if sufficient development land for predicted long-term needs can be shown to exist in the vicinity.[2]

Exceptional Circumstances

5.5   Our consultees basically agreed with the Environment Committee approach to permanence. None suggested Green Belts were immutable. There were circumstances, it was suggested, in which Green Belts could be altered. Most stressed the need to consider alterations within the process of development plan preparation and review. A number of local authorities interviewed wanted further advice on what might constitute exceptional circumstances. At present the local authority makes a reasoned case in a structure plan alteration or replacement. The Examination in Public Panel then forms a view. The discretion to decide what constitute exceptional circumstances resides with the Secretary of State who may alter the policies in the plan. In this way the national interest in sustaining the policy, and its consistency, is managed.

5.6   Within our case study areas there are a number of examples where exceptional circumstances have been argued. The main triggers for proposed changes have been changed economic circumstances (particularly the need for attractive greenfield sites for employment purposes), sub-regional growth demands (for example, in conjunction with development near airports), and demands for new housing. More locally, infilling to new by-pass roads has also caused some proposals for change. The Department has accepted a number of specific propositions, but not the view that exceptional circumstances justify a general re-assessment of the boundaries of an approved Green Belt across a whole County.

5.7   The outcomes of a number of recent cases are listed in Table 5.1. The main reasons for proposed deletions have been economic circumstances, such as sub-regional growth related to Gatwick Airport (land in Surrey), regional economic imbalance (Dartford, Kent) and shortages of land for high technology-related jobs (Cambridge). In the West Midlands a range of high quality sites have been released from the Green Belt, and the same has occurred in Wakefield. In Hertfordshire four significant proposals for deletions from approved Green Belt have been handled through the Structure Plan process. The need for housing land is more difficult to argue as an exceptional circumstance than other uses. In the case of Stevenage (Hertfordshire) land was deleted from the Green Belt because there was no white land in the District, whilst in Dacorum a proposal to release land on the edge of Hemel Hempstead was rejected, the

Table 5.1: Exceptional Circumstances in Structure Plans

argument	area	outcome
Proposed Green Belt Deletions		
uniquely extensive area of glasshouse dereliction	Broxbourne Herts	accepted, 1988 Structure Plan
no allowance for long-term development needs, housing	Stevenage Herts	accepted, 1988 Structure Plan
housing needs of District	Dacorum Herts	not accepted, 1988 Structure Plan
4000 dwellings on low density housing area, infrastructure improvements, protect areas of conservation importance elsewhere, Grange Estate	East Dorset Dorset	not accepted, 1990 South East Dorset Structure Plan, First Alteration
Proposed Green Belt Additions		
encroachment into the countryside; coalescence	East Herts Herts	not accepted, 1992 First Alteration
coalescence, protect countryside, control expansion of Markyate; regeneration of Luton	Dacorum Herts	not accepted 1992 First Alteration
control expansion of Royston	North Herts Herts	not accepted, 1988 Structure Plan
control growth of Alderholt, coalescence argument	East Dorset Dorset	not yet decided
manage growth in relation to Stanstead Airport; at Bishops Stortford	East Herts Herts	accepted, with large area of white land, 1988 Structure Plan
Others		
shortage of land and sites with potential for high tech industry associated with University	City of Cambridge Cambridgeshire	accepted, Replacement Structure Plan 1989
achieving balance between east and west of Region, changed circumstances, mixed uses	Dartford Kent	accepted, Structure Plan, Second Alteration 1990
sub-regional growth needs associated with Gatwick growth, lack of alternative areas for longer-term large scale development	Horley Surrey	accepted, 1989 Structure Plan, First Alteration

Source: Structure Plan Approval Letters

Department stating '... the fact that there is pressure for development does not constitute the exceptional circumstances which warrant altering the Green Belt'.[3] However, where housing needs cannot be accommodated entirely within existing urban boundaries, some revisions to Green Belts in local plans have been accepted. Development in South Staffordshire in the early 1980s, and on the southern edge of Macclesfield, may be prominent cases here.[4]

5.8   Some Authorities, such as Cheshire and Hertfordshire, have sought policies which would allow the small-scale revision of Green Belt boundaries, as part of the local plan preparation process. The view is that these are matters which are not of structural importance. Whilst allowing minor technical adjustments, to take account of appeal decisions or drafting errors, the Department have not been prepared to accept there is a small-scale level of adjustment which can be allowed as a general rule, and which is left to local discretion. The dangers of acceptance would be the risk of continuous nibbling at Green Belt in short-term policy reviews. Judgements on how far alterations proposed in District Local Plans may be regarded as of structural importance will continue to be made, in the last resort, by Regional Offices of the Department, in the absence of more precise guidance.

5.9   Current guidance suggests that Green Belt boundaries in approved local plans can be altered only exceptionally.[5] This has been interpreted as a requirement at the district level to justify exceptional circumstances on a site by site basis. The situation is now arising where development requirements, agreed in a Structure Plan, are accepted by all parties to imply the alteration of Green Belt boundaries in a specific district at the next review of the local plan. In this circumstance, the district is being asked to prove exceptional circumstances when it is, in effect, merely searching its urban boundaries and development insets for the least environmentally-damaging sites. In South Staffordshire this situation has occurred following approval of the Structure Plan in 1990. What is being sought is assurance that there are no reasonable alternatives to the alteration of the Green Belt, by developing other sites in towns or villages contained by and beyond the Green Belt. This follows the advice in PPG 2.

5.10   Priorities for land release, when development requirements have been established, are listed in the West Midlands Regional Guidance. They state:

•   as much development as possible, subject to other policies, should be on sites within the present built-up areas;

•   for development which has to be outside the present built-up areas, as much as possible should be in areas not covered by Green Belt policies;

•   for development which cannot be located in the above two categories, as much as possible should be accommodated through the careful drawing of Green Belt boundaries in areas where they have not yet been fully defined either in adopted local plans or development plans;

- only if a deficiency remains should alterations be contemplated to Green Belt boundaries which have already been defined in adopted local plans or the former development plans.[6]

These priorities appear an acceptable way forward which could be usefully deployed in other areas.

New Green Belts

5.11   Although not specifically stated in guidance, it is also necessary for local authorities to prove exceptional circumstances for new Green Belts. This is because Green Belt policy has always been regarded as a special one, with its unique presumption against development. Experience of past cases suggests authorities are required to establish why the normal processes of development control are not sufficient to secure their current development intentions. It may be concluded that development pressures are not sufficient to necessitate Green Belt. These were the basic points made in the Department's recent rejection of the proposal for a Green Belt around Hull, in Cleveland, and in the rejection of a 100 sq km extension of Green Belt in East Hertfordshire, both in 1992.[7] Given the technical and political difficulties in altering Green Belts, once confirmed, Authorities have been asked how far introduction of the policy will unnecessarily restrict future room for manoeuvre, and whether other policies could achieve the same results. In response Authorities cite the simplicity, robustness and enforceability of the Green Belt as a policy instrument, and its ability to secure its objectives over the longer-term. This inter-generational element, for example the promise of protecting the scale and setting of a historic city for the foreseeable future, has a powerful appeal to planners and locally-elected representatives.

5.12   In the case of the recent proposal to create a new Green Belt around Norwich, the Eastern Region Office considered the following issues should be addressed by the parties:

- the scale of changes (changed circumstances) since the last review of the Structure Plan, which might justify the policy being introduced at this time;

- whether the adverse effects of current development and other trends are those which the Green Belt instrument is designed to counter;

- whether other policies would be appropriate, especially given the importance attached to approved policies in development plans in the 1991 Act; and

- whether Green Belt would be too inflexible, compromising other objectives, such as those of allocating a ready supply of industrial and other development land.[8]

Future proposals for new Green Belts should be tested against the above criteria.

Safeguarded Land and Long-Term Needs

5.13   Only six of the sixteen Districts studied had safeguarded land (white land) in formally adopted plans. As progress is made in UDPs and district-wide local plans, a greater number of Authorities are introducing such land (see Table 5.2). The overall impression, however, is that most local authorities would prefer to rely on the possible alteration of Green Belts each time their plans are reviewed, thus avoiding the use of the safeguarded land mechanism. There are two basic situations here:

- where the Structure Plan states that the Green Belt is long-term (that is, is intended to apply for longer than the plan period), but this *does not* necessitate the definition of safeguarded land on the inner edge of the Green Belt; and

- where the long term concept suggests that safeguarded land *will* be required, because the capacity for redevelopment and intensification in urban areas is limited.

Table 5.2:   Safeguarded Land in Local Plans: Case Study Districts *

	in adopted plans	in plan proposals
no	10	7
yes	6	9

* England only

5.14   Examples of the former situation include Wolverhampton and Enfield, where it is argued that the redevelopment of sites within the urban envelope will suffice for local needs. Sheffield does not have safeguarded land in its approved Green Belt Subject Plan of 1983. Local policy makers would now like to have the room for manoeuvre that safeguarded land would have provided. Barnsley has no safeguarded land, it being argued that the District has plenty of land allocated for development and not taken up. In many ways the Green Belt is the 'real countryside' which remains.

5.15   In South East Dorset it was accepted that development requirements to 2001 could be accommodated within urban areas. It is stated:

'... He ... (the Secretary of State) ... considers that the present boundaries of the Green Belt should be broadly maintained and does not accept the Panel's view that land should be safeguarded for development after 2001'.[9]

The approved plan does not refer to long-term needs, but states that the built-up area of Bournemouth-Poole cannot continue to expand, and that the inner boundary of the Green Belt will therefore be regarded as its definitive limit for the foreseeable future. The relevant policy states that the inner boundary of the Green Belt 'will *generally* follow the edge of the main urban area'.[10] The Draft Verwood Local Plan (1991) interprets this policy as generally precluding the provision of 'white land' to allow for future outward growth around the edges of the built-up area beyond the Plan period.[11]

5.16   Where safeguarded land, or its equivalent, is provided the guidance states that normal development controls should be applied, and development plans should clearly state what the policies for such land are.[12] Table 5.3 gives examples of policy wordings adopted and proposed in plans. In Wakefield the areas of 'Presumption Against Development' (PAD) are seen as land which may be required to meet longer-term development needs. As long as adequate supplies of allocated land remain the PAD land will not be regarded as potential development land. The 388 hectares of PAD land, if developed at past rates, would last 25-30 years. In Macclesfield the circumstances of possible release of proposed 'Unallocated Land' are listed as:

•   a review of the Structure Plan;

•   where development cannot reasonably be sited within urban limits; or

•   where the land is not also required for open space.[13]

In Oxford proposed 'Safeguarded Land' between the urban area and the Green Belt is regarded as an extra designation, also being protected for landscape or open space purposes. Only parts of it may be regarded as not contributing to Green Belt purposes.[14]

5.17   Development control policy in safeguarded areas is as strict, or more strict, than in Green Belt. For example, in PAD areas in Wakefield, only development which is necessary for the operation of existing uses is seen as acceptable. Some sport and recreation facilities, and institutional uses, would not be regarded as acceptable. It is most common, however, for the same policy as in the Green Belt generally to be applied to safeguarded land. The current view of the Department, however, is that 'presumption against' policies should be avoided outside Green Belt areas.

5.18   Although Green Belts are regarded as long-term, Governments have always resisted placing a specific time, in terms of years, on the concept. This, again, preserves an area of discretion within which discussions on the need for, scale and type of safeguarded land can take place. A number of local authorities and consultees would prefer a specific time period to be stated in guidance. This would give a firmer indication of the scale of safeguarded land required. It would also help persuade local elected representatives, where doubt exists, that, the provision of such land is necessary. Most discussions of the concept, by Inspectors at inquiries, or in local authority literature, suggest 20-30 years equates to long-term, assuming structure plans look 10-15 years ahead. The House Builders Federation and York City Council recently re-iterated these arguments in relation to the York Green Belt.[15] If this is the case local authorities defending a Green Belt policy with no safeguarded land would need to be very sure about the possible adverse effects of intensification in their urban areas over such a period.

Long-Term Green Belts

5.19   A number of consultees felt the situation regarding safeguarded land, and the lack of firmer definition of the concept of 'long-term', unsatisfactory. Many saw it as creating delay as each new generation of planners re-learned the largely unwritten ground rules. Few, however, could chart a more appropriate way forward. The planners interviewed more often than not wanted safeguarded land. Where it did not exist they saw problems being stored up for the future. Local councillors, however, were not so willing to see safeguarded land in plans, especially if this required the politically unpalatable task of altering current boundaries (see para 5.13).

5.20   It appears that commitment to the concept of safeguarded land has varied through time. No reference to it was made in the 1955 Circular. The need to operationalize the long-term notion was the main reason for the production of the 1957 Circular. One of the main precursors of the 1984 Circular was the wish to remind local authorities of the need to avoid keeping land permanently open unnecessarily. The guidance on development plans in PPG 12, although referring to 'the proper definition' of Green Belt boundaries, stresses issues of the certainty of boundaries, rather than their long-term nature. The statement in PPG 2 that land will only 'in some cases' need to be safeguarded for longer-term needs has been the invitation for some to avoid addressing the full implications of the long-term issue locally.

Table 5.3: Safeguarded Land in Local Plans: Policy Wording

Wakefield

Presumption Against Development

'... development will be restricted to that which is necessary for the operation of existing uses together with such temporary uses as would not prejudice the possibility of long term development'

(Policy OL4, Draft Wakefield UDP, Volume 2, 1991)

Dacorum

Area of Special Restraint

'... until such time as the land allocated as 'Area of Special Restraint' is shown to be needed in an assessment of development land availability, or a review of this plan, there will be a presumption against development (other than would be allowed in the Green Belt) whether for the construction of new buildings, the extension or change of use of existing buildings, or the change of use of land'.

(Policy 2A, Dacorum District Plan, 1984)

Macclesfield

Unallocated Land

'... There will be no development on those areas of land between the urban limits and the inner boundary of the Green Belt which have not been allocated for development unless it can be shown that:

• additional development is required, as a result of a review of the County Structure Plan, to meet the development needs of the Macclesfield area post 2001;

• such development cannot reasonably be sited within the urban limits; and

• the land is not required for open space purposes'.

(policy GC7, paragraphs 4.21-4.22, Macclesfield Draft Local Plan, 1992)

5.21   Inadequacies in Regional Guidance, and structure plans, are often cited as a reason for the inability to define long-term Green Belts at local level. Regional Guidance does not look far enough ahead, with sufficient spatial detail, to guide County authorities, it is claimed. In turn, many Structure Plans, by the time they are approved, have run half of their course. Some Structure Plans investigated in this research, approved in 1992, only cover the period to 2001.

5.22   Three further arguments against safeguarded land were put to us. It was suggested that safeguarded land would attract much extra speculative activity, and its maintenance would therefore be impossible. There was little evidence however to demonstrate this. Although in East Dorset a small area of white land had been developed on appeal as soon as defined in a local plan, in Hertfordshire, where development pressures were stronger, Areas of Special Restraint in Dacorum and Broxbourne had been successfully defended. Second, it was argued that, with the new-found certainty resulting from the application of Section 54A principles, local authorities could operate a more secure plan-led system with regular five-yearly plan reviews. This more certain plan-making process would make it unnecessary to have safeguarded land, as in the past. Third, the safeguarded land may not be appropriately located. In Wakefield the land safeguarded in plans in the mid-1980s has not proved adequate for the siting requirements of employment-related activities in the early 1990s.

5.23 The general desirability of having a long-term perspective, especially where long lead times are prevalent as in the case of development projects, was stressed by some consultees. Others felt safeguarded land was an important safety valve for accommodating unforeseen needs or circumstances more effectively than otherwise would be the case. Taking the principle that the Green Belt instrument *manages* urban development, rather than stopping it, it may be argued that local plans should *normally* have safeguarded land. Local planning authorities should be required to justify why such land would *not* be needed. An increasing concern to avoid over-intensification in urban areas, both nationally and locally, makes it desirable for all local authorities with Green Belts to have safeguarded land. Important transport arguments may also enter the picture here (see Chapter 6). If safeguarded land is not proposed in plans local authorities, unlike now, should be required to explain how the character of suburban residential areas would be protected over the plan period.

5.24 Safeguarded land in plans should comprise areas and sites where development may occur in the longer term. It should be located where any development would be well integrated with existing development, and well-related to public transport and other infrastructure. The land should be genuinely capable of development if required, for example, not involving major reclamation for which funds have yet to be allocated. Valuable natural and built features, including landscape and wildlife sites, and historic buildings, should be protected. Also the stress placed on the need for a range of locations in land allocations for housing, as suggested in PPG 3, has implications for safeguarded land.[16] It would seem desirable to avoid all safeguarded land being in one location in a district.

Permanence - the Choice?

5.25 The above discussion suggests two scenarios. In the first the principles in paragraph 5.23 would obtain. Development plans would contain provisions for white land for long-term needs looking perhaps 20 years ahead. The aim would be to remove the need for short-term boundary changes in revisions to plans. This logic would create a high level of permanence for approved Green Belts. The second scenario would involve not defining safeguarded land between built-up areas and the Green Belt, as in Scotland (see para 7.43). As a result the need to reconsider Green Belt boundaries at each review of the development plan, say every ten years, would be increased. The level of permanence of approved Green Belts in this option would therefore be lower. Whatever the scenario selected the approach would need to be consistently applied across the relevant Green Belt as a whole. Where the second scenario is chosen the provision of white land would best become a normal requirement in development plans. If such land was not included in a development plan the local authority would need to justify the special circumstances that had led to this decision.

Main Findings and Recommendations

5.26 *Exceptional circumstances for the alteration of approved Green Belts in structure plans have most often been substantiated for employment-related development.*

Some of the exceptions agreed in structure plans were already agreed in Regional Guidance; others were argued more locally. Most refer to high amenity, well-located sites, intended for high technology or other 'leading edge' firms. The Department has challenged the number, size and location of such sites where local authorities have interpreted the guidance over-generously. It would appear counterproductive for local authorities to specify what 'exceptional circumstances' might be in policies in structure plans. Local authorities should, however, set out to demonstrate exceptional circumstances if they wish to alter boundaries in a structure plan, and not merely argue that the normal process of review can allocate new supplies of land. Changes to Green Belt boundaries should be considered in relation to structure plan alteration and replacement, and not first at district plan level. General policies which allow almost continuous small-scale review of boundaries should also not be allowed as these devalue the concept [5.5-5.10].

5.27 *Structure plan policies allowing for the general small-scale alteration of Green Belt boundaries by districts, as part of the local plan process, are not acceptable.*

The argument advanced in favour of such policies is that there is a level of Green Belt boundary alteration which is not of structural importance. Whilst minor technical adjustments, to allow for appeal decisions and drafting errors are clearly acceptable, there is a risk, if such policies were accepted, that Green Belt policy would proceed entirely by continuous 'nibbling' at short-term policy reviews [5.8].

5.28   *Where exceptional circumstances have been demonstrated in altering a Green Belt boundary in a structure plan, it may be unnecessary to require districts to also prove exceptional circumstances for the release of land on a site by site basis.*

This argument surrounds what it is necessary to prove to secure the alteration of an agreed Green Belt boundary in a local plan. If the circumstance is a ruling on a district housing land total, which all parties at the EIP accept implies Green Belt changes, a general locational steer for the district in the structure plan may be appropriate. Also the district should only have to show that the sites chosen are better than other sites in the district (see para 9 of PPG 2) not that there are exceptional circumstances independent of those demonstrated in the structure plan. This situation may increasingly occur as boundaries in some district-wide plans require alteration [5.9].

5.29   *There is a need to set out the criteria to be satisfied for the establishment of new Green Belts, or major extensions to existing ones.*

Proposals for new Green Belts continue to be made. However Green Belts should be seen as a policy instrument to be used only exceptionally, when other development control policies have proved inadequate. They should fulfill Green Belt purposes. Authorities should assess how appropriate such a measure would be to the problems of the locality concerned, and how far circumstances had changed rendering an alteration to policy necessary. Clear evidence should be sought by the Department on these points [5.11-5.12].

5.30   *There is a strong case for making safeguarded land ('white land'), or its equivalent, a normal requirement in development plans.*

Only one half of the local authorities studied had white land or its equivalent in plans, although the number proposing to include white land in new district plans was higher. It is important in terms of sustainable development to have a long-term view on the direction of development in localities. This should also aid infrastructure provision and the negotiation of community benefits. A new emphasis on avoiding town cramming, put forward in advice in PPG 3, and a concern to protect urban greenspace, suggests development outside existing urban boundaries may be the most suitable option in many circumstances. The need to minimise travel also suggests that mixed use peripheral or corridor developments, well related to public transport routes, may provide the opportunity to minimise the growth of traffic and accompanying emissions. Where no white land had been included in plans local authorities regretted its absence. There would appear no advantage in placing a specific time period, in terms of years, on the phrase 'long term'. However, it would be most useful if the phrase referred to well beyond the plan period [5.13-5.25].

5.31 *The issue of the extent of, and policies to be applied in, white land should be clarified.*

Circular 14/84 states that the normal processes of development control will apply in white land. Advice in Circular 50/57 suggests a model policy whereby the same land use prescription should be applied as in the Green Belt. Some authorities prefer a development control policy which suggests no development should occur which would prejudice later comprehensive development. White land should be capable of development if needed in the medium term. Policies in the interim should protect wildlife and landscape features and recreational access. Such land should be well related to infrastructure and existing and planned public transport facilities [5.23-5.24; 6.18].

It is recommended that:

R.29 *Where exceptional circumstances for the alteration of Green Belts have been substantiated in structure plans these should not need to be established again at site level [5.9].*

R.30 *Where new Green Belts are being proposed local authorities would need to demonstrate what major changes in circumstances had made the adoption of this exceptional measure necessary, and why normal development control or other policies would not be adequate [5.11-5.12].*

R.31 *Green Belt boundaries should be regarded as enduring well beyond the plan period. The provision of safeguarded land would be a normal requirement in development plans for Green Belts, unless local authorities could demonstrate where development would be located over the succeeding twenty years [5.19-5.25].*

R.32 *If a local authority is not proposing to provide white land in its plan it should justify the circumstances that have led to this decision [5.19-5.25].*

R.33 *Development control policy in white land should state that no development should occur which would prejudice later comprehensive development. Policies should, in particular, protect wildlife and landscape features, and existing access for recreation [5.24].*

R.34 *White land should be well related to existing and planned infrastructure including public transport facilities [5.24].*

References

1. DOE (1988a) <u>Green Belts</u>, PPG 2, paras 7 and 11; DOE (1984) <u>Green Belts</u>, Circular 14/84, para 4.

2. House of Commons Environment Committee (1984) <u>Green Belt and Land for Housing</u>, HC 275-I, paras 18-25.

3. DOE (1986) <u>Hertfordshire Structure Plan</u>, Proposed Modifications, para 3.7.

4. DOE (1992a) <u>Cheshire Replacement Structure Plan</u>, Approval Letter.

5. DOE (1988) op. cit., para 6.

6. DOE (1988b) <u>Strategic Guidance for the West Midlands</u>, PPG 10, para 12.

7. DOE (1992b) <u>Cleveland Structure Plan, Second Alteration</u>, Approval Letter.

8. Norfolk County Council (1989) <u>Green Belt</u>, Technical Report, Norfolk Structure Plan, Norwich Area, p 5.

9. DOE (1990) <u>South East Dorset Structure Plan</u>, First Alteration, Approval Letter, para 5.6.

10. Dorset County Council (1990) <u>South East Dorset Structure Plan</u>, First Alteration, policy 1.3.

11. East Dorset District Council (1991) <u>Verwood Local Plan</u>, Deposit Draft, para 3.26.

12. DOE (1988a), op. cit., para 11; DOE (1984) op. cit; para 4.

13. Macclesfield Borough Council (1992) <u>Macclesfield Local Plan</u>, Draft.

14. Oxford City Council (1992) <u>Oxford 2001 - Oxford City Local Plan Review</u>, paras 2.18-2.19.

15. House Builders Federation (1992) <u>Statement on White Land</u> to Ryedale Local Plan Inquiry round table discussion, Leeds, HBF.

16. DOE (1992c) <u>Housing</u>, PPG 3, paras 45-49.

TRANSPORT AND VEHICLE EMISSIONS

The Context

6.1 People and economic activities have been leaving urban areas for some decades, and the early results of the 1991 Census show people continuing to leave the largest cities. Dispersal also continues in the outer parts of city regions to small rural villages and towns beyond Green Belts. Some people are 'pushed' out of the cities by poor environmental conditions, high costs and congestion. Others are moving after consciously choosing a rural-based lifestyle. This is made possible by the relatively low cost of private car travel. The opportunities of increased personal mobility, as a result particularly of Motorway and trunk road construction, have reinforced this trend.

6.2 The inner and outer fringes of the Green Belts have become some of the most attractive parts of city regions, particularly to development investors. Major traffic generators, such as office and commercial developments and superstore shopping centres, have been attracted to Motorway corridors such as the M25, M42 and M62. As a result we now see more extensive and complex patterns of daily commuting, and other forms of travel across the Green Belt zones around the major cities. However, as existing road space fills, this lifestyle will become more difficult to sustain.

6.3 As people move out of cities, encouraged by opportunities for greater mobility, it does not always follow that accessibility is increased or even maintained. Land use activities become more dispersed and, through distance, car dependency is increased. This gives rise to two interrelated effects. First, travel distances to most activities increase. Secondly, there is a growth in 'escort' style journeys where car drivers are required to convey other members of the household to and from different activities. This can severely restrict 'free time' for both individuals and the household as a whole.

6.4 Not surprisingly therefore transport accounts for one quarter of all carbon dioxide emissions in Britain, and private car use makes up 90 per cent of all road travel.[1][2] Journey to work is only a quarter of the picture, with leisure journeys comprising 44 per cent of the total and rising. National forecasts, produced in 1989 suggest, if sufficient roadspace existed, there could be two and a half times as much traffic on the roads by 2025.[3] Given such scenarios, and the increasing problems of congestion, attention has been directed to the need for more sustainable patterns of urban development and energy use.

6.5 The scale of travel is influenced by a wide range of personal and behaviourial factors. Individual preferences, motivations and choices are themselves constrained by income, family structure and age. In the absence of a fundamental change in transport policy we can expect to see people travelling further in greater numbers of private vehicles. As road space in cities becomes more congested, the relative attraction of uncongested rural roads will grow, reinforcing counter-urbanisation trends. Reductions in rural services, such as

98

shops, banks and schools will lead to increases in travel from villages to nearby urban areas. The land use planning system cannot reverse these trends. However, a number of respected commentators believe that, *in combination with other fiscal and transport management measures*, land use planning policies have a role to play.[4]

Transport and Urban Form

6.6 There is an emerging consensus over the need to integrate land use and transport planning so as to encourage development patterns which minimise the need to travel. This applies internationally, through the agreement on Agenda 21 at the Rio Earth Summit, and at the European level through the recent Green Paper on Transport and the Environment.[5] At national level research on the reduction of transport emissions through planning has been carried out by the Department, following a commitment in the White Paper, *This Common Inheritance*.[6] In recent policy guidance the Government has made clear its intention to work towards ensuring that development and growth are sustainable. Planning decisions, it states, '... should not deny future generations the best of today's environment'.[7] The land use planning system clearly has a long-term influence through its powers to determine the locations and juxtapositions of uses. However, the role of land use planning and containment policies is not clear cut. We should be cautious in making exaggerated claims for any particular pattern in the absence of more detailed research.

Previous Work

6.7 Work on the relationship between urban form and energy use is coarse grained and speculative. However, the following *tentative* conclusions emerge from work carried out so far:

- Measures such as road pricing, the supply and pricing of car parking spaces and public transport enhancement (especially 'new' quality modes such as Light Rail and Guided Busways) are the most powerful ways of influencing the level of travel by private car, particularly in the short term;

- Physical land use policies have a lesser role, and will only act over the longer term. Experimental analysis carried out by Rickaby at the regional scale suggests perhaps a ten to fifteen per cent saving in fuel use may be achieved by land use changes alone over a twenty-five year period.[8]

- The physical separation of activities is the most important factor in generating the need to travel. Therefore 'compactness', in the form of contained development at reasonably high densities, will lead to lower vehicle trip lengths and frequencies.[9] It will also increase the likely attractiveness of public transport, offering the prospect of relatively short high frequency journeys.

- Compactness and containment become a problem when there is insufficient road space, and congestion problems overtake the benefits of proximity. There are no size rules for this, although Barton mentions cities of 250,000 people.[10] To an extent, in any event, congestion is a somewhat relative phenomenon being a function of perception of the acceptability of delay as much as a measured reality. Therefore perceptions of congestion may occur in much smaller settlements. However, it is only in London at present and major cities such as Leeds (700,000) in the near future where the 'throughput' of people is likely to begin declining as a result of congestion.[11]

- An alternative way of reducing the physical separation of activities would be to '... decentralise some jobs and services and relate then to residential areas'. This would comprise concentrations of jobs and services either in suburban or urban fringe areas. This is the 'dispersed concentration' model favoured by Owens.[12]

- A variant on the above would be to focus mixed development along radial corridors served by public transport extending out from existing urban boundaries; and the promotion of policies for higher densities along public transport routes within urban areas.[13]

- Within large urban areas more interspersal of uses could be encouraged. This would imply mixed use zoning. However, if transport is not made more expensive, this could lead to greater outer city movement between what would become competing centres. There would also be the problem of the protection of suburban living environments from business and other activities.

- Work based on National Travel Survey data suggests that transport energy consumption per person in towns over 25,000, with good local services and a variety of employment, is only two thirds that of small villages of less than 3,000 population, and is lower than that for London. This implies that relatively large satellite towns would, on this criterion, be a relatively energy efficient form of development.[14]

- Policies of small village expansion, or sprawl (defined as scattered or very low density rural development), would be more costly in energy terms.

- A limited amount of evidence is emerging to suggest that new settlements (freestanding or adjacent to existing urban areas), linked by high quality forms of public transport and associated traffic management, can be designed to encourage a high level of use of public transport.[15] The dispersal strategy in Leeds District is proposing 1,000 dwellings at Micklefield, partly within existing Green Belt, but adjoining the Leeds-Selby railway line.

6.8   At present these can be no more than indicative prescriptions. They point towards the following criteria being of greatest benefit:

- compactness and containment of development;

- minimisation of the distance between activities;

- the promotion of more autonomous satellite towns;

- the avoidance of sporadic development, and tight constraints on development in small villages; and

- the use of clear (transport) accessibility criteria in determining planning applications.

Role of the Green Belt

6.9   Green Belts have, through their history, 'worked with the grain' of these ideas. For example, the containment of development is an immediately observable outcome of the policy. As a result densities in urban areas have been kept up, this being aided by the redevelopment and re-cycling of urban land. Land use statistics suggest that 42 per cent of new development is being carried out on land previously used for another purpose.[16] As a result the distance between activities in towns has been kept lower than it otherwise would have been. How far this has resulted in lower fuel use is dependent on the efficiency and effectiveness of urban public transport, cycle routes or other forms of transport in particular circumstances.

6.10   The issue of distances between activities at a sub-regional or regional scale is difficult to assess. When Green Belt policy was being fashioned in the 1950s the Town and Country Planning Association suggested the width of Green Belts should be sufficient to reduce wasteful daily commuting, and assist in the creation of economically self-contained satellite towns in the countryside beyond.   In practice the scale of separation of home and work has far outstripped the average width of Green Belts. The degree of self-containment of the New Towns beyond the London Green Belt for example grew in the 1960s and early 1970s, but has been swamped by the general growth in travel since.[17] An important conclusion of Elson's National Study in 1986 was that Green Belts had not been strong enough to affect the scale of counter-urbanisation, but had shaped dispersal into compact physical forms.[18] Ever-increasing distances between homeplaces and work have been sustained by the cheapness and efficiency of the road system and the private car as a mode of travel.

6.11   Dispersed concentration, referred to in paragraph 6.7, implies the promotion of areas of mixed land use in suburban areas or the urban fringe. Most local authorities have however adopted very firm policies on the release of sites on the inner edges of Green Belts. They have not consciously planned 'self contained suburbs,' but have allowed gradual accretion by infill and rounding off. The development of 'windfall sites' has depended on site-specific economic factors rather than any transport rationale. Green Belt policy has restricted any bold initiatives to create corridor growth, or very large mixed use peripheral developments. If, by doing this, it has pushed development beyond the Green Belt then this is an adverse effect of the policy if extra car borne travel has resulted. Because of the geographical configuration of many districts choices between alternative locations for development on this sub-regional scale are rarely being addressed.

6.12 The creation of satellite towns has been made possible using the Green Belt, among other policy instruments, in some areas. There is however, a need for *very firm* peripheral restraints on the major town or city, and a relatively buoyant local economy, to create sufficient growth to be moulded by the planning system. The Oxford Green Belt is 34,000 hectares in extent, and has been operated as a five mile band around the City since 1962. One of the purposes of the settlement strategy for Oxfordshire is to concentrate development in four country towns (Witney, Bicester, Banbury and Didcot) at the same time controlling development on the edge of the City. Although there has been growth inside Oxford, and on its edge, development has been successfully promoted in the country towns such that those closest to Oxford are approaching the 20,000 population level. Jobs have increasingly located within them, and their town centres have been improved with good shopping facilities. A degree of autonomy has been created. This appears to approximate the 'decentralised concentration' model seen as robust by Owens, although the dominance of Oxford, and the lack of transport investment, has meant that commuting problems remain. Also it has taken many years for the policy to take effect. (The transport implications of the policy to expand country towns beyond the Oxford Green Belt are currently being investigated in an ESRC-sponsored project at Oxford Brookes University).

6.13 The idea of restricting sprawl is central to Green Belts, and to wider countryside planning. In our case study areas the scale of growth proposed within inset villages has been conservative in numerical terms. Sprawl in the countryside has not been allowed to occur, although there is a steady trickle of building conversions to residential use in widely scattered locations.[19] Overall local authority actions have largely removed the worst excesses of this high cost form of development. This must be counted as a success of Green Belts.

Implications for Green Belt Policy

6.14 Although we should be wary of making simplistic assertions there is an emerging view that consistently pursued policies for urban containment, over the long term, could provide the opportunity for the restraint of traffic growth. Green Belts have intrinsic appeal because they are capable of implementing long-term settlement strategies, once decided. It is the settlement policy (for example, urban containment) which carries the implications for transport, not the Green Belt policy instrument. (Containment policies operate for example in broadly the same way around Leicester and Nottingham, but only the latter has a Green Belt). There is a need to link Green Belt policy more clearly to settlement strategy and choices. In this way it will develop a rationale in regional and sub-regional planning. Scottish Office advice on Green Belts makes the relationship clear. Plans should it states, in defining Green Belts, '... relate the demand for all forms of development to a long-term settlement strategy for the plan area taking a realistic view of all the locations where demand can be met'.[20]

6.15 The West Midlands Regional Forum of Local Authorities is addressing issues at this scale and has developed four scenarios for discussion, prior to the preparation of new Regional Guidance. Where locations for housing growth to achieve sustainability are discussed it poses the question:

'... Should these locations be in balanced communities including further new towns beyond the Green Belt, thereby minimising the need for travel if a balance can be achieved, *or* should they be in transport corridors within commuting distance of the main employment centres in order to encourage the use of public transport, but at the risk of increasing car borne traffic?'

A 'social needs' scenario, which would attempt to retain existing jobs and generate new jobs in areas easily accessible to those in greatest need, would focus new development in and around the Birmingham and Coventry conurbations. This would imply significant Green Belt land releases '... on the edges of the conurbations and adjoining main towns and in transport corridors'.[21]

6.16 When developing a long-term settlement strategy in Structure Plans, local authorities are faced with deciding the appropriate balance between:

- infill and intensification in urban areas;

- peripheral development, or some form of corridor growth;

- additions to rural villages or small country towns; and

- new settlements.

Government guidance leaves some room for doubt as to the priorities between these alternatives. Local authorities are encouraged to give emphasis to the re-use of suitable vacant land within urban areas for housing. At the same time a balance is to be struck between the need for development and the interests of conservation by avoiding the sacrifice of green spaces in urban areas. New development in rural areas is to be '... sensitively related to the existing pattern of settlement having regard to the need to protect the countryside'.[22] New settlements are only to be contemplated after a long list of criteria have been satisfied. These imply it will be unlikely if many are approved. One criterion states that new settlements will only be approved where the alternative of peripheral expansion is less satisfactory.

6.17   Since 1990 policies have moved to downplay the importance of new settlements, and to raise the importance of maintaining green space in urban areas, referring to the need to avoid exceeding local environmental capacities, 'town cramming'. This suggests the balance between urban intensification and green field peripheral development is the most important one to be struck in plans. With a greater emphasis on liveability in urban areas more development will be pushed to urban peripheries.[23] Also, with small settlement expansion also seen as costly, urban peripheral development will remain the prime option. This choice would be reinforced if the development included a mixture of uses, and could be related to existing bus or light rapid transit schemes. Where new development is related to very high quality public transport provision it might comprise separate new settlements along a rail route rather than a continuous corridor development extending from an existing urban area. This option, if it were to occur, would involve locating new settlements in Green Belts.

6.18   The major implication of the transport arguments in this Chapter is that authorities should take account of the need to promote sustainable patterns of development in drawing long-term Green Belt boundaries. Elevating the importance of sustainability may involve the re-drawing of Green Belt boundaries in some areas. Local authorities will also need to search for white land areas in peripheral locations well-related to public transport routes.

Main Findings and Recommendations

6.19   *Contained patterns of development can support policies which are designed to reduce the need to travel.*

The literature reviewed, and expert opinion, suggests containment policies can assist in creating more sustainable patterns of development. The influence of land use planning is likely to be long-term. Shorter term reductions in the growth of pollution are more likely through public transport enhancement, and such measures as the pricing of road and car parking space. Green Belts are important because they halt costly private car-dependent sprawl, creating compact forms of development, thus minimizing the distance between activities [6.9-6.13].

6.20   *Green Belts allow issues of the relative concentration or dispersal of activities at the sub-regional level, and their transport implications, to be clearly addressed.*

Because most Green Belts cover a number of local authority areas they can implement decisions made on the balance between urban intensification, peripheral development and additions to small freestanding towns and villages, at sub-regional level. Scottish Office advice makes this sub-regional role more explicit than advice in England, stating that in defining Green Belts plans authorities should relate the demand for all forms of development to a long-term settlement strategy for the plan area [6.14-6.16].

6.21 *Where there is a requirement for the development of greenfield sites, principles of sustainable development may conflict with policies for the retention of existing Green Belt boundaries.*

If Green Belt boundaries are too tight, in the absence of urban infill new development will be pushed beyond them. If Green Belts are too wide the distance between activities will be unnecessarily increased. The result will be wasteful extra journeys, often by private car. Given these problems, well-contained urban peripheral developments and, occasionally, free-standing settlements along public transport corridors within and beyond city fringes, may be the preferred 'models'. If principles of sustainability are to be given greater importance in the future then the re-drawing of the inner boundaries of some Green Belts may be necessary. These principles will need to extend to the definition of white land [6.14-6.17].

It is recommended that:

R.35 *Local authorities should take account of the need to promote sustainable patterns of development when drawing up Green Belt boundaries in development plans [6.14-6.17].*

R.36 *The boundaries of white land should also create the potential for compact forms of development well-related to public transport [6.14-6.18].*

R.37 *Green Belt boundaries should represent the outcome of a considered judgement on the sustainability attributes of development in urban areas, development beyond the Green Belt, or development by additions to towns and villages within it [6.14-6.16].*

R.38 *The possibility of freestanding new settlements located along very high quality public transport corridors in the Green Belt should be evaluated in deciding on settlement strategies [6.17].*

References

1. The best general account of the relationship between transport demands and urban form is Breheny, M. (1992) <u>Sustainable Development and Urban Form</u>, London, Pion. See also Owens, S. (1991) <u>Energy Conscious Planning</u>, London, CPRE.

2. Rickaby, P.A., J. P. Steadman and M. Barrett (1992) 'Patterns of Land Use in English Towns: Implications for Energy Use and Carbon Dioxide Emissions', in Breheny, M. (ed.) (op. cit), p 195.

3. Countryside Commission (1992) <u>Trends in Transport and the Countryside</u>, CCP 382, Cheltenham, Countryside Commission.

4. See, for example, Banister, D. (1992) 'The Congestion Gap: Planning and Technical Solutions', paper to Cambridge Econometrics Annual Conference, Cambridge, July; Owens, S. (1991) op.cit.; Rickaby et al (1992), op.cit.

5. EC Transport and Environment Commission (1992) <u>The Impact of Transport on the Environment</u>, Brussels, EC.

6. See DOE (1993) <u>Reducing Transport Emissions Through Planning</u>, London, HMSO; HM Government (1991) <u>This Common Inheritance</u>, Cmnd 1200, London, HMSO.

7. DOE (1992) <u>Development Plans and Regional Planning Guidance</u>, PPG 12, London, HMSO, para 1.8.

8. Rickaby, P.A., et. alia., op.cit.

9. See University of Reading and David Lock Associates (1993) <u>Alternative Development Patterns, New Settlements</u>, (unpublished, London, DOE, Appendix 2).

10. Barton, H. (1992) 'City Transport: Strategies for Sustainability', in Breheny, M. (ed.) (1992) op. cit., pp 197-216.

11. Steer Davies Gleave (1991) <u>Leeds Transport Strategy</u>, Leeds, SDG.

12. Owens, S. (1991) op. cit.

13. Barton, H. (1992) op.cit.

14. Banister, D. (1992) 'Energy Use, Transport and Settlement Patterns', in Breheny, M. (ed.) (1992) op.cit., pp 160-181.

15. Steer Davies Gleave (1992) <u>East Leicester Transport Choice Strategy</u>, Leeds, SDG; Steer Davies Gleave (1992) <u>Midmeredales (Hull) Guided Bus Pilot Project</u>, Leeds, SDG.

16. DOE (1992) Land Use Change in England No 7, Statistical Bulletin (92)4, London, DOE.

17. Breheny, M. (1992) 'The Contradictions of the Compact City: A Review', in Breheny, M. (ed.) 1992, op. cit.

18. Elson, M.J. (1986) Green Belts: Conflict Mediation in the Urban Fringe, Heinemann, London, p 252-3.

19. See Chapter Two, and Appendix C.

20. Scottish Development Department (1985) Development in the Countryside and Green Belts, Circular 24/1985, Edinburgh, SDD.

21. West Midlands Regional Forum of Local Authorities (1992) The West Midlands: Your Region, Your Future, Making the Right Choices, Paper No 2, Stafford, WMRFLA; paras 7.19 and 7.80.

22. DOE (1992) Housing, PPG 3, London, HMSO.

23. New Homes Marketing Group (1990) New Homes and a Better Environment, London, HBF.

7.   GREEN BELTS IN SCOTLAND

Introduction

7.1   This Chapter considers the role of the Green Belts around Edinburgh and Glasgow, and relates this to the advice in Circular 24/1985. The information is based on interviews with the Regional Council, Edinburgh City, Midlothian, Eastwood and Motherwell Districts and the Scottish Office Environment Department (SOEnD). The work carried out on Green Belts in Scotland comprised *policy case studies*. Detailed development control analysis or assessment of appeals was not carried out. Also there was no wide-ranging programme of interviews with conservation and development interests, as in the study of Green Belts in England. The findings relate therefore to the major parameters of Green Belt policy only, in the context of a possible up-dating of Scotish Office Circular 24/1985.

7.2   In 1990 there were five approved Green Belts in Scotland, totalling some 165,000 hectares (Table 7.1) (Scottish Office, 1991).[1] Scotland's total area of Green Belt has fluctuated through the years, most significantly with the abandonment of the Dundee Green Belt and a major reduction in the Aberdeen Green Belt in the eighties. In August 1992, proposals for new Green Belts in the Central Region, around Stirling, Dunblane and Alloa, were approved.[2] In September 1992 the Secretary of State for Scotland approved some exceptional housing land release in the Greater Glasgow Green Belt, and a significant Green Belt extension around Ayr, Prestwick and Troon.[3] Green Belt policy, originally put forward in Circular 14/1960, is currently operated under Circular 24/1985.[4] In conjunction with general policy guidance on development in the countryside, this sets out the three main purposes of Green Belts in Scotland as:

- to maintain the identity of towns by establishing a clear definition of their physical boundaries and preventing coalescence;

- to provide countryside for recreation or institutional purposes of various kinds; and

- to maintain the landscape setting of towns.

Defining Green Belts

7.3   The general location of Green Belts, and development control policies to be applied within them, are proposed in structure plans, prepared by the Regional Authorities. These are, in turn, approved by the Secretary of State for Scotland. The structure plan, it states in Circular 24/1985, should '... set out the urban settlement structure necessary to meet the demographic, economic and social needs of the area' within the plan period. Outwith the settlement

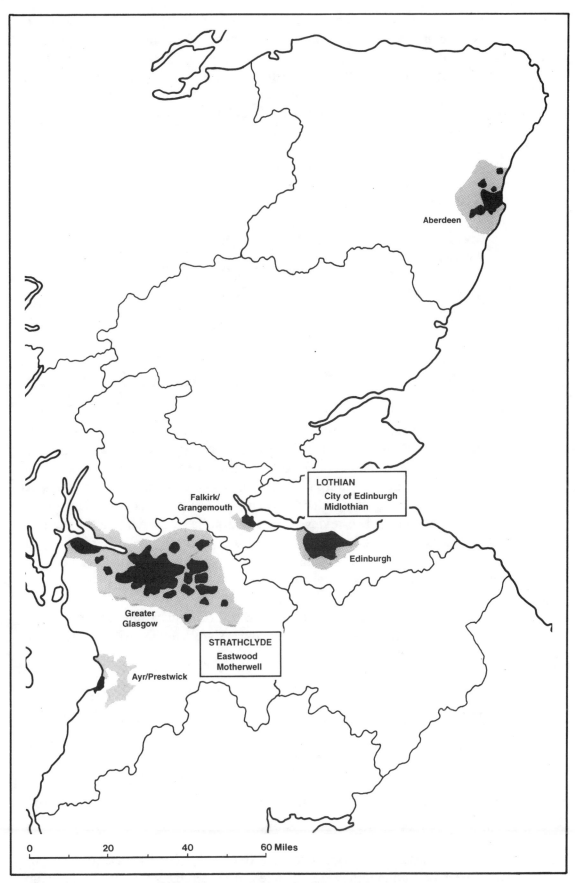

Figure 7.1: Green Belts in Scotland.

109

structure thus defined authorities may, where there are strong development demands adjacent to large towns and cities, strictly control development by Green Belt policies.[5] There is no discussion of the precise longevity of the Green Belt, and there are no provisions for the possible inclusion of white land, or a similar policy, in development plans. Circular 24/1985 states that towns and villages within Green Belts should not be allowed to expand beyond the detailed limits established in local plans.

Table 7.1: Area of Approved Green Belts 1990

green belt	hectares
Aberdeen	23,664
Ayr/Prestwick	2,853
Falkirk/Grangemouth	3,495
Greater Glasgow	120,000
Lothian	14,600
total	164,612

Source: Scottish Office (1991) Scotland: Land Use and Physical Features, Edinburgh, SO.

7.4   Circular 24/1985 was introduced at a time when countryside policies were seen as too restrictive. The Circular suggests that the 'stability and endurance' of Green Belt policies could only be expected where '... a balance between containment and growth of urban development can be sustained on a long term basis'.[6] In relating this rather Delphic phrase to structure plans, local authorities are advised to review Green Belt policies by relating the demand for all forms of development to a long term settlement strategy for the plan area, taking a realistic view of all the locations where the demand can be met. Such reviews, it is stated, might involve:

- identifying land on the inner boundaries of, and within settlements in, Green Belts which is no longer making a significant contribution to Green Belt objectives;

- identifying the scope for infill in towns and villages within Green Belts; and

- bringing into use derelict land, or land with little or no inherent agricultural value, in towns or villages within Green Belts.

Where derelict land, or land of no agricultural value, is not to be developed it should be subject to environmental improvement.[7]

7.5   Thus, while Ministers in Scotland have frequently stated their strong support for Green Belt policy, they do not rule out some change as part of structure plan reviews. There is concern that local authorities put forward any such proposals on a well-researched basis, for example looking at all locations where demand can be met. But, at the same time, once reviews have been incorporated into structure plans, further adjustments to boundaries should only be needed, it is suggested, in exceptional circumstances. This implies that changes proposed in any structure plan review would need to satisfy this criterion.

Development Control

7.6   The advice suggests there should be a general presumption against any intrusion into Green Belts. Paragraph 4 (iv) states:

> '... approval should not be given, except in very special circumstances, for the construction of new buildings and the extension or change of use of existing buildings, for purposes other than agriculture, horticulture, woodland management and recreation, or establishments and institutions standing in extensive grounds or other uses appropriate to the rural character of the area'.

There are no elaborations relating to tourism, or any mention of farm diversification. Minerals are not mentioned in the Circular, and there is no discussion of how far development plans might be permitted, or not, to elaborate the basic wording relating to development control contained in the guidance.[8]

7.7   Regional Councils have the power to call-in any application of strategic importance for their own decision. In the case of the Edinburgh Green Belt, for example, a notification system exists whereby Districts inform Lothian Regional Council of all applications in the Green Belt. Applications are differentiated by their significance in terms of the Structure Plan's Green Belt policy. Applications considered significant are notified to other authorities in the Region before permission is granted. In the case of applications considered non-significant this is only done after the event. The Secretary of State for Scotland also has power to call-in applications from either of the other levels. This power has only been used in a very small number of major cases. Called-in applications normally go to a public local inquiry. In some Green Belt areas the relevant local authorities have concluded Green Belt Agreements, essentially codes of practice to ensure the uniform interpretation and implementation of Green Belt Policy between authorities (see para 7.3).

The Edinburgh Green Belt

Aims

7.8   The Edinburgh Green Belt extends to a depth of between two and three miles around the City, and has been in existence since the mid 1950's. The Green Belt, formally approved in 1956, has the following aims:

111

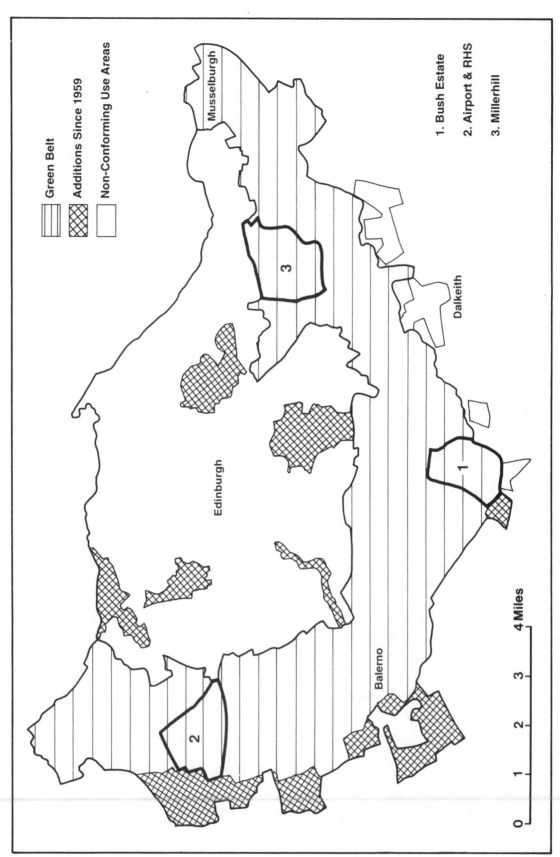

Figure 7.2: Edinburgh Green Belt.

Green Belt

Additions Since 1959

Non-Conforming Use Areas

1. Bush Estate
2. Airport & RHS
3. Millerhill

Musselburgh

Dalkeith

Edinburgh

Balerno

0 1 2 3 4 Miles

- to limit the further expansion of the City;

- to prevent the merging of built-up areas;

- to prevent the use of agricultural land for development, and

- to preserve and enhance the landscape setting of the Capital.[9]

7.9   In 1974 the Scottish Office approved extensions in the form of green areas in the City, including Holyrood Park, the Braid Hills and Corstorphine Hill. All but one of these are detached from the main peripheral area of Green Belt, but perform a function as major elements of what has been termed 'the landscape within the City structure' (see Figure 7.2). At the same time some 940 acres (380 ha) of land was taken from the inner edge of the Green Belt for housing. The major changes since this time occurred in 1988. Following a boundaries review in that year some 94 hectares of land were deleted from the inner edge of the Green Belt, but 500 hectares were added to its outer edges around the town of Balerno, to the south west, and in other outer areas. Urban envelopes around some smaller settlements in outer areas were also defined.[10]

The Green Belt Agreement

7.10   As part of the approved first Lothian Structure Plan in 1979 the Regional Council agreed to provide further guidance for local plans, and develop a code of practice for development control in the Green Belt. This led to the conclusion, in 1983, of the Edinburgh Green Belt Agreement. Apart from giving detailed definition to Green Belt boundaries the Agreement covers:

- development control in the Green Belt; where it states that permission will not be given for new development or redevelopment other than for agriculture, forestry, active recreation or other uses appropriate to a rural area, *except that which can be shown to be necessary and of strategic significance and for which no suitable alternative location exists outwith the Green Belt.* This follows structure and local plan policy.

- environment; where it states that any planning consents for new development or for alterations to the use, size or appearance of existing development in the Green Belt, *will contain provisions to improve the landscape and architectural quality of development within the Green Belt.*

- urban envelopes (inset settlements); here any consents *will contain appropriate provisions to improve views of the settlement from elsewhere in the Green Belt.*

- landscape enhancement; here a programme of remedial landscaping will be adopted by member authorities.

- non-conforming developments: the 1979 Structure Plan accepted there were a number of major uses, already in the Green Belt, whose further development may be justified. These are the Edinburgh University Research Centre at Bush, the Airport and Royal Highland Showground, Heriot Watt University at Riccarton and the Millerhill Railway Marshalling Yards. The Agreement states that the expansion requirements of these uses will be considered in relation to their *strategic significance*.[11] (Authors' emphasis).

7.11 The Agreement, most importantly, created a consultation process to aid uniformity of decision-making. Any application contrary to Green Belt policy objectives, or for the expansion of an existing non-conforming use, is circulated to other authorities for comment. The other authorities can make their views known to the circulating authority. If matters remain unresolved the application is referred to a meeting of the Joint Planning Liaison Committee, at which elected representatives of all Green Belt authorities are represented. Failure to agree at this stage may lead to call-in by the Regional Council or, after notification, by the Secretary of State. There has been no formal monitoring of the Agreement. A report by Lothian Regional Council, however, suggests that some authorities have encouraged a more liberal approach to certain types of applications, especially those for change of use and extensions to existing properties. This may relate, in particular, to the non-conforming use areas, the Regional Council stating '... the full potential of the major non-conforming uses has not been inhibited by Green Belt policy'.[12]

The Lothian Structure Plan - First Review 1985

7.12 The First Review of the Structure Plan took place at around the time of the publication of Circular 24/1985. It retained the original purposes of the Edinburgh Green Belt, and reinstated the development control principles from the 1983 Green Belt Agreement. (These do not, of course, fully accord with the 1985 Circular). The submitted plan suggested that land for housebuilding over the Plan period to 1996 was to come from a mixture of:

- infill within urban areas, and

- the development of greenfield sites beyond the existing built-up area.

The approved Structure Plan considered that if, in addition to the existing land supply, 450 dwellings per year came forward as infill within the Edinburgh built-up area, there would be no need to take any more Green Belt land for development until after 1991. However if, by this date, no alternatives were available it was recognised that the release of some Green Belt land for housing might be necessary.[13] A number of local plans had already begun to identify environmentally undistinguished areas of Green Belt for possible development. In order to identify 'stable long-term boundaries' the Scottish Office approval letter for the 1985 Plan instructed the local authorities to carry

114

out an expeditious review of Green Belt boundaries, along the lines suggested in Circular 24/1985. This was completed in 1988 and proposed, at detailed level:

- extensions to the Green Belt of some 200 hectares; and

- deletions of some 183 hectares, on the inner boundaries within the City by-pass, or alongside outer settlements.

7.13   The accepted Green Belt boundaries around Edinburgh should remain stable at least until the end date of the Structure Plan. As the Review states; 'This ... refers to policy requirements to 1996, and the new Green Belt boundary should endure to that date. If subsequent Structure Plan alterations or reviews decide that new development land is needed, the settlement strategy will have to be reviewed'.[14]

Success of Policy Objectives

7.14   The effectiveness of the Green Belt policy was discussed by the Regional Council in papers published in 1989, and is further debated in papers forming part of the current review.[15]

7.15   The objective of containing urban growth has become more difficult to sustain as demands for lower density housing, industrial, commercial and retail space have continued. In the last ten years infill development in Edinburgh has run ahead of the predicted 450 dwellings per annum specified in the Plan, but this is now putting pressure on the character of existing good quality living environments in the City. As a result the Edinburgh City Centre Local Plan has an approved anti-intensification policy for residential areas.[16] The lack of any white land or its equivalent suggests the likely revision of Green Belt boundaries at each Plan review. This has, in practice, occurred. So far the changes to the inner boundary, whilst of medium scale, appear not to have seriously impaired the basic purposes of the Lothian Region Green Belt.

7.16   The role of the Green Belt in preventing coalescence with nearby settlements has assumed greater importance through time. Some development has leapfrogged what is, in UK terms, quite a narrow Green Belt, to such areas as South Queensferry, Balerno and Dalkeith. The construction of the Edinburgh by-pass has placed extra pressures on Green Belt land, not all of which have been resisted.

7.17   Although overall the need to prevent the loss of agricultural land to development has lessened, large parts of the Edinburgh Green Belt are of prime agricultural quality. This Green Belt objective therefore remains important. Finally, in a number of areas urban fringe pressures have had an impact on farmed landscapes, as have intrusions from new infrastructure, such as roads. A number of the prominent landscape features within Edinburgh, are regarded as virtually sacrosanct, and a subtle pattern of ridgelines and secondary landscape features provide visual containment, thus 'fitting' the City into its setting. This issue was discussed at length in the South East Edinburgh Local Plan.[17]   Landscape improvement has also been the theme of the Edinburgh Green Belt Initiative.[18]

Effectiveness of the Edinburgh Green Belt

7.18   The basic aims of limiting the further physical expansion of the City, and preventing coalescence, have clearly been achieved.   Although minor incursions have been made to the south of the City, and somewhat larger ones to the west, the containment provided by the by-pass has proved effective here. The Green Belt is a narrow cordon which acts to channel development to particular locations within other parts of Lothian. There have been significant additions to the outer edge of the Green Belt through time. An important debate is arising as to whether any large-scale new development which can be justified should go beyond the Green Belt, or be accommodated as a peripheral expansion to the City itself, in land which is now Green Belt. Transport, vehicle emission and infrastructure cost arguments could to be marshalled in favour of the peripheral development solution (see Chapter 6).

7.19   A second major issue relates to 'high amenity' sites. The Scottish Office National Planning Guideline of 1985 relating to individual high amenity sites states '... Structure Plans should include policies that reflect the special needs of high technology industries in terms of high amenity, environment and accessibility'.[19]   These attributes may often be present in Green Belt locations, as the 1988 Edinburgh Boundary Review suggests. The Review also indicates that, once allocated, such sites should remain within the Green Belt, thus offering greater control over future growth.[20] One high amenity Green Belt site has been released at Melville Gate near Dalkeith, but has been developed subsequently for office use. The new Use Classes Order provides little certainty for local authorities that sites initially allocated or used for high technology activities will remain in such use. There are considerable pressures from Scottish Enterprise and the Local Enterprise Companies for a continual supply of such sites.[21]

7.20   The economic fortunes of Midlothian District have been constrained for many years by lack of infrastructure, especially roads. The situation has now improved with the Edinburgh by-pass dissecting the Green Belt south of the City.   As a result Midlothian are seeking new high amenity sites for employment within the Green Belt, and adjacent to main by-pass junctions. These were recommended in a Study *Midlothian - Towards 2000*, recently completed for the Council by consultants.

7.21   Areas of non-conforming use are also a problem. These comprise large sites where it is considered the growth of well-established uses should not be unduly inhibited. All remain within the Green Belt notation, that is, 'washed over'. They are shown in Figure 7.2, and are listed in paragraph 7.3. Policy

116

states that further development of these uses will be considered '... in relation to their strategic significance for Green Belt principles'. In some instances this may not be a problem. It is relatively clear-cut to distinguish the necessary operational requirements of Edinburgh Airport from opportunistic proposals (eg. petrol filling stations, hotels and retail outlets) seeking a competitive advantage by developing a site near the Airport. The policy is less clear where educational, institutional and business uses are concerned. Expansion is a particular issue. For example, in relation to the Heriot-Watt (HW) Riccarton campus, the Ratho, Newbridge and Kirkliston Local Plan states that '... the expansion requirements (of the University) within their existing boundaries will be supported provided they can be shown to be of strategic significance'.[22] The original HW site was regarded as an exceptional circumstance within the Green Belt. It now comprises new University buildings with Science Park additions. Phase one was within the site and users were controlled by a Section 50 Agreement. Phase two did not have an agreement, but was still within the relevant curtilage. Phase three has been approved on new greenfield land outside the relevant curtilage, but with a Section 50 Agreement. In the case of Bush Farm, in Midlothian District, a consultant study has suggested the development of a University agricultural research establishment in large grounds as a 'Technopole', along the lines of a similar development near Nice, France. Permission has been granted for 'high tech' and related uses beyond the area of the grounds immediately around the House, although it is likely this will become office development.

7.22 A third issue relates to sites of strategic significance in the Green Belt. The approved Lothian Structure Plan refers to allowing, within Green Belts, only uses appropriate to a rural area, except those which can be shown as *necessary*, and of *strategic significance*, and for which no alternative location exists. One example of the use of these arguments is approval of the siting of the new Edinburgh Southern General Hospital in the Green Belt. Also there are currently four competing football stadia proposals in the Edinburgh Green Belt. These relate to new grounds for Hearts and Hibernian Football Clubs. The proposals also include leisure uses and other forms of built development. They have been called-in for decision by the Regional Council, and may be treated as sites of strategic significance which cannot be easily fitted into the urban area.

7.23 Both the non-conforming use areas, and the sites of strategic significance, have the potential to erode the Green Belt from within. It could be argued they result from defects in the original definition of Green Belt boundaries. For sites of such scale and importance exclusion from the Green Belt, as insets, might be a course of action leading to less uncertainty and conflict. If the aim is not to inhibit the economic potential of such areas, it seems inappropriate that they remain in Green Belt. Those who perceive the Green Belt in landscape terms think it logical to retain the non-conforming uses within Green Belt so that any contribution to the high quality landscape around Edinburgh can be retained and enhanced as development proceeds.

Other Issues

7.24 The Regional Council record a steady flow of small-scale developments in the Green Belt, many of which are adjudged to have little impact on its open rural appearance (for example riding stables, barn conversions and small hotel extensions). However, a number of issues relating to development control are important here. Firstly, the Circular refers to 'recreation' as an acceptable Green Belt use. This is, in practice, generally interpreted as outdoor recreation. However for large schemes, with major job impacts, other priorities may obtain. A large indoor 'Tropical World' scheme, with a major car park, was supported by Midlothian District and the Regional Council. The words of the Circular could be improved to clarify recreation issues such as the extent and type of ancillary buildings allowable, or levels of use. Secondly, the interpretation of 'very special circumstances' in the Circular (para 4.iv) is left to the Regions, and has not been systematically monitored by the Scottish Office.[23] More information is needed here, by an analysis of development control decisions and appeals.

7.25 Thirdly, farm diversification has not to date been seen by The Scottish Office and its Agriculture Department as a problem in Green Belt policy terms, although Lothian Regional Council were less sanguine about this. This should be further investigated. Fourthly, policies on the re-use of redundant farm buildings should be clarified. The policy here (although not written down) is to allow conversion or refurbishment to residential use. The Guidance, however, does not refer to the attitude to changes to other uses, and this should be remedied. Finally, in the approved Lothian Structure Plan there is a presumption against mineral working in the Green Belt. Minerals (and waste disposal) are not referred to in the existing Scottish Office Guidance. Consideration should be given to policy on these topics.

Central Region Green Belts

7.26 The Structure Plan for Central Region, approved in August 1992, contains a number of new 'separating' Green Belts in the area of Falkirk, Bridge of Allen, Stirling, Dunblane and Alloa. The Green Belts are justified on two grounds:

- to prevent coalescence, and

- to protect the landscape setting of towns.

In drawing up boundaries in local plans, the Plan states a need to limit Green Belts '... only to the key strategic areas of land requiring long-term protection'.[24] This may mean that the Green Belt boundary may not be contiguous with the edge of the current built-up area, allowing scope for future development beyond 2001. Green Belt policy is intended not only to protect the landscape settings of towns such as Falkirk and Stirling, but also areas of countryside forming the setting of heritage features of natural and/or regional importance, such as the site of the Battle of Bannockburn and Cambuskenneth Abbey.

7.27 The development control guidelines approved in the Structure Plan also contain new wording. They state:

> '... with the exception of development required for farming and forestry, or tourism and recreation purposes that require a countryside location, (but excluding urban forms of development such as hotels, time share developments or holiday villages), new development in the Green Belt will be firmly resisted'.[25]

The reference to tourism purposes that require a countryside location appears unique. Of more general importance is the mention of 'requirement for a countryside location' as a criterion for decision-making.

The Greater Glasgow Green Belt

Aims

7.28 The Greater Glasgow Green Belt is some 120,000 hectares in extent, nearly ten times as large as the Edinburgh Green Belt (see Figure 7.3). First proposed in the *Clyde Valley Plan* of 1946, the Green Belt around Glasgow has been established and added to in a range of development plans since 1958. The reasons for designation have, however, remained the same:

- to check the future growth of built-up areas;

- to prevent neighbouring towns from merging;

- to preserve the special character of towns, including their landscape setting;

- to protect agricultural land from development; and

- to preserve landscape character and provide for the enjoyment of the countryside.[26]

The Renewal Strategy

7.29 In a Regional Report in 1976 the Regional Council contended that it was no longer necessary to promote policies of continued overspill of people and jobs from the Conurbation. If unchecked, processes of decentralisation would exacerbate the decline of urban areas and impede their regeneration. The Secretary of State agreed, in response, that action to deal with shortages of employment and inner city deprivation must be based on a new *urban renewal* strategy. This would seek to utilise existing physical and social infrastructure, and promote the development of vacant and derelict urban land. The 1979

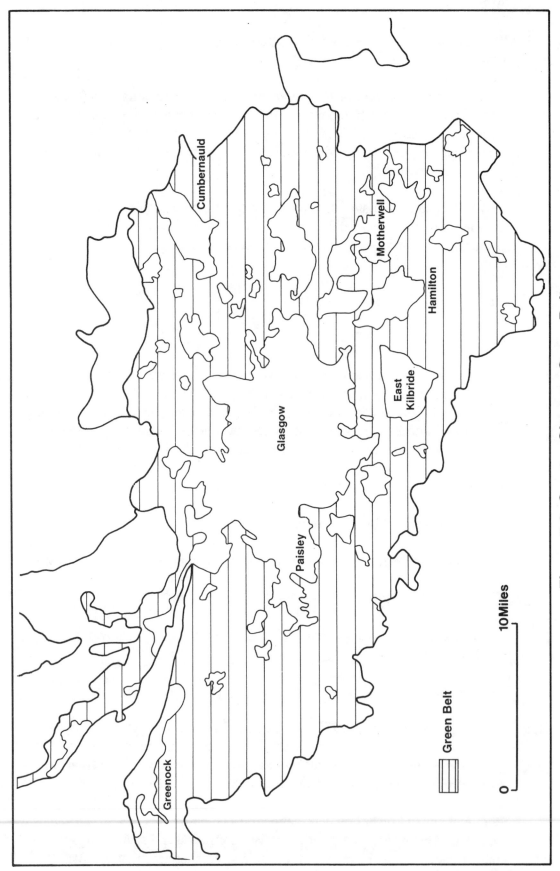

Figure 7.3: Greater Glasgow Green Belt.

Green Belt

0   10Miles

Cumbernauld

Motherwell

Hamilton

East Kilbride

Glasgow

Paisley

Greenock

Structure Plan laid out this strategy, and the complementary role of Green Belt as a policy instrument. Urban renewal would be assisted by:

- the provision of an adequate supply of development land;

- the identification of development opportunities, particularly for employment uses; and

- the conservation and improvement of the environment.

7.30 The Renewal Strategy utilises Green Belt in a strong supporting role to ensure that:

- future greenfield land releases are related to an identified need for new land whilst achieving wider social benefits;

- speculative pressure for urban expansion into the countryside does not jeopardise the process of renewal; and

- action to upgrade the environment on the urban fringe can proceed with confidence.[27]

Monitoring evidence suggests that during the 1980s the Green Belt assisted in focusing new development onto brownfield sites. The second update of the Structure Plan in 1986 noted an increased proportion of private sector housing completions on redevelopment sites, the level growing from 27 per cent in 1981 to 60 per cent in 1985. By 1985 some two thirds of industrial completions were on recycled land. The annual release of greenfield land had decreased from around 400 hectares in the 1970s to around 50 hectares in the 1980s.[28]

7.31 The principle at work was that of maintaining a *balance* between urban redevelopment and greenfield development using Green Belt as a regulator. The Regional Council has therefore sought to retain the Region's competitiveness by continuing to provide a range of attractive development opportunities, particularly for employment, in urban peripheral locations. Circular 24/1985 is interpreted in the 1986 Written Statement as follows:

'... The settlement strategy seeks to ensure that there is an appropriate scale, quality and distribution of land to meet likely future demands for development. This is achieved through opportunities arising from the recycling of redundant urban land, supported where necessary with the planned expansion of urban areas into greenfield sites. At any one time, the required balance varies'.[29]

The need for land release from the Green Belt has been considered in the context of biennial updates of the Structure Plan submitted to the Secretary of

State for Scotland. To date these have been modified and approved in the light of objections without recourse to EIP.

The Last Five Years

7.32 By 1988 the Regional Council concluded that the economic strength of the City and conurbation was such that a greater measure of greenfield housing, 'high amenity' industrial development, and out of centre retail and office uses could be accommodated. Two factors came together in the 1990 Update:

- a reduction in the rate at which brownfield sites were being brought forward, partly due to reduced support for land renewal from the Scottish Development Agency; and

- a calculation that the sites for 33,000 dwellings previously programmed for development in Greater Glasgow and Lanarkshire by 1997 would need to be boosted by a further 13,000 to meet revised demands.

To achieve this the 1990 Update proposed that the Green Belt should contribute sites for 6,000 dwellings from around twenty selected locations, on the basis that many of the less difficult brownfield sites had been used, and that the bringing on-line of many of those which remained was likely to be erratic and unpredictable. The Regional Council's selection of Green Belt release locations was based on a consideration of Green Belt quality (in terms of purposes and landscape prospects), accessibility, infrastructure, effectiveness for development by 1997, marketability, distribution and housing choice. SRC sought to avoid options with an excessive carry-over after 1997 which might divert attention from urban renewal, but some of the chosen locations contained a specified longer term capacity. The releases totalled around 200 hectares.[30] It is notable that the basic locations were selected as suitable and practicable by the Regional Council and approved in the Structure Plan Update. They were not passed down as numbers of dwellings required on a district-wide basis. In approving this Update, and its exceptional provisions for land release, the Secretary of State for Scotland set out the criteria for release so that they could be applied to any other locations required after reassessing the land supply. Precise site boundaries are to be identified through the various districts' local plans and development control.[31]

7.33 Strathclyde Regional Council contend that the greenfield land releases do not constitute a change in policy direction. However Eastwood District, a prosperous commuter suburb to the south west of Glasgow, scheduled to receive the largest new allocation in approved Green Belt, has considerable reservations over the policy. They had successfully retained Green Belt boundaries in the District, defined in four local plans, over the 1980-86 period. In the draft District Local Plan (1992) however, Green Belt land releases have reluctantly been proposed to accord with Regional guidelines. The District is now concerned that the degree of permanence implied by Green Belt

122

designation in the past will be more difficult to uphold in the future. Some 80 hectares of land have been identified for release south of Newton Mearns. The District is keen to retain control and co-ordination over any development, rather than allowing land release by appeal. The draft District Plan therefore contains a set of criteria to be followed by developers, including a requirement for extensive structural tree planting along the Green Belt boundary, and provision for the extension of a proposed Light Rapid Transit network into the sites.[32]

Employment Sites

7.34   Employment sites have, on occasion, also been provided in the Strathclyde Green Belt. This follows production of the National Planning Guideline on High Technology Industry in 1985 (see para 7.19). A working party identified a number of sites in the Strathclyde Green Belt, and at least one of them at Erskine (the Compaq site) received permission in 1987. The 1990 Structure Plan Update suggests that three other proven Green Belt sites exist for single industrial or business users. During 1992 a further single user site has been proposed in Motherwell District as part of land to be released to form a Lanarkshire Enterprise Zone, in response to the announced closure of the Ravenscraig Steel Works. This process of site selection and approval, and the lack of subsequent control through the General Development Order, has been criticised. It has been suggested that the schemes have compromised the coalescence and landscape conservation purposes of Green Belts in the region, and in some cases land has been sold by the Scottish Development Agency without covenants restricting future activities to high technology use.[33] In addition to single user high amenity sites the most recently approved Structure Plan includes around 35 hectares of land, previously in the Green Belt, for industrial and business use.

7.35   Circular 24/1985 refers to the need for local authorities to take a *long term* view of the demand for all forms of development and resulting settlement strategy before defining Green Belt boundaries.[34] No reference is made to white land or its equivalent. In Strathclyde there is no white land. The 1986 Structure Plan Update discusses the reasons why. Basically it is contended that if land was to be excluded from the Green Belt for long-term needs:

- there would be problems in controlling the rate at which it was released;

- a two-tier Green Belt would be created which would undermine the simplicity of the Green Belt concept; and

- most damagingly, such a scheme would undermine the prospect for upgrading and re-instating the urban fringe by creating uncertainty about the value of remedial action to improve landscapes in the area of interim status.[35]

The Secretary of State has indicated, in correspondence with Strathclyde, that 'long term' means *ten years or more*. The 'stability and endurance' of Green Belt referred to in the Circular is intended to relate to that period. In Strathclyde there is no overall plan period. The Regional Council have varying plan periods for different issues. For example housing provision is planned over a seven year period. The Regional Council take the view that Green Belt policy should provide control *indefinitely*, but that there should be flexibility to move the inner boundary of the Green Belt as the strategy is updated.

Development Control

7.36　Strathclyde Regional Council (SRC) operate a strategic overview role in development control. There are very few applications, possibly 15 a year, called in by SRC. These are normally in Green Belt. Hospital sites have been released, notably one in Eastwood District. The Regional Council treat hospital sites embedded in the edge of urban areas as brownfield sites, and others as greenfield sites. They claimed few problems. Eastwood District however would prefer a Scottish version of DOE Circular 12/91 relating to the re-use of redundant hospital sites. Golf courses are regarded as acceptable uses, although 'fairway housing' is invariably ruled out. SRC recently opposed a new hotel in the Green Belt on the grounds that an adequate supply of accommodation was available elsewhere.

7.37　Eastwood, which is one of the most strict Districts by reputation in terms of development control, has the following policies in its draft Plan:

- allowing farm diversification to new farm uses in selected parts of the Green Belt, as long as there are no adverse environmental impacts;

- establishing a presumption against quarrying, sand and gravel extraction and peat working;

- allowing the conversion of derelict farm buildings to residential uses, subject to a range of criteria:

- supporting forestry planting where water courses, landscape and recreational access will not be harmed or restricted; and

- restricting wind turbine developments to areas where landscape and heritage resources, including locally-important views, will not be affected.[36]

Conclusion

7.38　Although the policy wording may have some difference, it appears the overall outcome of the operation of Green Belt policy in the Glasgow Conurbation is not dissimilar from other areas across the UK. The Green Belt was established in a comprehensive manner at strategic level in 1979, since when large numbers of local plans have added a patchwork of not fully complete detail. In 1985 the Circular invited local authorities to take a new long-term look at Green Belts and review boundaries if necessary. Over the period 1980-91 relatively little land was taken from the 1979 Green Belt. The changes accepted in 1992 are relatively small (200-300 hectares) given the full extent of the Green Belt. The conurbation-wide view of the Regional Council has clearly assisted in the selection of sites for development in suitable locations.

Main Findings and Recommendations

7.39   Green Belt purposes in Scotland remain limited. For example, checking sprawl is not specifically listed as a purpose in the Green Belt guidance; neither is preventing encroachment into the countryside. Urban regeneration, and protection of the historic character of towns, are also not mentioned. It may be worth considering whether creating a clearly-defined boundary, and preventing coalescence, are broad enough and sufficient purposes to cover the range of circumstances in which Green Belt policy might be applied in the future. The new Structure Plan for the Central Region defines Green Belts in limited areas where the prevention of coalescence is a problem, and in (wider) areas where the protection of the countryside is important to the landscape setting of towns. If the Lothian Region were to adopt only the Circular 24/1985 purposes this would take away their current Green Belt objective of limiting the further expansion of the City. In other words a Green Belt around Edinburgh based on coalescence and landscape arguments only might take a different form, and might not, in theory be a continuous belt around the City. The objective of providing for recreation has proved confusing to some. It is not always clear that if retaining the open nature of the Green Belt is important, there is a need to qualify the general term 'recreation'. In the Central Region Plan of 1992 tourism uses are discussed and ruled out. In strict terms the current guidance mentions landscape, but not the retention of openness *per se*. This might be referred to under the second purpose, if considered an important criterion.

7.40   The landscape objectives of the policy may cause problems when the Green Belt needs to be reviewed. Although, for the general public, the idea of protecting attractive landscape features accords with their intuitive views of what a Green Belt should be, local authorities can use them to suggest that boundaries are literally permanent. In this case the development option of peripheral development can be closed off. Whilst no-one would find it desirable to take attractive rural land for development, there can be disputes over the relative landscape value of land in the 'middle' categories, when development possibilities are being examined. One likelihood is that the landscape protection and coalescence objectives may come to conflict, for example, where visually undistinguished land forms a narrow gap between two settlements whose separate identity is valued by local residents. There is a logical inconsistency here, and the guidance should perhaps suggest what

125

general procedure should be employed in selecting land for development, when required, at Structure Plan reviews.

7.41 The recently approved Central Region Structure Plan has approved a number of Green Belts, in diagrammatic form as yet, to prevent coalescence, and protect the landscape setting of towns. It is likely that these will be more in the nature of a set of green wedges, green gaps (or green barriers on the Clwyd County Council model) rather than all-encompassing peripheral Green Belts. This form of Green Belt has been put forward as a more appropriate instrument where economic regeneration is also important, for example in the discussion over new Green Belts in Wales.[37]

7.42 The role of Green Belts in complementing urban regeneration has reached a more sophisticated level in the Strathclyde Region than elsewhere in the UK. The philosophy should be reproduced in Guidance, together with the importance of the role of Scottish Enterprise in guaranteeing a flow of usable brownfield land. This could form a useful model for future co-operation between the new Urban Regeneration Agency and local authorities in England.

7.43 In practice the Green Belt is not complemented by a white land policy. Although the Guidance refers to long term settlement policy, in Lothian the possibility and scale of any adjustment to the Green Belt is decided at the same time as the Plan is reviewed. This does not make Green Belt issues less contentious. Indeed, it appears to encourage quite widespread speculative activity by developers trying to second guess change. If a developer can obtain permission by this method (s)he can effectively force the hand of the Local Authority. White land gives the local authority a stronger hand in the land allocation process, perhaps more appropriate in what is now an increasingly plan-led system. It should be noted in Strathclyde the Scottish Office have stated that long term, for the purpose of Green Belt policy, should be seen as a period of ten years or more beyond the end date of the Structure Plan.

7.44 Pressures from the development agencies, and local economic circumstances, suggest that high amenity sites for specific prestigious users are likely to be sought in Green Belt areas. In strict terms there is therefore a conflict between Circular 24/1985 and the 1985 High Technology National Guideline. One approach is to keep such sites, if allocated, within the Green Belt to assist in controlling their future physical expansion. The second would be, as in England, to suggest that 'very special circumstances' require to be proven before they are approved. The third would be to exclude them from the Green Belt as insets. The equivalent here would be the Strategic Planning Guidance for the West Midlands, and Yorkshire and Humberside, which has been issued by Department of the Environment Regional Offices on this topic. In this instance, when approved, the sites are excluded from the Green Belt.

7.45   Non-conforming use sites vary in character, some being essential infrastructure such as the airports, whereas others (such as Bush House near Edinburgh) are essentially office uses in extensive grounds. They remain within the Green Belt, not as insets. Their boundaries therefore are not clear. Even where local plans states that the *de facto* boundaries should not be breached, this has occurred. The criterion that developments should be judged on their strategic significance seems an unnecessary complication. Such developments could be seen as 'very special circumstances'. However, as this latter formulation implies greater discretion to local authorities, the SOEnD may need to be more interventionist, to protect the consistency of Green Belt policy if such a change was introduced. If local government re-organisation removes the Regional tier, this course may be dictated anyway. Alternatively these sites, might be made insets in Green Belts, if the prevention of physical expansion is judged a problem.

7.46   Provision for institutional purposes, also referred to in Circular 24/1985, raises other issues. It may be argued that it is sufficient to regard institutions as an acceptable use within the Green Belt. To elevate provision for institutions to a purpose for defining Green Belt allows the argument to be made that Green Belts could be seen as a reserve area for uses that cannot be fitted into the City. Put another way it would be a purpose of the Edinburgh Green Belt to provide for uses such as the Southern Hospital, it would become an acceptable use, as opposed to one argued under 'exceptional circumstances'. This might generate a wide range of speculative applications.

It is recommended that:

RS.1   *Checking sprawl, retaining the openness of the countryside, and protecting the setting and special character of historic cities should be considered as additional Green Belt purposes [7.8; 7.14-7.17; 7.28; 7.39-7.41].*

RS.2   *The role of Green Belts in urban regeneration, and their effectiveness in managing the balance between large site land release in urban and greenfield areas, should be referred to in guidance [7.29-7.33; 7.42].*

RS.3   *Given that Green Belts in Scotland do not have associated areas of white land, guidance should give the criteria which would be employed in selecting any land necessary to be released from the Green Belt in reviews of development plans [7.3-7.5; 7.12; 7.35;7.42].*

RS.4   *Consideration should be given to resolving the conflict between Circular 24/1985 and the 1985 High Technology Guideline. Very special circumstances should have to be demonstrated for the release of large employment sites in Green Belts [7.19-7.20; 7.23; 7.34; 7.44].*

RS.5   Consideration should be given to treating the so-called 'non-conforming use areas' (Lothian Green Belt) as insets within the Green Belt [7.10-7.11; 7.21; 7.23; 7.45].

RS.6   Uses not seen as appropriate to the rural character of the Green Belt, but seen as necessary and of strategic significance (eg. football stadia, new hospitals), should only be approved in the Green Belt in very special circumstances [7.10; 7.22-7.23; 7.46].

RS.7   Consideration should be given to promoting guidelines for the re-use of redundant hospital and other large sites in Green Belts, along the lines of DOE Circular 10/91 [7.22; 7.36; 7.46].

RS.8   It should be made clear that the use of land for both outdoor sport and recreation is appropriate in Green Belts [7.24; 7.27; 7.36].

RS.9   A statement on the attitude to farm diversification proposals in Green Belts should be made [7.25; 7.37].

RS.10   A policy for the re-use of redundant agricultural buildings, in terms of acceptable new uses, should be put forward [7.25; 7.37].

References

1.   Scottish Office (1991) <u>Scotland: Land Use and Physical Features</u>, Fact Sheet 19, Edinburgh, SO.

2.   Scottish Office (1992) <u>The Structure Plan for Central Region: Central 2000</u>, approval letter, Edinburgh, SO.

3.   Scottish Office (1992) <u>Strathclyde Structure Plan 1990 Update</u>, Approval Letter, Edinburgh, SO.

4.   Scottish Development Department (1985) <u>Development in the Countryside and Green Belts</u>, Circular 24/1985, Edinburgh, SDD.

5.   Ibid., annex, para 4.

6.   Ibid., para 6.

7.   Ibid., para 7.

8.   Ibid., para 4 (iv).

9.   Lothian Regional Council (1989a) <u>Edinburgh Green Belt: Background</u>, Green Belt Information Note 1, Edinburgh, LRC.

10.   Lothian Regional Council (1985) <u>Lothian Region Structure Plan</u>, Written Statement, Edinburgh, LRC.

11.   Lothian Regional Council (1983) <u>Edinburgh Green Belt Agreement</u>, Edinburgh, Lothian Regional Council, Edinburgh, East Lothian and Midlothian District Councils.

12.   Lothian Regional Council (1989b) <u>The Edinburgh Green Belt Agreement</u>, Green Belt Information Note 3, Edinburgh, LRC.

13.   Lothian Regional Council (1985) op.cit.

14.   Ibid.

15.   See Lothian Regional Council (1989a) and (1989b) op.cit; also Lothian Regional Council (1989c) <u>Edinburgh Green Belt Survey and Review 1980</u>, Green Belt Information Note 2, Edinburgh, LRC; Lothian Regional Council (1989d) <u>Green Belt Improvement Programme and Green Belt Initiative</u>, Green Belt Improvement Note 4, Edinburgh, LRC; Lothian Regional Council (1991) <u>Lothian Region Structure Plan Review</u>: Discussion Papers, Edinburgh, LRC.

16.   Edinburgh District Council (1992) <u>Central Edinburgh Local Plan</u>, Edinburgh, EDC.

17. Edinburgh District Council (1990) <u>South East Edinburgh Local Plan</u>, Written Statement, Edinburgh, EDC.

18. Edinburgh Green Belt Trust (1991) <u>The Enhancement of Edinburgh's Green Belt as the 'Front Garden of Scotlands Capital'</u>, Business Plan, Edinburgh, EGBT.

19. Scottish Development Department (1985b) <u>High Technology: Individual High Amenity Sites</u>, Edinburgh, SAD.

20. Lothian Regional Council (1988) <u>Green Belt: Review of Boundaries</u>, Edinburgh, LRC.

21. Lothian Regional Council (1991) op.cit.

22. Edinburgh District Council (1985) <u>Ratho, Newbridge and Kirkliston Local Plan: Written Statement</u>, policy 2.a.

23. Scottish Development Department (1985) op.cit., para 5 iv.

24. Central Regional Council (1992) <u>Central 2000: The Structure Plan for Central Region</u>, Stirling, CRC., para 7.1a.

25. Ibid., policy ENPO.4, as amended by the Scottish Office Environment Department.

26. Strathclyde Regional Council (1988) <u>Structure Plan Update (1988)</u>, Written Statement, p 57.

27. Strathclyde Regional Council (1979) <u>Strathclyde Structure Plan</u>, Glasgow, SRC.

28. Strathclyde Regional Council (1986) <u>Structure Plan Update (1986)</u>, Written Statement, Glasgow, SRC.

29. Ibid., p 24.

30. Strathclyde Regional Council (1990) <u>Structure Plan Update (1990)</u>, Written Statement, Glasgow, SRC.

31. Scottish Office (1992) <u>Strathclyde Structure Plan: 1990 Update</u>, Approval Letter, Edinburgh, SO.

32. Eastwood District Council (1992) <u>District Plan</u>, Consultation Draft, para 2.19.

33. Coon, A. G. (1989) 'High Technology Versus High Amenity', <u>Scottish Planning Law and Practice</u>, <u>29</u>, p 7.

34. Scottish Development Department (1985) op. cit., paras 6 and 7.

35.   Strathclyde Regional Council (1988) op.cit., para 2.33.

36.   Eastwood District Council (1992) see paras 9.19 and 9.20.

37.   Assembly of Welsh Counties (1992) <u>Strategic Planning Guidance in Wales</u>, Topic Reports, pp 69-79 'Green Belts'.

Appendix A: The Research Team and the Steering Group

The Research Team

Project Director

Professor Martin Elson
Oxford Brookes University

Project Principals

Stephen Walker
Oxford Brookes University

Jeremy Edge
Weatherall Green and Smith

Research Associates

Roderick Macdonald
Oxford Brookes University

Linda Morgan
Woodrow Wilson School of Public and International Affairs, Princeton University (intern placement with Oxford Brookes University and Department of the Environment)

Janet Toulson
Weatherall Green and Smith

Elizabeth Wilson
Oxford Brookes University

Specialist Transport Advice

Russell Kilvington
Steer Davies Gleave

Stephen Holman
Steer Davies Gleave

Other Assistance

Research assistance for specific tasks was provided by Jo Hardman and Stewart Glasser of Oxford Brookes University, and Simon Harrison and Daniel Parry-Jones of Weatherall Green and Smith. The project Secretary/Administrator was Jane Robinson.

The Steering Group

Richard Wakeford   Chairman
Planning and Development Control Directorate

Des Coles   Nominated Officer
Planning and Development Control Directorate

Cathryn Evans (previously Siobhan Kearney)
Planning and Development Control Directorate

Elizabeth Davies
Directorate of Planning Services

Sheila Edmunds (Keith Nix)
North West Regional Office

Roger Kelly
Scottish Office Environment Department

Robert Lowenstein
Directorate of Planning Services

Sue Todd
West Midlands Regional Office

Michael Wellbank
President, Royal Town Planning Institute

Neil Whitehead
London Regional Planning

Roger Wilson
The Planning Inspectorate

Corresponding Members

Lindsay Roberts
Welsh Office

Clive Robbins
Directorate of Rural Affairs

1.   Literature Search

Introduction

B.1   This Appendix provides a commentary on a range of Green Belt policy issues arising from the literature search. The paper begins by setting out a number of 'starting points', outlining some basic characteristics of the Green Belt concept.   It then outlines the achievements of Green Belt as a policy instrument, before discussing a range of criticisms Green Belt policy has attracted over recent years.   Appendix G deals with land use and environmental policies within Green Belts. The reference material used largely refers to the post-1988 period, that is, following the production of PPG 2.

Development of the Concept

B.2   Green Belt policy was first introduced nationally in 1955. Since that time it has undergone a number of changes, with the production of amended advice in 1957, 1984 and 1988. The planning and development contexts within which Green Belt has operated have clearly altered greatly over its thirty five year life.

B.3   In 1955 Green Belts were deployed to assist in the dispersal and decentralization of population, particularly from the larger cities. They were part of a three-pronged attack on regional planning problems which included the dispersal of population to new and expanded towns, the deployment of Green Belts, and the redevelopment (at lower densities) of urban areas. As a result Circular 42/55 stressed 'checking the further growth' of large built up areas, and the prevention of coalescence. Preserving 'the special character of a town', the third purpose, was used to justify Green Belts around Oxford, Cambridge, York and Chester. It is notable Green Belts were not envisaged as stopping development; they were seen as shaping development into particular forms. A government booklet published in 1962 stated this well, noting Green Belts were '... a means of shaping the expansion of a city on a regional scale and not just an attempt to combat the forces making for growth' (DOE,1988).

B.4   Although the 1960s and 70s saw considerable pressures on Green Belts, from expanding leisure demands as well as from urban development, Government advice was not altered. Despite the popular appeal of the idea of Green Belts as a means of protecting landscape, and providing for recreation, these were not introduced as new purposes. Green Belts were retained and expanded in structure plans introduced following local government re-organisation in 1974.

B.5   In the late 1970s new priorities entered the scene. As people left the cities in large numbers their economies declined and inner city services deteriorated. In other areas economic restructuring was rapid leading to the loss of jobs in basic industries such as iron and steel, coal extraction and other manufacturing.

In 1984 a fourth objective 'assisting urban regeneration' was included in the Green Belt advice. This did not imply that urban regeneration could be effected by peripheral Green Belt restraint on its own, but the reduction in greenfield development sites implied by the policy would assist in directing the attention of land developers and service providers to re-using urban sites. Green Belt restraint was in practice, complemented by a wide range of urban regeneration measures, such as the creation of Urban Development Corporations, area-based Partnerships and Task Forces.

B.6 The guidance published in 1988 was, uniquely, not the subject of prior public consultation. It added 'safeguarding the surrounding countryside from further encroachment' to Green Belt purposes. This was the first reference to a *rural* objective for Green Belts, the previously accepted objectives being urban, and directed towards the town. This may reflect the removal of the agricultural presumption in 1987. The aim of protecting the character of towns was now to apply to *historic* towns. This might be interpreted as a clarification and limitation of the scope of the concept, given some of the proposals to surround small freestanding towns with Green Belts, made in the early 1980s. By 1988 the original objective of 'checking further growth' had been altered to that of 'checking unrestricted sprawl', thus avoiding the association of Green Belt with the notion of stopping growth.

B.7 In 1991 Michael Heseltine announced the intention of the Government to develop a more positive thrust to the Green Belt policy. This would entail investigating the possibility of adding two new purposes to the existing functions of Green Belts. These would be to:

- enhance and improve the natural beauty of the countryside adjoining cities; and
- increase opportunities for the quiet enjoyment of the countryside.

The 'greening' theme has been taken up in a number of Ministerial speeches in the last three years. It is worthy of note that in the White Paper *This Common Inheritance* the Green Belt is listed under policies with a conservation theme. Also PPG 12 sees Green Belt among policies with 'conservation and the environment as their common flavour' (DOE, 1992).

B.8 By 1990 the area of approved Green Belt had grown to 1,550,000 hectares, some 12 per cent of England. This was over double the area covered by agreed Green Belt in 1979, but only 20 per cent greater than the area covered by *de facto* Green Belt policies at that date. A number of new Green Belt proposals were being handled by the Department in 1992. The largest included new areas:

- around Hull, and separating Hull from Beverley in North Yorkshire;
- around Telford in Shropshire (an area currently defined as an Area of Special Restraint for Housing);

- across South Hampshire from the New Forest in the west, to the West Sussex border in the east;
- around Norwich, Norfolk;
- an area north east of Leeds; and
- an area in East Hertfordshire.

B.9   A number of starting points emerge from this discussion;

- the 1955 concept was *never literally a stopper*, and the wording has been further softened subsequently;
- the Green Belt is an *instrument* of urban and regional policy; it remains capable of delivering a pre-determined pattern of development and restraint on a sub-regional scale. What the pattern is must be decided through Regional Guidance and structure plans;
- through most of its history the aims of Green Belt have been *urban*; they are not related to the quality of the landscape or of agricultural land;
- the Green Belt is *always deployed with other polices*; at present Green Belt is central to planning advice, as our review of current PPGs shows. Particularly important links exist with PPGs 3, 4, 7 and 17;
- there are a range of significant *proposals for new Green Belts;*
- finding ways and means of promoting Green Belt *as an instrument supporting conservation and environmental aims* is a current concern.

The Achievements of Green Belt

B.10   Green Belts have, particularly over the past 10-15 years, attracted strong support from Ministers. There is cross-party agreement on the value of the policy. In a recent statement to the RICS study on Green Belts the County Planning Officers' Society gives the policy strong support, as do the District Planning Officers in an article by Haslam in 1991 (CPOS 1990 (unpublished); Haslam, 1991). The Consumers Association conducted a household survey of 2,300 adults in 1989 which demonstrated very strong support for the policy among the general public, even in areas with relatively high unemployment. Those surveyed thought preserving the special character of the countryside, and providing green space for people to enjoy, were the most important reasons for setting up Green Belts. Also only slightly more people (37 per cent) agreed than disagreed (34 per cent) with the statement that the Government is fully committed to protecting the Green Belt. Table 1 gives more information (Consumers Association, 1989). Whilst accepting these comments we should perhaps be wary of how far the public are appraised of the current objectives, and physical extent of Green Belts.

Table B1:   'Which' Magazine Survey of Green Belts: What Do Consumers Want?

- Four out of five people agreed that Green Belts should be protected at all costs - while less than one in five agreed that controls on development should be relaxed.
- The idea that there's so much pressure on space these days we can't afford to keep all Green Belt land open got little support - only 27 per cent agreed while over 54 per cent disagreed.
- Only one in three people agreed that Green Belts should be used to provide more housing at a cost ordinary people could afford.
- Three out of five people did not support the idea of allowing more industry or office development in the Green Belt, even if it creates new jobs. Even in regions with higher unemployment rates, more people disagreed than agreed.
- Shopping centres got even shorter shift - only 15 per cent agreed there was nothing wrong with building them in the Green Belt, while 61 per cent disagreed strongly.
- People thought preserving the special character of the countryside and providing green space for people to enjoy were the most important reasons for setting up Green Belts. They gave these higher priority than the 'official' aims of the Green Belt.

(Source: Consumers Association, 1989)

B.11   The two major *national* studies of the Green Belt are those carried out by the House of Commons Environment Committee in 1984 and Martin Elson in 1986. The House of Commons investigation concluded, '... Green Belts have a broad and a positive planning role: that of open spaces whose presumption against development can better shape urban areas, particularly on a regional scale' (House of Commons Environment Committee, 1984). They supported the anti-coalescence and character preservation objectives of Green Belts, but found the issue of checking further peripheral growth more difficult. They felt difficult judgements had to be made over the feasibility of further development within urban areas, before the tightness of Green Belt boundaries could be agreed.   The Committee supported the addition of 'assistance to urban regeneration' as a purpose of Green Belts. They also recommended the need to give Green Belt status to pockets of land within conurbations, stating this should be explicitly spelt out in guidance.

B.12   In *Green Belts: Conflict Mediation in the Urban Fringe,* now published seven years ago, Elson concluded that the following are seen as the basic outcomes of Green Belt policy:

a) *Green Belts have 'managed' the process of decentralization into specific physical forms.*

Here it was concluded Green Belts have retained the openness of the land. They have cut the rate of conversion of open land to below 0.1 per cent per annum, and allowed the worst excesses of scattered development to be avoided. What they have *not* done is greatly affect the pace and rate of decentralisation. In short they are 'shapers' not 'stoppers'.

b) Green Belts have contained patterns of new development.

This has been done in the interest of economy and access to existing urban services. It appears peripheral development, taking account of existing sewer runs, public transport routes and school provisions, is the most economic form of development in terms of incremental public sector borne costs. This set of arguments is part of the 'sustainable development' debate in the 1990s, but was seen by local authorities as an economic imperative in the 1970s and 1980s.

c) Green Belts have ensured separation between urban areas, thus retaining their much-valued identities.

This proved to be an intangible, but important, benefit to many local residents. The avoidance of coalescence is a very clear principle in UK planning, and can be seen very strongly when scanning appeal decision letters. As a result, however, many of the narrower gaps between towns have become communication corridors, often with a consequent deterioration in their visual appeal. The retention of such 'gaps' has aided the modernisation of strategic communication patterns, but with an emphasis on car-borne travel.

d) Green Belts have retained valuable agricultural land and other space extensive uses.

The retention of open land in the urban fringe by Green Belt policy has assisted agriculture, in conjunction with restrictions on the development of agricultural land of good quality. Green Belt controls have also assisted mineral producers by keeping land open for aggregate extraction near to major sources of demand. A similar rationale obtains for opencast coal production.

e) Green Belts have retained accessible land in pleasant surroundings nearer to people living in cities than would otherwise have been the case.

Green Belts have retained basic recreation resources, especially for informal recreation. In the case of the London Green Belt about 9 per cent of the area is in leisure use. There may be distance and cost problems for London inner city residents in reaching the Green Belt, but in areas such as Tyneside, Merseyside and Greater Manchester a wide cross section of users are found. In Greater Manchester and the West Midlands the penetration of Green Belt into and between urban areas in the form of green wedges and river valleys has greatly assisted access. The Department has, however, always resisted separate green wedge policies within Green Belts.

f) Green Belts create a degree of clarity in policy which reduces excessive bureaucracy, and associated costs.

Green Belts are the most clear-cut policy instrument in planning. They specify precise geographical areas where the basic presumption is against development, and where the onus is on the applicant to make a particular case for a scheme. As a result, the physical extent of speculative applications is reduced, an outcome supported by Government warnings to major developers that attempts to overturn Green Belt policy by *ad hoc* schemes may attract the award of costs at appeals. This must reduce processing costs and make the system more manageable, particularly if accompanied by a consequent reduction in the number of planning appeals (Elson, 1986).

The Possible Costs of Green Belt

B.13 Criticism of Green Belt policy is both polemical and research based. Much of it is part of a wider critique of planning. Some of the work is merely assertion of what the outcomes of Green Belt policy have been, without any backing of empirical information. It should be recalled that Green Belts are but one *instrument* of urban and regional policy, dealing mainly with its physical aspects. For example Green Belts designed to check sprawl may be well suited to such a task if quite narrow. Green Belts to improve recreation access, or give identity to major city neighbourhoods, might need to give greater emphasis to green wedges and 'green chains' in their definition. It is difficult to generalize, and to attribute outcomes to one particular policy, in complex urban fringe situations.

B.14 Overall, eight areas of criticism of Green Belt policy have been isolated. They suggest application of the policy has led to:

- increases in land costs and house prices;
- ineffectiveness in tackling sub-regional problems;
- diversion of development into the deeper countryside;
- urban intensification;
- increases in travel and CO_2 pollution;
- inflexibility, and difficulties in alterating boundaries;
- strictness in terms of development control; and
- an inability to allow growth where needed.

Each is discussed in turn. Issues of recreation demand and potential, landscape and wildlife are discussed in Appendix G.

Increases in Land Costs and House Prices

B.15 This argument has been made in relation to containment policy generally (Evans 1988), and Green Belt policy specifically (Business Strategies Ltd., 1989). The argument made by Evans relates to housing only and suggests

139

with continuing demands for housing land, and restricted supply, prices have been artificially raised. The Department's index of housing land prices shows land values rose 1,000 per cent between 1969 and 1985, against a 400 per cent increase in the general Retail Price Index. The increase in land prices, it is argued, has then fed into increases in house prices. This has led to reduced plot sizes, and has caused developers to build higher proportions of flatlets and terraced dwellings than otherwise would have been the case (Evans, 1991). This theme is supported by work investigating the economic effects of the planning system in the mid-1980s (Cheshire, 1991), and is polemically supported by a range of groups including the House Builders Federation (HBF, 1986) and the Adam Smith Institute (ASI, 1988).

B.16   A study by Business Strategies Ltd for ARC Properties attempted to isolate the costs of the London Green Belt. Making a number of crude assumptions about the physical distribution of population around the South East without Green Belt policy, it then compared this to a crude index of the coverage of Green Belts by District. This resulted in the view that in the absence of Green Belt controls the population of the South East 'would be able to shift inwards by approximately 7.6 miles'. The study concluded that a sum equivalent to three per cent of Gross National Product is consumed sustaining the London Green Belt, with new home owners paying £6 a week more in mortgage servicing costs than would otherwise be the case (BSL, 1989). In their response to the *RICS Green Belt Working Party* the CPOS suggest it is difficult to disentangle the separate effect of Green Belts on land prices, instancing the level of earnings, mortgage availability (credit), and property rents as other important factors (CPOS, 1990). Research recently commissioned by the Department on the relationship between land and house prices, concluded the release of significantly greater amounts of land 'on a national scale and over a considerable period of time' would not have a major effect on house prices (Gerald Eve, 1991). Land and house prices are determined at the local level where a large number of local and site-specific factors come into play. Research by the Joseph Rowntree Foundation has suggested that releasing large amounts of land including Green Belt, is not an effective way of reducing house prices or widening access to home ownership (Bramley et al, 1993). The 1988 Green Belt booklet acknowledges the general issue of land prices stating '... there are bound to be sharp increases in the value of building land if the need for more land encounters the restrictions implicit in Green Belt policy'; and 'land prices have risen sharply' wherever permission to build could be obtained (DOE, 1988, p.32).

Ineffectiveness in Tackling Sub-Regional Problems

B.17   Decentralization has spread economic activity and housing around broad areas of lowland Britain. New patterns of accessibility created by 'Green Belt' Motorways such as the M25 and M42 have increased the relative attractiveness of the outer city region. An 'edge city' is in the making. The countryside is an increasingly attractive location for service and small manufacturing employment (Newby, 1991). Where one service centre dominates a subregion, as in the cases of Oxford or Edinburgh, extra daily commuting along radial routes in likely to be the resulting pattern. Otherwise complex interactions between work, home, school and leisure will develop between settlements of widely different sizes within and across what Steeley terms the 'Aegean Sea' of the Green Belt (Steeley, 1990). A main criticism is that planning policies (particularly Green Belts) 'have contained the physical but not the functional growth of cities' (Simmie et alia, 1992, p.45). Herington suggests 'Green Belts...essentially 'stoppers' of urban growth around large (and a few smaller) cities,...are located too close to the metropolitan cores to have any impact on the dispersed outer parts of the regional cities which now extend over much of lowland England' (Herington, 1991, p.125). Cherry has also recently made this point (Cherry, 1992). What are needed, it is asserted, are new forms of strategy for the outer parts of city regions which are seen as increasingly separate, in demographic, social and economic terms from the metropolitan cores.

B.18   This could imply, as an alternative, the extension of Green Belt type coverage systematically across broader areas so as to deliver more coherent decisions; a form of regional planning. The RSA study suggests Green Belts are poor tools for regional planning (RSA, 1990). However others, such as the House of Commons Environment Committee, argue they are one of the *only* tools capable of channelling and shaping development at a sub-regional scale. Even in the free market-led scenario painted by David Lock, Green Belts, possibly narrower than those already in existence, are seen as desirable to limit town and city growth, with accompanying development at selected points elsewhere (Lock, 1989, p.35). What is being reflected here is the ineffectiveness of the administrative system to deliver regional planning. Simmie and his colleagues summarize the issues well '... many of the possible advantages of compact settlement planning, by policies of local physical containment, have been subverted by the inability to plan for the whole functional extent of individual cities. In many cases, conflicts between the two major tiers of English local authorities...have contributed to this problem' (Simmie, et alia, 1992, p.46).

Diversion of Development into the Deeper Countryside

B.19   This set of arguments extends from those in the previous two paragraphs. Shoard argues that holding on to every inch of Green Belt could create more environmental problems than it solves. Some of the 'scruffiest, dreariest semi-urban countryside in England' is protected by Green Belts. Yet 'try to build on the edge of a town or village and however suitable the site, a howl of protest will go up from residents out to defend their views and property values'. Green Belt has grown out of control, it is claimed, so there is a basic danger when development requirements in an area have been established, 'real' countryside beyond the Green Belt will be developed. Would it not have been better she suggests 'for the unprepossessing fields of Tillingham Hall to go under concrete rather than...more remote and attractive countryside?' (Shoard, 1988). This polemical material finds echoes in current practice. A parallel argument led to the CPRE supporting peripheral development on the City of York, rather than a new settlement or settlements beyond a York Green Belt, during the recent debate on sub-regional planning in the area (CPRE, 1991). This argument is also linked to the popular notion that poor quality land in the Green Belt should be developed (ASI, 1988; Phoenix Group, 1989). It is also seen as one of the reasons why the Dundee Green Belt was abandoned in Scotland. The ability of planning authorities to control sporadic development beyond Green Belts however appears not to be in doubt given the continual overlaying of conservation policies which countryside planning now represents (see Newby, 1991).

B.20 A secondary argument here contends Green Belt land uses can intercept development pressures that would otherwise go further afield. This rationale is referred to by the Countryside Commission in its study *'Planning for a Greener Countryside'* (Countryside Commission, 1989), and has recently been cogently re-iterated by Kirby. He states '... unless Green Belts can fulfil their recreational, and access potential, and satisfy a wider variety of urban leisure demands, it may not be possible to conserve our finest landscapes - the National Parks and AONBs' (Kirby, 1990, p. 238). There is however, little evidence to support the view that Green Belt could intercept such demands. Many would not see the National Parks and the urban fringe as substitutable locations for recreation. Indeed, experience of Green Belt recreation may encourage visitors to explore further afield, and may generate greater amounts of long distance leisure travel through the countryside as a result (Countryside Commission, 1992). More information is required on this range of issues.

Urban Intensification

B.21 Since the early 1980s, and particularly after publication of the House of Commons Environment Committee Report on *Green Belt and Land for Housing*, Government advice has emphasised development in urban areas in order to assist in the protection of Green Belts. The re-use of urban land has been a constant theme, with the establishment of land registers, and the alteration of derelict land reclamation priorities to reflect 'hard' end uses. Planning policies have encouraged higher densities in housing areas, with local authorities constantly exceeding those prescribed in earlier 1970s plans. Starter homes, and houses for single person households, were encouraged to locate on small infill sites at very high densities. A study by Roger Tym and Partners showed one quarter of all sites developed in South East England were urban infill sites (R. Tym, 1987). More recent evidence from the Department of the Environment shows 42 per cent of all new housing being developed on sites not previously in agricultural use (DOE, 1992).

B.22 Evans argues that land scarcity, leading to premium values for urban infill sites, has led to much intensification of use. Houses on large plots have been re-developed, backland development has occurred, and allotments and sports grounds have been turned over to built uses (Crockett, 1990). Private sports grounds have been particularly at risk as companies sought to realize assets, either to stay in business or as part of rationalizations or closure plans (Bedford, 1991). This form of 'town cramming' (as it has become known) has also included major retail and warehouse development, adding new traffic flows to already congested roads. The visual quality of many residential neighbourhoods has been eroded, and urban wildlife and conservation values, often greater than in 'prairie agriculture' areas in the countryside, have also reduced. The residents of many new houses built since 1981 are unhappy about their size and facilities, according to a recent study from the Building Research Establishment (BRE, 1992). In order that new housing development should link better with its landscape setting, the New Homes Environment Group have suggested more generous space allocations for housing sites (NHEG, 1989). Urban wildlife planners would also like to see densities kept down. The Friends of the Earth report *Reviving the City* suggests, in the interests of sustainable development:

- the retention of existing urban open space;
- the creation of 'natural' open spaces, which would have low management requirements;
- the retention of school and water authority sites;
- the linking up of sites physically, into 'green chains'; and
- the creation of new urban forestry areas, to assist in reducing pollution (Elkin, T. et. alia, 1991).

It is clear that this would require some loosening of the existing urban fabric in most of our towns and cities, and a reduction in the density of new development (Millward, 1990).

Increased Travel and CO_2 Pollution

B.23   This is a complex issue, and there is no published research on the relationship between Green Belt policy and propensity to travel. Interviews conducted by the London Research Centre, in an RTPI-sponsored study on the relationship between transport change and planning policy, suggest Green Belt policy might lead to extra travel (RTPI, 1991). This view has also been expressed in comment on the Department's decision on the Chester Green Belt, and in correspondence from the President of the RTPI to the Minister (Basden, 1991). If tight Green Belts lead to the 'displacement' of new houses beyond them, in the absence of a job move, individuals and households may be accepting higher travel. However, as the County Planning Officers Society point out, there are many complex factors at work here. In general terms higher incomes and greater leisure time lead to more travel, as has the growth of the company car as a 'perk' in the 1980s (CPOS, 1992).

B.24   In areas dominated by one centre, such as Oxford, it appears development beyond Green Belts may have led to greater travel. This may have been 'traded' for the pleasantness of life in small county towns. However as jobs also decentralize patterns of movement become more complex. If the communications of an area are car-based very considerable extra travel appears

143

likely to be generated. The idea of avoiding coalescence, which is built into Green Belt policy, may make 'corridor' development, which many favour for its public transport service possibilities, more difficult to achieve. Overall freestanding new settlements could be expected to score poorly on criteria of car travel generation, in contrast to urban peripheral development. Green Belt policy may, by firstly retaining compact urban areas; and secondly allowing a measured amount of urban peripheral development, provide an excellent basic framework for further measures designed to reduce aggregate travel. The view that containment assists in creating sustainable patterns of development in transport terms, is the main conclusion of recent work (Breheny, 1992). There is an upsurge of work suggesting that development along public transport corridors can be appropriate in terms of transport emissions efficiency. A recent study by Ecotec identifies the conflict with designated Green Belt (Ecotec, 1993, p.62 and pp.88-89), and the discussion on emerging regional guidance in the West Midlands makes the same point (Saunders, 1993).

Green Belt is Inflexible

B.25   In this critique Green Belt tends not to be treated as an instrument of policy, but as a policy in itself. Newby suggests that Green Belt has become in economists' jargon 'a positional good' with powerful local groups protecting its inviolability. This situation is evidenced by protestations that Green Belts are 'permanent'. Permanence becomes translated by local planners with Green Belts into boundaries contiguous with the end date of the plan period (that is, they have no white land provision). This is most often based on the notion that future development land will be found exclusively in existing urban areas. Breheny puts the politics behind this situation well: '... put crudely, it is a question of whose quality of life will suffer most; urban dwellers, suffering already and faced with further town cramming; or rural dwellers, protective of their own and the environment's interests' (Breheny, 1990).

B.26   The second issue is the time taken to approve detailed Green Belt boundaries in plans in the first place. This extends to the problems of altering Green Belts, both by establishing exceptional circumstances, and in making alterations even when indicated in Regional Guidance or approved structure plans (see Simmonds, 1988). This is partly dictated by the nature of the system whereby local authorities propose policy, and Government can only alter intentions by a relatively cumbersome process of intervention at later stages in the plan process. It is also conditioned by the wide range of interests involved, all with a right to comment and participate, in the process of arriving at a decision. The relative tardiness in defining Green Belt industrial sites in the West Midlands is a case in point (WMJDT, 1992).

The Land Use Prescription in Green Belts is too Strict

B.27   The basic land use prescription within Green Belts has altered little since 1955. Development is basically restricted to uses ancillary to agricultural production.

During the production-driven years of the 1970s and early 1980s this suited farmers well. However CAP controls, and high levels of indebtedness, have caused farmers to seek diversification of their enterprises. Farmers have thus come more into contact with planners, as well as into conflict with the countryide conservation lobby (Marsden, 1992). Although Government supports diversification in the countryside generally in PPG 7, policy on building re-use varied significantly in Green Belt areas. Ironically, therefore, the farmers best located for urban markets find their diversification possibilities most limited.

B.28   Clearly, the success of diversification in new agricultural enterprises is dependent on the enterpreneurial skills of individual farmers. The new enterprises selected may not always be a 'good neighbour', and can include scrapyards, garages, transport businesses and various forms of contracting (Elson, 1987). A survey by Ilbery in the Warwickshire Green Belt discovered the range of diversification enterprises shown in Figure 2. He found that tenancy agreements, availability of capital, and Green Belt policy had acted as the main constraints on diversification in the study area. He states: '... Within Green Belt areas, planning permission is normally refused for the construction of new buildings or for changes in the use of existing ones. Garden centres and farm shops are classed as commercial activities and their development is also restricted. However, when considering planning applications the relevant authority distinguishes between activities which are ancillary to farm operations and farm shops/garden centres where some or all of the products are 'bought in' from other suppliers; the latter will not normally be granted planning permission. One third of the farmers were dissatisfied with such land use constraints' (Ilbery, 1988). Such restrictions may have eased since this survey was carried out in 1987, but no detailed evidence exists to substantiate such a proposition.

B.29   Planning restraints in the deeper countryside may also have become more severe over recent years. A combination of local protectiveness, and the increasing scale of conservation designations, are some of the factors considered relevant. The proper development of employment in the more truly rural areas may be denied by restrictive policies, frequently championed by newcomers. As Newby states '... Powerful local coalitions now exist in many rural areas to keep out any kind of development, including that which is necessary to maintain the vitality of the local economy. Thus the idea, if not the formal designation, of Green Belts has spread out over vast areas of rural England. We now live in the age of Nimby. This is all the more tragic given that the future growth of rural communities will not be provided by agriculture, nor even by forestry, but by manufacturing and service industries, especially those in the high technology sector which do not need to be based in towns' (Newby, 1991). Green Belts were, in the past, regarded as being distinguishable from policies in the remainder of the countryside by their more severe restraints. The 1988 booklet suggests for example '... in the rural areas beyond the Green Belt it may be necessary at some time to allocate areas for building which might be quite extensive' (DOE, 1988). Green Belts were seen

145

as a special policy measure to tackle very strong development pressures in urban fringes. Does it matter if this distinction is removed?

Table B2: Farm Diversification in Birmingham's Green Belt*

1. Direct Marketing Industrial

   - farm gate sales
   - farm shop
   - pick your own schemes
   - delivery rounds

2. Accommodation

   - bed and breakfast
   - holiday accommodation
   - caravan/camping sites

3. Recreation

   - horse riding/stables
   - water sports
   - shooting
   - informal recreation
   - special events/attractions
   - farm tours

4. Commercial/Small

   - farm catering
   - fish farming
   - stud farm
   - craft centre
   - cattery/kennels
   - dairies
   - cheese/ice cream making
   - packing and bottling

5. Others

   - dumping
   - building lets
   - land lets
   - farm woodland

(Total: 120 farms)

* The study area was in the Meriden Gap, and was entirely within the West Midlands Green Belt.

Source: Ilbery, 1988.

Green Belts Have Not Allowed Economic Growth Where it is Needed

B.30 This argument is made in the Regional Studies Association report. It suggests, as a 'rigid national planning policy', Green Belt is rarely modified to suit regional or local economic needs. The blanket restraint of Green Belts, subject to certain exceptions, is applied irrespective of location, regional development needs or the interests of industrialists (RSA, 1990, pp 14-16). Simmie extends this argument to growth regions, suggesting containment policies reduce the possibility of promoting economic growth in conjunction with such developments as the Channel Tunnel, and associated opportunities in Southern England and Northern France. He states '... a crucial outcome of the continuation of land use containment policies combined with inadequate communication and transport systems, particularly in South East England, could therefore be to drive economic growth south of the Channel rather than north of Watford' (Simmie, 1992).

146

B.31 Elson's national study revealed that Green Belts *were* looser in areas where economic growth was a more urgent necessity. It was concluded '... it appears that Green Belts have been used in the South East around London, in parts of the West Midlands, and south of Manchester, to *check* sprawl and concentrate development in certain locations. In the conurbations north of Birmingham they appear to have been used as a *shaping* device, with little significant deflection of activity (especially economic activity)' (Elson, 1986, p 258). The Structure Plan process, in particular the Examination in Public, provides a forum for balancing assessed development requirements with pre-existing policies. The process of preparing Regional Guidance provides a similar function. Thus we find the recent release of Green Belt in North West Kent, in the West Midlands Green Belt, north of Cambridge, and along the M62 corridor in response to locally asserted needs. Questions remain over whether such releases are the correct size, or whether it has taken too long to remove them from the Green Belt.

B.32 Perhaps more contentious is whether large Green Belt releases near to historic towns should be pursued as a valid way of promoting sub-regional growth. This was, and remains, the situation around Chester. It might be argued that releases of land near Chester would result in further locational re-adjustment in the North West Region, but little growth. Also, as development occurred around the periphery of Chester, the increased activity generated would undermine its historic character. This is an urban policy argument, about the balance between utilizing prime environmental assets in the interests of the economy, or relying on ordinarily attractive commercial environments. Basically the planning system does not appear as restrictive as the Regional Studies Association claim. In no areas does an embargo on the development of new land for employment uses exist. The redevelopment of sites in urban and countryside areas provides a constant flow of 'windfall' development sites. Redundant hospital sites, over fifty of which may arise in the London Green Belt alone, are a case in point.

2. Green Belt Bibliography

Contents

1. General

2. Specific Areas

3. Urban Fringe Issues, Recreation and Sport

4. Community Forests

5. Golf Courses

6. Green Belt Management, Nature Conservation, Area Management, Groundwork

7. Hospital Sites

8. Transport and CO_2

9. Development Control

10. Comparative Studies

Note: This bibliography covers material published since PPG 2 was released in January 1988.

1. *General*

Adam Smith Institute (1987) An Environment for Growth, London, ASI.

Adam Smith Institute (1988) The Green Quadratic, London, ASI.

Anon (1988) 'The Green Belt Hinders Progress', Shop Property, March 26-29.

Baker, N. and J. Wiggin (eds.) (1987) This Pleasant Land? - A New Strategy for Planning, London, Phoenix Group.

Blunden, J. and N. Curry (eds.) (1988) A Future for Our Countryside, Oxford, Blackwell.

Bond, R. (1992) 'Urban Sprawl Special - Stretching to the Limits', Surveyor, 20 August, pp 8-11.

Bramley, G. and W. Bartlett (1993) Planning, The Market and Private Housebuilding, Housing Research Findings No 72, York, Joseph Rowntree Foundation.

Building Employers Confederation (1990) Urban Stall, London, BEC Economic and Public Affairs Department.

BSL Business Strategies (1989) The Costs of the Green Belt, Bristol, ARC Properties.

Cherry, G. (1992) 'Green Belt and the Emergent City', Property Review, 1, 3, pp 91-101.

Council for the Protection of Rural England (1992) Our Common House: Housing Development and the South Easts' Environment, London, CPRE.

CPRE (1992) Home Cooking - Environmental Ingredients to Save the South East from Over-Development, leaflet, London, CPRE.

County Planning Officers Society (1990) Response to the RICS Green Belt Working Party, Unpublished.

Clifford, S. (1989) 'Ideas on the Fringe: People and Places' The Planner, 75, 3, pp 29-31.

Commission of the European Communities (1990) Green Paper on the Urban Environment, Brussels, EEC.

Crockett, D. (1990) 'Suburban Redevelopment - An Appraisal of Recent Pressures and Policy Responses in an Outer London Borough', The Planner, 76, 31, pp 11-14.

Department of the Environment (1988) The Green Belts, London, HMSO.

Elson, M. J. (1986) Green Belts: Conflict Mediation in the Urban Fringe, London, William Heinemann.

Elson, M. J. (1991) 'Green Belts and Growth Management - The UK Situation', National Growth Management Leadership Conference, Thousand Friends of Oregon, Oregon, USA.

Elson, M. J. (1992) Green Belts - A Symbol of Green Planning?, Landscape Design, February, pp 11-13.

Evans, A. (1988) No Room - No Room : The Costs of The British Town and Country Planning System, London, Institute of Economic Affairs.

Evans, A. W. (1991) 'Rabbit Hutches on Postage Stamps : Planning, Development and Political Economy', Urban Studies, 6, pp 853-870.

Eve, Gerald and Department of Land Economy, University of Cambridge (1992) The Relationship Between House Prices and Land Supply, London, HMSO.

Hall, C. (1991) 'Green Belts or Greed Belts?', The Planner, 77, p 7.

Haslam, M. (1990) 'Green Belts and the Future - A View from the Districts', The Planner, 76, 34, pp 14-16.

Healey, P., McNamara, P., Elson, M. J. and A. J. Doak (1988) Land Use Planning and the Mediation of Urban Change, Cambridge, CUP.

Herington, J. (1991) 'How to Deal with Urban Shorelines', Town and Country Planning, 60, 4, pp 124-6.

Horsman, R. (1988) 'Shades of Green', paper to Landscape Institute/RTPI Conference, Green Belts and the City - Poverty or Pleasure, London, RTPI.

House of Commons Environment Committee (1984) Green Belt and Land for Housing, First Report for Session 1983-4, HC 275-1, London, HMSO.

Lock, D. (1989) Riding the Tiger : Planning in the South of England, London, Town and Country Planning Association.

New Homes Environment Group (1990) More Homes and a Better Environment, London, HBF.

Phoenix Group (1989) Green Belts or Green Gardens?, London, Phoenix Group.

Regional Studies Association (1990) Beyond Green Belts - Managing Growth in the 21st Century, London, Jessica Kingsley.

Royal Institution of Chartered Surveyors (1992) 'Report of the RICS Green Belt Working Party', Chartered Surveyor Monthly, Planning and Development Bulletin, 1, 7, pp 1-5.

Scottish Development Department (1985) Development in the Countryside and Green Belts, Circular 24/85, Edinburgh, SDD.

Shoard, M. (1988) 'Lie of the Land', Environment Now, July, pp 50-51.

Shucksmith, M. (1990) Housebuilding in Britain's Countryside, London, Routledge.

Simmie, J., S. Olsberg and C. Tunnell (1992) 'Urban Containment and Land Use Planning', Land Use Policy, 9, 1, pp 36-46.

Simmie, J., S. Olsberg and C. Tunnell (1992) Planning Outcomes in the UK, Working Paper 3, Planning and Development Research Centre, University College London, UK.

Sinclair, G. (1992) The Lost Land: Land Use Change in England 1945-1990, London, CPRE.

Which Magazine (1989) 'The Green Belt', Which, August, pp 338-41.

Whitehead, J.W.R. (1998) 'Urban Fringe Belts : Development of an Idea', Planning Perspectives, 3, 1, pp 47-58.

Young, K. (1989) 'Rural Prospects', in British Social Attitudes, 5th Report, Aldershot, Gower, pp 155-74.

2. *Specific Areas*

Assembly of Welsh Counties (1991) Strategic Planning Guidance in Wales : Interim Report on Green Belts, Newport, AWC.

Assembly of Welsh Counties (1992) Strategic Planning Guidance in Wales, Topic Reports, Mold, Clwyd County Council, pp 69-79.

Caldwell, N. (1991) 'Green Belts for Wales' in Welsh Office (1991) Green Belts for Wales?, Cardiff, WO.

Campaign for the Protection of Rural Wales (1990) How Green Was My Valley?, Welshpool, CPRW.

Civic Trust for Wales (1991) Green Belts - A Critical Review, Cardiff, CTW.

Elson, M. J. (1992) 'Green Belts - Political Priorities and Policy Responses', The Planner, 78, 9, pp 10-11.

Fladmark, J. (1989) The Countryside Around Towns in Scotland : A Scottish Programme of Partnership and Action, Perth, Countryside Commission for Scotland.

Garbutt, J. M. (1989) Green Belt Renegotiation in the Outer Metropolitan Area, Working Paper 114, School of Planning, Oxford Polytechnic.

Hall, P. (1989) London 2001, London, Unwin Hyman.

Leeds City Council (1990) The Control of Development in the Green Belt, Leeds, LCC.

London and South East Regional Planning Conference (1989) Countryside, Background Paper for Regional Strategy, RPC 1504, London, SERPLAN.

London and South East Regional Planning Conference (1990) A New Strategy for the South East, RPC 1789, London, SERPLAN.

London Planning Advisory Committee (1989) Green Issues - A Report by the Topic Working Party, Romford, LPAC.

Norfolk County Council (1990) Green Belt - Technical Report, Norfolk, NCC.

Oxford City Council (1990) The Oxford Green Belt - A Consultation Paper, Oxford, OCC.

Saunders, D. (1993) Regional Planning Guidance for the West Midlands - Report on Birmingham Conference 1993, Stafford, West Midlands Regional Forum.

Simmons, M. (1988) 'Keeping the Green Belt Up To Date - The Case of North West Kent', The Planner, May, pp 14-16.

Welsh Office (1991) Green Belts for Wales? : Strategic Planning Guidance in Wales, Cardiff, Welsh Office.

West Midlands Joint Data Team (1992) Black Country Sector - Premium Employment Locations - First Monitoring Report, Solihull, WMJPT.

West Midlands Regional Forum of Local Authorities (1992) The West Midlands: Your Region, Your Choice, Making the Right Choices, Stafford, WMRFLA.

3. *Urban Fringe Issues, Recreation and Sport*

Broom, G. (1992) 'Our Priceless Countryside - The Context', in Our Priceless Countryside, CRRAG Conference Proceedings, Bristol, CRRAG, pp 21-23

Cheshire, P. (1991) 'Managing Change, the Role of Market Incentives' in A Brief for the Countryside in the 21st Century, London, Royal Society of Arts, pp 18-22.

Council for the Protection of Rural England, NHTPC and ADC (1990) Planning Control over Farmland, London, CPRE.

Council for the Protection of Rural England (1991) Sport and Recreation - A Response to the Government's Draft Planning Policy Guidance Note, London, CPRE.

Country Landowners Association (1989) Enterprise in the Rural Environment, London, CLA.

Countryside Commission (1987) New Opportunities for the Countryside : Report of the Policy Review Panel, CCP 224, Cheltenham, Countryside Commission.

Countryside Commission (1989) Planning for a Greener Countryside, CCP 264, Cheltenham, Countryside Commission.

Countryside Commission (1990) 'Green Belt - Grey Belt?', Countryside Commission News, 46, Nov-Dec.

Countryside Commission (1991) Caring for the Countryside - Policy Agenda for England in the 1990's, CCP, Cheltenham, Countryside Commission.

Countryside Commission (1992) Enjoying the Countryside : Policies for People, CCP 371, Cheltenham, Countryside Commission.

Countryside Commission, English Nature, London Ecology Unit, London Wildlife Trust (1991) Green Capital : Planning for London's Greenspace, CCP 344, Cheltenham, Countryside Commission.

Countryside Commission for Scotland (1987) The Countryside Around Towns in Scotland - A Review of Change 1976-1985, Perth, CCS.

CPOS, MPOS, DPOS (1990) Planning in the Urban Fringe, Initial Report of the Joint Special Advisory Group, Middlesborough, SAG.

CPOS, MPOS and DPOS (1992) Planning in the Urban Fringe, Final Report of the Joint Special Advisory Group, Middlesborough, Cleveland County Council.

DOE (1992) Action for the Countryside, London, HMSO.

Elson, M. J. (1987) 'The Urban Fringe : Will Less Farming Mean More Leisure', The Planner, October, pp 19-22.

Elson, M. J. (1991) Green Belts for Wales - A Positive Role for Sport and Recreation, Sports Study No 5, Cardiff, Sports Council for Wales.

Elson, M. J. (1993) 'Sport and Recreation in the Green Belt Countryside' in Glyptis, S. (ed) Leisure and the Environment, London, Belhaven Press.

English Tourist Board (1988) Visitors in the Countryside - Rural Tourism : A Development Strategy, London, ETB.

Exeter University (1991) Patterns, Performance and Prospects in Farm Diversification, Agricultural Economics Unit, Exeter, UOE.

Harrison, C. (1991) Countryside Recreation in a Changing Society, London, TMS Partnership.

HM Government (1989) Planning Permission and the Farmer, London, HMSO.

HM Government (1992) Action for the Countryside, London, HMSO.

Ilbery, B. W. (1988) 'The Development of Farm Diversification in the UK : Evidence from Birmingham's Urban Fringe', Journal of the RASE, pp 21-35.

Land Capability Consultants (1991) Damaged Land in the Urban Fringe, Romford, LPAC.

McLaughlin, B. (1992) 'Agriculture and Rural Strategy: Diversification in the Farming Industry', The Planner, 78, 21, pp 12-15.

National Economic Development Council (1991) The Planning System and Large Scale Tourism and Leisure Developments, London, NEDC.

Newby, H. (1988) The Countryside in Question, London, Hutchinson.

Newby, H. (1990) 'A Vision for the Countryside' in A Brief for the Countryside in the 21st Century, London, Royal Society of Arts.

Pacione, M. (1990) 'Development Pressure in the Metropolitan Fringe', <u>Land Development Studies</u>, <u>7</u>, 2, pp 69-82.

Phillips, P. (1992) 'New Strategy Needed for Tacky Fringe', <u>Planning</u>, <u>993</u>, pp 14-15.

Pryce, G. (1992) 'The Case for the Urban Fringe', <u>The Planner</u>, <u>78</u>, 13, pp 8-10.

Royal Society of Arts (1990) <u>A Brief for the Countryside in the 21st Century</u>, London, RSA.

Rural Development Commission, English Tourist Board and Countryside Commission (1992) <u>The Green Light - A Guide to Sustainable Tourism</u>, London, RDC.

Sports Council (1992) <u>A Countryside for Sport - A Policy for Sport and Recreation</u>, London, Sports Council.

Steeley, G. (1990) 'An Aegean of Cities', <u>Town and County Planning</u>, <u>59</u>, Dec, 33.

Willis, K. et. al. (1992) <u>Urban Development in the Rural Fringe : A Decision Analytic Framework and Case Study of the Newcastle Green Belt</u>, Countryside Change Unit Working Paper 31, Newcastle, University of Newcastle Department of Agricultural Economics and Food Marketing.

Winter, M. and A. Rogers (eds.) (1988) <u>Who Can Afford to Live in the Countryside?</u>, Occasional Paper No. 2, Centre for Rural Studies, Royal Agricultural College, Cirencester.

4. *Community Forests*

Bishop, K. (1991) 'Community Forests : Implementing the Concept', <u>The Planner</u>, <u>77</u>, 18, pp 6-10.

Bishop, K. (1992) 'Assessing the Benefits of Community Forests : An Evaluation of the Recreational Use Benefits of Two Urban Fringe Woodlands', <u>Journal of Environment Planning and Management</u>, <u>35</u>, 1, pp 63-76.

Bishop, K. (1992) 'Creating Community Forests - Problems and Opportunities', <u>Tree News</u>, Summer.

Burton, I. (1992) 'Community Planning Down in the Forests', <u>Planning</u>, <u>970</u>, p 8.

Clark, J. C. (1991) 'The First Year of a Community Forest', <u>Landscape Design</u>, No. 203, pp 21-24.

Council for the Protection of Rural England (1991) <u>Community Forest Charter</u>, London, CPRE.

Countryside Commission (1989) <u>Forests for the Community</u>, CCP 270, Cheltenham, Countryside Commission.

Countryside Commission and Forestry Commission (1991) <u>Forests for the Community</u>, CCP 340, Cheltenham, CC.

Kirby, M. (1989) 'Greening the Green Belts : The Community Forest Concept', <u>County Landowner</u>, <u>63</u>, 2, pp 24-25.

Kirby, M. (1990) 'Environmental Protection in Areas of Development Pressure', <u>Town and Country Planning</u>, <u>59</u>, 9, pp 236-8.

Minter, R. and M. Johnston (1989) 'Forests for the Community', <u>Housing and Planning Review</u>, <u>44</u>, 5, pp 22-3.

Pitt, J. (1991) 'Community Forest Cities of Tomorrow', <u>Town and Country Planning</u>, <u>60</u>, 6, pp 188-190.

Pitt, J. (1991) 'The Fast Lane of Urban Fringe Forest Economics', <u>Urban Forest Economics</u>, pp 189-204.

South Yorkshire Community Forest (1992) <u>Community Forest Plan and Opportunities Document - Executive Summary</u>, Sheffield, South Yorkshire Community Forest.

Staffordshire County Council et. alia (1992) <u>Forest of Mercia Plan</u>, Draft Consultation Plan, Stafford, SCC.

Thames Chase (1992) <u>Thames Chase Plan : Draft for Consultation</u>, Brentwood, Thames Chase.

5. *Golf Courses*

Chatters, C. (1989) 'Golf : Growth in a Vacuum', <u>Ecos</u>, <u>12</u>, pp 21-5.

Countryside Commission (1992) <u>New Golf Courses - Countryside Commission Policy</u>, CCP 365, Cheltenham, Countryside Commission.

Essex Planning Officers Association (1990) <u>The Essex Golf Report</u>, Chelmsford, ECC.

Hurst, G. (1989) <u>The Demand for Golf</u>, RAGC of St. Andrews, St. Andrews, RAGC.

Nature Conservancy Council (1989) <u>On Course Conservation - Managing Golf's Natural Heritage</u>, Peterborough, NCC.

Sports Council (1993) <u>Study of Golf in England</u>, London, The Sports Council.

Surrey County Council (1992) <u>Guidelines for the Development of New Golf Courses in Surrey</u>, Kingston, SCC.

6. *Green Belt Management, Nature Conservation, Area Management and Groundwork*

Ash Environmental Partnership (1988) <u>The Greenbelt Company: Concept Feasibility Study</u> (with Touche Ross and Co.), unpublished.

Collis, I. (1990) 'Groundwork - Fact and Fiction', <u>Ecos</u>, <u>11</u>, 4, pp 34-42.

Countryside Commission and English Nature (1991) <u>Green Capital: Planning for London's Greenspace</u>, CCP 344, Cheltenham, Countryside Commission.

Edinburgh Green Belt Trust (1991) <u>The Enhancement of Edinburgh's Green Belt as the Front Garden of Scotland's Capital</u>, Business Plan 1992-4, Edinburgh, EGBT.

Johnson, P. (1988) 'The Development of Groundwork', <u>Town and Country Planning</u>,

Jones, P. (1988) 'The Growth of the Groundwork Movement', <u>Housing and Planning Review</u>, <u>43</u>, 1, pp 14-16.

Jones, P. (1990) 'Groundwork Projects', <u>Planning Outlook</u>, <u>33</u>, 1, pp 62-64.

Knightbridge, R. (1988) 'Groundwork and Nature Conservation', <u>Ecos</u>, <u>6</u>, p 3.

Tyldesley, D. and I. Collis (1990) 'Nature Conservation and Local Government - A Review of Progress', <u>Ecos</u>, <u>11</u>, 4, pp 13-19.

7. *Hospital Sites*

Falk, N. (1988) 'New Approaches for Green Belt Planning', <u>Town and Country Planning</u>, <u>57</u>, 6, pp 186-3.

Smith, R. (1988) 'Shenley Park - Very Special Circumstances', <u>Housing and Planning Review</u>, <u>43</u>, 6, pp 8-10.

Smith, R. (1988) 'Community Planning for a Garden Village', <u>Town and Country Planning</u>, <u>57</u>, 12, pp 344-8.

8. *Transport and Co_2*

Association of County Councils (1991) <u>Towards a Sustainable Transport Policy</u>, London, ACC.

Banister, D. (1992) 'Energy Use, Transport and Settlement Patterns' <u>in</u> Breheny, M. (ed.) <u>Sustainable Development and Urban Form</u>, Pion, London.

Basden, A. (1991) 'Cramping our Style', <u>Town and Country Planning</u>, <u>60</u>, 10, pp 294-5.

Breheny, M.; T. Gent and D. Lock (1992) <u>Alternative Development Patterns - New Settlements</u>, London, HMSO (unpublished).

Countryside Commission (1992) <u>Trends in Transport and the Countryside</u>, CCP 382, Cheltenham, Countryside Commission.

Ecotec Research and Consulting (1993) <u>Reducing Transport Emissions Through Planning</u>, London, HMSO.

Elkin, T., D. McLaren and M. Hillman (1991) <u>Reviving the City : Towards Sustainable Urban Development</u>, London, FOE and PSI.

London Research Centre (1991) <u>Traffic Growth and Planning Policy</u>, London, RTPI.

Newman, P. and J. Kenworthy (1989) 'Gasoline Consumption and Cities - A Comparison of U.S. Cities with a Globa Survey', <u>Journal of the American Planning Association</u>, <u>55</u>, 1, pp 24-37.

Owens, S. (1986) 'Strategic Planning and Energy Conservation', <u>Town Planning Review</u>, <u>57</u>, 1, pp 69-86.

Owens, S. (1991) <u>Energy Conscious Planning</u>, London, CPRE.

Owens, S. (1991) 'Energy Efficiency and Sustainable Land Use Patterns', <u>Town and Country Planning</u>, February, pp 44-5.

Rickaby, P. A. (1987) 'Six Settlement Patterns Compared', <u>Environment and Planning B: Planning and Design</u>, <u>14</u>, pp 193-223.

Rydin, Y. (1992) 'Environmental Dimensions of Residential Development and their Implications for Local Planning Practice', Journal of Environmental Planning and Management, 35, 1, pp 43-61.

Steadman, P. (1980) Configurations of Land Uses, Transport Networks and their Relation to Energy Use, Milton Keynes, Open University.

Steer Davies Gleave (1991) Leeds Transport Strategy, Leeds, SDG.

9. *Development Control*

Ede, B. (1990) 'The Stockley Park Project', Landscape Design, 187, pp 42-7.

Hares, D. (1992) 'Lakes from Wasteland', Landscape Design, February, pp 24-26.

Lichfield, D. (1992) 'Parkland Offers Pleasing Prospects for Green Belts', Planning, 991, p 7.

Millichap, D. (1990) 'Courts called in to decide on conflicting belt policies', Planning, 13.7.90.

Williams, M. (1989) 'How to obtain planning permission in the green belt', New Law Journal, 139 (6430), 1476, 1501, 1504.

3.   **Planning Policy Guidance**

PPG 2 - Green Belts

1. The Government attaches great importance to Green Belts, which have been an essential element of planning policy for more than three decades. The objectives of Green Belt policy and the related development control policies set out in 1955 remain valid today.

2. The first official proposal 'to provide a reserve supply of public open spaces and of recreational areas and to establish a green belt or girdle of open space' was made by the Greater London Regional Planning Committee in 1935. New provisions for compensation in the 1947 Town and Country Planning Act allowed local authorities to incorporate green belt proposals in their first development plans. The codification of Green Belt policy and its extension to areas other than London came in 1955 with an historic circular inviting local planning authorities to consider the establishment of Green Belts. That process of local initiation and central approval continues today. It has resulted in the approval of 15 separate Green Belts, varying in size from 1,200,000 acres around London to just 2,000 acres at Burton-on-Trent.

3. The Green Belts approved through structure plans now cover approximately 4,500,000 acres, 14% of England. The general extent and location of the designated areas are given in the table and map overleaf.

Purposes of Green Belts

4. Green Belts have five purposes:

- to check the unrestricted sprawl of large built-up areas;
- to safeguard the surrounding countryside from further encroachment;
- to prevent neighbouring towns from merging into one another;
- to preserve the special character of historic towns; and
- to assist in urban regeneration.

5. Green Belts also have a positive role in providing access to open countryside for the urban population. Such access may be for active outdoor sports or for passive recreation. Outdoor leisure pursuits are likely to occupy an increasing proportion of the Green Belts if, as currently expected, the land needed for food production decreases.

6. Green Belts often contain areas of attractive landscape, but the quality of the rural landscape is not a material factor in their designation or in their continued protection.

Designation of Green Belts

7. The essential characteristic of Green Belts is their permanence and their protection must be maintained as far as can be seen ahead.

8. Green Belts are established through development plans. Their general extent has now been fixed through the approval of structure plans and many detailed boundaries have been set in local plans and in old development plans.

9. One the general extent of a Green Belt has been approved it should be altered only in exceptional circumstances. If such an alteration is proposed the Secretary of State will wish to be satisfied that the authority has considered opportunities for development within the urban areas contained by and beyond the Green Belt. Similarly, detailed Green Belt boundaries defined in adopted local plans or earlier approved development plans should be altered only exceptionally. Detailed boundaries should not be amended or development allowed merely because the land has become derelict. On the outer edge of a Green Belt, readily recognisable features, such as roads, streams or belts of trees, should be used to define the boundaries.

10. Where detailed Green Belt boundaries have not yet been defined, local planning authorities are urged to complete this task. It is necessary to establish boundaries that will endure and they should be carefully drawn so as not to include land which it is unnecessary to keep permanently open. Otherwise there is a risk that encroachment on the Green Belt will have to be allowed in order to accommodate future development.

11. When local planning authorities prepare new or revised structure and local plans, and proposals affecting Green Belts should be related to a time scale which is longer than that normally adopted for other aspects of the plan. They should satisfy themselves that Green Belt boundaries will not need to be altered at the end of the plan period. In some cases this will mean safeguarding land between the urban area and the Green Belt which may be required to meet longer term development needs.

Control Over Development

12. The general policies controlling development in the countryside apply with equal force in Green Belts, but there is, in addition, a general presumption against inappropriate development within them.

13. Inside a Green Belt, approval should not be given, except in very special circumstances, for the construction of new buildings or for the change of use of existing buildings for purposes other than agriculture and forestry, outdoor sport, cemeteries, institutions standing in extensive grounds, or other uses appropriate to a rural area.

14. Structure and local planning policies should make no reference to the possibility of allowing other development in exceptional circumstances. Nor should the visual amenities of the Green Belt be injured by proposals for development within or conspicuous from the Green Belt which, although they would not prejudice its main purpose, might be inappropriate by reason of their siting, materials or design.

15. Minerals can be worked only where they are found. Their extraction need not be incompatible with Green Belt objectives, provided that high environmental standards are maintained and that the site is well restored.

16. Green Belts contain a large number of substantial and attractive agricultural buildings which, with normal repair and maintenance, can be expected to last for many years. When these are no longer needed for farming, the planning authority will need to consider whether they might be appropriately re-used for other purposes which help to diversity the rural economy. Redundant buildings can provide suitable accommodation for small firms or tourist activities or can be used as individual residences. The re-use of redundant buildings should not be refused unless there are specific and convincing reasons which cannot be overcome by attaching conditions to the planning permission.

17. In the next few years many older hospitals located in Green Belts are likely to become redundant. In planning for the future of these buildings and their sites the aim should be to use them for purposes compatible with the Green Belt, which can include institutional uses. The size, layout and form of the buildings may, however, make them unsuitable for such purposes. In such cases it will be necessary to consider whether circumstances exist that would warrant the change of use of the buildings or the construction of new buildings.

18. In some cases it may be possible to convert the existing buildings for housing or other uses, perhaps with some demolition of ancillary buildings. But if that is not a practical solution then the future of the buildings and the site, and the possibility of redevelopment, will need to be carefully considered. Putting the sites to beneficial use will be preferable to allowing the buildings to remain empty and the site to become derelict. Guidelines to assist local planning authorities in preparing policies for the sites and in dealing with planning applications follow.

Circular 12/91 - Redundant Hospital Sites

1. In the next few years many older hospitals located in Green Belts are likely to become redundant. In planning for the future of these buildings and their sites the aim should be to use them for purposes compatible with the Green Belt, which can include institutional uses. The size, layout and form of the buildings may, however, make them unsuitable for such purposes. In such cases it will be necessary to consider whether very special circumstances exist that would warrant the change of use of the buildings or their replacement by new buildings. It is important that the site is considered as a whole and that an assessment of the opportunities for re-use for purposes compatible with the Green belt is made as early as possible in the process of closing a hospital.

2. In some cases it may be possible to convert the existing buildings for housing or other uses, perhaps with some demolition of ancillary buildings. But if that is not a practical solution then the future of the buildings and the site, and the possibility of redevelopment, will need to be carefully considered.

Putting the sites to beneficial use will be preferable to allowing the buildings to remain empty and the site to become derelict. Any proposals for altering or demolishing listed buildings or which affect their settings should be considered in the light of the advice in DOE Circular 8/87 - "Historic Buildings and Conservation Areas - Policy and Procedures".

3. Guidelines to assist local planning authorities in preparing policies for the sites and in dealing with planning applications are set out below. These guidelines apply both to cases in which an older hospital site is wholly redundant, and also to cases where part of a site is redundant and part is to be retained for for use or redevelopment as a smaller hospital. Proposals should of course be considered in the light of all material planning considerations - including, for example, the traffic implications of redevelopment - as well as the specific guidelines below.

Guidelines for the future use of redundant hospital sites in Green Belts

(a)   An assessment should be made as early as possible in the process of closing a hospital of the scope for re-using existing buildings. Re-use for purposes within the accepted Green Belt categories is the preferred option, especially where the buildings are of architectural or historical importance. There may in particular be scope for re-use by institutions requiring buildings standing in extensive grounds.

(b)   However, if there is little or no prospect of viable re-use within those categories, then other uses are preferable to allowing the buildings to remain empty or grossly under-occupied. The aim should be to provide for suitable uses by conversion of the existing buildings.

(c)   If the existing buildings, or part of them, are unsuitable for conversion, then the aim in any redevelopment should be ensure that the impact to the Green Belt is no greater than that of the existing development. The new buildings should not normally occupy a larger area of the site nor exceed the height of the existing buildings. For this purpose the relevant areas is the aggregate ground floor area ("footprint") of the existing buildings, excluding temporary buildings, open spaces with direct external access between wings of a building, and areas of hardstanding. The character and dispersal of proposed redevelopment will need to be considered as well as its footprint; for example many houses may together have a much smaller footprint than a few large hospital buildings, but may be unacceptable because their dispersal over a large part of the site and enclosed gardens may have an adverse impact on the character of the Green Belt, compared with the current use. The location of the new buildings should be decided having regard to the purposes of the conservation, and the need to integrate the new development with its surroundings (eg it may be more appropriate to site new development close to existing buildings).

(d)   If the assessment referred to in guideline (a) shows that re-use is not a realistic option, the health authority may choose to demolish buildings rather than leave them in a semi-derelict state pending decisions about redevelopment. In that case it will be necessary to keep suitable records for the purposes of guideline (c).

(e)   In cases of mixed redevelopment, partly for health service purposes and partly for other purposes, the test area embodied in guideline (c) will relate to the *total* development of the site, for all purposes; to enable this to be assessed, it will be particularly important that proposals for the partial redevelopment of a hospital site should be put forward in the context of comprehensive, long-term plans for the site as a whole. In granting any planning permission local authorities should consider the need for conditions to ensure that redundant buildings are demolished as new buildings are erected, thus keeping the total developed area under control.

(f)   In all cases one important aim of any conversion or redevelopment proposals for redundant hospital sites should be, where possible, to enhance the amenity value of the site as a whole, eg by preserving mature trees, keeping or laying out landscaped areas (with adequate provision for their maintenance), conserving natural habitats, and where practicable improving public access and providing new opportunities for outdoor sports or informal recreation. Local planning authorities should have regard to the desirability of preserving gardens and grounds of special historic interest; the English Heritage register of historic gardens lists sites of particular importance.

(g)   Conversion or redevelopment should not normally require additional expenditure by the public sector on the provision of infrastructure, nor should it overload facilities such as schools and health care facilities. Local planning authorities should take account of any additional infrastructure requirements (eg roads) which may have significant adverse effects on the Green Belt.

(h)   Local planning authorities should where appropriate include policies on these lines in their development plans.

4.   This circular is not considered to have any significant expenditure or manpower implications for local authorities.

5.   The advice in this circular replaces that in paragraphs 17 to 18 of Planning Policy Guidance Note 2, "Green Belts". The new advice will be incorporated in PPG 2 when that is next revised. DOE Circular 12/87 is hereby cancelled.

Circular 14/84

1. The Government continues to attach great importance to Green Belts which have a broad and positive planning role in checking the unrestricted sprawl of built-up areas, safeguarding the surrounding countryside from further

encroachment, and assisting in urban regeneration. There must continued to be a general presumption against inappropriate development within Green Belts. The Government reaffirms the objectives of Green Belt policy and the related development control policies set out in Ministry of Housing and Local Government Circular 42/55.

2. Structure plans have now been approved for most parts of the country and these identify the broad areas of the Green Belt. Detailed Green Belt boundaries are now being defined in local plans and in many cases these are based on Green Belt areas defined in earlier development plans approved prior to the introduction of structure and local plans. This process of local plan preparation is continuing and this circular includes advice on the definition of detailed Green Belt boundaries in local plans.

3. The essential characteristic of Green Belts is their permanence and their protection must be maintained as far as can be seen ahead. It follows from this that:

(a)   Once the general extent of a Green Belt has been approved as part of the structure plan for an area it should be altered only in exceptional circumstances. If such an alteration is proposed the Secretary of State will wish to be satisfied that the authority has considered opportunities for development within the urban areas contained by and beyond the Green Belt. Similarly, detailed Green Belt boundaries defined in adopted local plans or earlier approved development plans should be altered only exceptionally.

(b)   Where detailed Green Belt boundaries have not yet been defined in earlier approved development plans or in adopted local plans - for example, where approved structure plans have extended the area of the Green Belt to include areas previously referred to as "interim" Green Belt, it is necessary to establish boundaries that will endure. It is especially important that these boundaries of Green Belts should be carefully drawn so as not to include land which it is unnecessary to keep permanently open for the purpose of the Green Belt. Otherwise there is a risk that encroachment on the Green Belt may have to be allowed in order to accommodate future development. If Green Belt boundaries are drawn excessively tightly around existing built-up areas it may not be possible to maintain the degree of permanence that Green Belts should have. This would devalue the concept of the Green Belt and also reduce the value of local plans in making proper provision for necessary development in the future.

4.   Since the protection of Green Belts must be maintained, planning authorities in defining detailed Green Belt boundaries in local plans will need to relate their proposals to a longer time scale than is normally adopted in plans for new development. While making provision for development in general conformity with the structure plan they should satisfy themselves that Green Belt boundaries will not need to be altered at the end of that period. In some cases this will mean safeguarding land between the urban area and the

Green Belt which may be required to meet longer term development needs. The normal process of development control serves this purpose and authorities should state clearly in structure and local plans the policies that they intend to apply in those areas over the period covered by the plan.

5.   It is particularly important that full use is made of opportunities for bringing back into use areas of neglected or derelict land and for recycling urban land, including obsolete industrial sites and buildings unlikely to be required in future for their original purpose. The development of such sites can make a valuable contribution to inner city renewal and reduce the pressures on undeveloped land. The maintenance of effective Green Belt policy will assist in this.

6. Well defined long-term Green Belt boundaries will help to ensure its future agricultural, recreational and amenity value, whereas less secure boundaries would make it more difficult for farmers and other land owners to maintain and improve their land. Local planning authorities can assist in this by working together with land owners and voluntary groups to enhance the countryside, and especially those areas of land within the Green Belt, or adjacent to it, which are suffering from disuse or neglect. This is particularly important in parts of the Green Belt that are close to existing urban development, or between urban areas within conurbations, and which can be especially vulnerable to neglect or damage. Such areas may form an important part of the Green Belt and, if so, need to be protected and maintained, but in considering whether to include such areas within the Green Belt, where detailed boundaries have not yet been established, authorities should also consider carefully whether the land could be better reserved for future development and thus ease the pressure on the other land that should have the long-term protection of the Green Belt. Once the detailed boundaries have been fixed they should not become derelict. The overall aim should be to develop and maintain a positive approach to land-use management which *both* makes adequate provision for necessary development *and* ensures that the Green Belt serves its proper purpose.

7. For convenience the two earlier circulars on Green Belts (MHLG Circulars Nos 42/55 and 50/57) are reproduced in the Annex to this circular. The policy advice that they contain remains valid but insofar as they relate to the earlier development plan system they are out-of-date and are replaced by the present circular.

PPG 1 (1992) General Policy and Principles

The town and country planning system is designed to regulate the development and use of land in the public interest. The system has served the country well. It is an important instrument for protecting and enhancing the environment in town and country, preserving the built and natural heritage, conserving the rural landscape and maintaining Green Belts (para 2).

'... The Planning system, and the preparation of development plans in particular, can contribute to the objectives of ensuring that development and growth are sustainable' (para 3).

'... Such plans, which should be consistent with national and regional planning policy, provide the primary means of reconciling conflicts. Although their provisions are not prescriptive, they are intended to provide a firm basis for rational and consistent decisions on planning applications and appeals' (para 17).

'... Where the development plan is material to the development proposal, and must therefore be taken into account, section 54A requires the application or appeal, to be determined in accordance with the plan, unless material considerations indicate otherwise. In effect, this introduces a presumption in favour of development proposals which are in accordance with the development plan' (para 25).

PPG 3 (1992) Land for Housing

'Development Plans should show how future requirements for new housing can best be met, having regard to other planning objectives, such as Green Belt policy' (para 8).

'In order to meet the requirement for new housing and at the same time maintain conservation policies, it is important that full and effective use is made of land within urban areas' (para 15).

'The contribution of urban sites to total housing provision has increased in recent years. Recent information on land use changes in England shows that nearly half of the land developed for housing was either previously developed or was vacant land in built-up areas' (para 17).

'Such settlements [new settlements] can only be contemplated where sites are not within a Green Belt' (para 32).

Annex A - Affordable Housing for Local Needs in Rural Areas

'... This guidance does not alter the general presumption against inappropriate development in the Green Belts. Green Belt policy remains as set out in Planning Policy Guidance Note 2' (para 11).

'Most Green Belt areas are by their nature close to the main conurbations, and conditions are not typical of the generality of rural areas to which this policy is addressed. Special considerations may, however, arise in some of the more extensive areas of Green Belt away from the urban fringe, particularly in areas where there are many small settlements and it may not be practicable or appropriate to define Green Belt boundaries around each one' (para 12).

'In some of these areas local planning policies already recognise that very limited development within existing settlements may be acceptable and consistent with the functions of the Green Belt. It is for local planning authorities to judge whether low cost housing development for local community needs would fall within the scope of such policies' (para 13).

'The release, exceptionally, for small-scale, low cost housing schemes of other sites within existing settlements, which would not be considered for development under such policies, would again be a matter for the judgement of the planning authority, having regard to all material considerations, including the objectives of Green Belt policy and the evidence of local need' (para 14).

PPG 4 (1992) Industrial and Commercial Development and Small Firms

'... Where an area of open countryside (eg a Green Belt) needs to be protected against encroachment buildings will not become more acceptable because their occupancy is restricted' (para 14).

PPG 5 (1992) Simplified Planning Zones

'... SPZs may not be set up in National Parks, Conservation Areas, AONBs, Green Belt, SSSIs, and any other areas specified in an order by the Secretary of State' (para 7).

PPG 6 (1988) Major Retail Development

'... Proposals for such development, which may be well over 100,000 sq ft and up to 1 million sq ft or more (10,000 - 100,000 sq m), have no place in the Green Belt, where there is a strong presumption against all inappropriate development' (para 15).

PPG 7 (1992) The Countryside and Rural Economy

Green Belts and the Urban fringe.

'... Green Belts are established through development plans, to check urban sprawl, safeguard the surrounding countryside, prevent neighbouring towns from merging, preserve the special character of historic towns, and assist urban regeneration. They cover some 15,500 square kilometres, about 12 per cent of England. There are none in Wales. Within Green Belts there is, in addition to the general policies controlling development in the countryside, a presumption against inappropriate development' (para 3.12).

'Despite the strict control of urban sprawl there are around some conurbations areas of "urban fringe" where land use conflicts and environmental problems arise. Urban fringe is not a designation, though some urban fringe areas are found within Green Belts. The urban fringe often accommodates essential but neighbouring functions such as waste disposal and sewage treatment, and contains areas of derelict land and damaged landscape and under-use land whose viability for agricultural use has been affected by urban pressures. It requires a positive approach to planning and management, aimed at securing environmental improvement and beneficial use of land, and increased public access, to provide an amenity for the residents of urban areas' (para 3.13).

PPG 8 (1992) Telecommunications

'... the nature of some telecommunications development may in some cases bring it into apparent conflict with established local and national planning policies. Masts antennas and other telecommunications developments may all need particular locations in order to work effectively, but these sites may be subject to special planning policies if for example they are in the Green Belt, National Parks...[etc]' (para 7).

'Planning authorities will need to be alive to special needs and technical problems of telecommunications developments and in many cases these will have to prevail over normal planning policies' (para 8).

PPG 9 (1989) Regional Planning Guidance for the South East

'... There are now approved Structure Plans covering the whole region and these together with the Greater London Development Plan, provide a framework of well-established land use policies. Many of these policies such as those concerning the conservation of the countryside and maintenance of the Green Belt will continue to apply over the period of this guidance and will be reaffirmed in successive structure plan reviews' (Appendix A, para 7).

'The phased development of Stanstead airport will need to be taken into account when considering the scale and location of provision for development in Essex and Hertfordshire. As the White Paper on Airports Policy said, any urban development associated with the airport must be provided for with great care (Cmnd 9542, para 5.31). The White Paper also referred, at paragraph 5.33, to the importance the Government attaches to existing policies for protecting agricultural land, Green Belts and the character of surrounding towns and villages, and the avoidance of pressure of demand for sporadic unplanned development' (Appendix A, para 6).

'To make adequate provision for orderly development in the surrounding counties [of London] particularly in those locations identified in structure plans ("growth areas") whilst safeguarding, with appropriate policies, Green Belts, AONBs, better quality agricultural land and other open countryside' (Appendix B, para 2(b)).

'This Government firmly supports rural conservation, although the degree of restraint must depend on local circumstances. There should continue to be the strongest restraint on development in the Metropolitan Green Belt, for which a depth of 12-15 miles is usually adequate. Outside the already approved Metropolitan Green Belt I would require special justification before approving its extension to a greater depth than this' (Appendix B, para 7).

'The general presumption against development in the Green Belt is not affected by the M25 and there should continue to be the strongest restraint on development there. The improved access which the Motorway provides will enhance the recreational value of the Green Belt' (Appendix C, para 3).

PPG 10 (1988) Strategic Guidance for the West Midlands

'... The West Midlands Green Belt has been established to check the unrestricted sprawl of large built-up areas, to safeguard surrounding countryside, to prevent neighbouring towns merging into one another, (a good example being the Meridian Gap separating Birmingham and Coventry), to preserve the special character of historic towns and to assist in urban regeneration. It also protects good agricultural land, preserves the quality of the landscape, provides opportunities for sport and recreation and helps nature conservation. Although the general area has been established in approved structure plans, there are large parts where detailed boundaries have yet to be defined. Where boundaries do exist little land has been left between the edge of the built-up areas and the Green Belt to meet development needs, yet there is little evidence that a tightly-drawn inner boundary of itself supports urban regeneration. Unitary Development plans must establish secure Green Belts which take proper account of the likely scale and pattern of development needs into the twenty first century'.

'Green Belts must be permanent and their protection maintained as far as can be seen ahead. A full-scale review of the West Midlands Green Belt is not warranted. Instead, local authorities are asked when preparing development plans to use the following process in determining where development needs should be met:

(a)   As much development as possible (subject to the regeneration strategy and the policy emphasis in the inner areas of each District) should be on sites within the present built-up areas;

(b)   For development which has to be outside the present built-up areas, as much as possible should be in areas not covered by Green Belt policies;

(c)   For development which cannot be located inside built-up areas or outside on land not in the Green Belt, as much as possible should be accommodated through the careful drawing of Green Belt boundaries in areas where they have not yet been defined either in adopted local plans or in the former development plans;

(d)   Only if a deficiency still remains after (a), (b) or (c) should alterations be contemplated to Green Belt boundaries which have already been defined in adopted local plans or the former development plans'.

'The identification of up to 330 hectares of land for high technology development by 2001 will inevitably have some implications for the Green Belt, and by that date up to 2,400 dwellings in Solihull, 1,400 in Birmingham and 700 in Wolverhampton may need to be built on land in categories (c) or (d) above; but housing development in the other Metropolitan Districts is unlikely to have a similar effect. In the Shire Counties, relaxing the requirement to accommodate migrant households within the Metropolitan Journey to Work Area should minimise any effects on the Green Belt. It is unlikely that development for purposes other than high technology industry or housing will be permitted in the Green Belt, except activities covered by paragraphs 12 to 18 of Planning Policy Guidance Note No 2'.

'In defining Green Belt boundaries, local authorities should relate their proposals to a longer time-scale than is normally adopted in plans for new development, though it may not be possible at this stage to foresee accurately the scale of development that is omitted from the Green Belt to meet potential long-term needs, it should be protected in the meantime by strong development control policies. Long-term needs alone are unlikely to justify changes to existing boundaries'.

'Green wedges are a distinctive feature of the West Midlands Green Belt. They assist nature conservation, help to maintain and improve the environmental quality of the urban areas, and provide vital recreational opportunities for residents or urban areas'.

'The best and most versatile agricultural land (in the West Midlands Metropolitan Districts, grades 1, 2 and, in some areas 3a of the MAFF Agricultural Land Classification) should not be built on unless there is no other land available for the particular purpose. Unitary development Plans should also take into account the Government's policies for the use of redundant agricultural buildings, the diversification of agricultural businesses, the establishment of farm woodlands and other structural measures to reduce surplus production'.

'Policies for the countryside, including positive action to conserve and enhance its attractiveness and maintain and improve public access, should where relevant be an integral part of Unitary Development Plans. In suitable cases, development can complement both agricultural and recreational uses. Development proposals should be based on a proper appreciation of the countryside resource'.

'The West Midlands must play its part in maintaining supplies of minerals for he construction industry within the Region. The unnecessary sterilisation of mineral resources by other forms of development should be avoided. Like other forms of development, mineral working is subject to Green Belt and agricultural land policies, but the need for minerals may sometimes be overriding, especially if satisfactory landscaping and restoration proposals can be included' (paras 11-18).

PPG 11 (1988) Strategic Planning Guidance for Merseyside

'... The main objectives of the Merseyside Green Belt are to check urban sprawl, safeguard valuable countryside and assist urban regeneration. Those objectives remain valid and will continue. There is no need for a general review of the Green Belt but the preparation of UDPs provides the opportunity to give precision to the detailed boundaries of the Green Belt where those have not yet been clearly defined. The aim must be to establish firm boundaries which will ensure the permanence of the Green Belt.

The policies governing the control of development in Green Belts are set out in Planning Policy Guidance Note No. 2 (January 1988) and Unitary Development Plans should conform to that guidance. The Councils should plan to make full use of land within the existing built-up areas, especially through bringing back into use neglected or derelict land. Such development as cannot be catered for within the present built-up area should be located in areas not covered by Green Belts. Wherever possible, land subject to other policy constraints, including those relating to the protection of the best and most versatile agricultural land and the need to protect the countryside for its own sake, should also be avoided. Alternations to Green Belt boundaries should be considered only when it can be clearly demonstrated that an area of land within the existing Green Belt boundary no longer makes a significant contribution to the objectives of the Green Belt'.

PPG12 (1992) Development Plans and Regional Planning Guidance

Green Belt Boundaries

'...   1.   The Secretary of State for the Environment notes with concern, that, in some areas of England, Green Belts that have been established in general terms in approved structure plans have not yet had their detailed boundaries defined in general local plans or in old subject plans.

2.   In preparing local plans, authorities should pay particular attention to the proper definition of Green Belt boundaries, sos that there is no uncertainty as to where Green Belt policies do and do not apply. In some parts of the country the detailed boundaries of Green Belts have not yet been formally determined. In determining detailed boundaries, authorities should take account of the advice given in PPG 2.

3.   Where existing local plans are being revised and updated, existing Green Belt boundaries should not be changed unless alterations to the structure plan have been approved, or other exceptional circumstances exist, which necessitate such revision' (Annex D).

PPG 17 (1991) Sport and Recreation

The Urban Fringe

'... Planning authorities should consider the scope for encouraging recreational facilities and increased public access to open land on the urban fringe, where this is compatible with existing uses. Subject to policies in local plans, protection or creation of open space for amenity, wildlife, conservation or recreational purposes is no less important than these areas than in inner urban areas.

In some areas of the urban fringe, sites for recreational use may act as an important buffer between agricultural and urban uses to protect crops from damage. Recreational opportunities may also arise in connection with new development in the urban fringe, such as business and industrial parks. Local planning authorities are asked to give sympathetic consideration to planning applications for afforestation initiatives in urban fringe areas, as proposed by the Countryside and Forestry Commissions, and for possible changes of use of agricultural land for suitable recreational pursuits. It is important, where possible, to enhance the "rights of way" network in these areas. Where proposals for recreation initiatives are considered, nature conservation interests in the area should be taken into account.

Green Belts

Planning policy for the Green Belts is set out in PPG 2. There is a general presumption against inappropriate development, but 'outdoor sport' is one of the uses of land which will often be appropriate on Green Belt land. The suitable conversion of redundant buildings may be needed to facilitate outdoor sport in the Green Belt. In very special circumstances, such sport may require the construction of small ancillary buildings, unobtrusive spectator accommodation, or other essential facilities. Local planning authorities should consider each application on its merits, bearing in mind the objectives of the Green Belts. Outdoor sport may offer a means of improving the environmental quality of Green Belt land, and there may be opportunities for redundant hospital sites (Circular 12/91)' (paras 32-34).

PPG 21 (1992) Tourism

'... Different considerations apply in the case of Green Belts since the designation of those areas is not related primarily to landscape quality but it is intended chiefly to restrict the outward expansion of the urban areas that they enclose. There is thus a general presumption against nearly all forms of new development within them and especially against large scale new development of any kind. Green Belt policy is explained fully in PPG 2' (para 5.14).

173

Holiday Caravans

'... Local planning authorities should take full account of the advice contained in PPG 2 on Green Belts' (Annex B, para 5.15).

MPG 1 Applications, Permissions and Conditions

'... in areas such as Green Belts, where amenity considerations are of great importance, mineral extraction may be acceptable as a temporary activity, restricted as it is by the expected life of the working. In order, however, that any such industrial type activity should not be excessive or prolonged, it may be necessary to impose conditions restricting such plant, machinery and buildings to use in connection with the treatment, dressing or processing of material produced only from the site' (para 107).

MPG 3 Opencast Coal Mining

'... Policy on Green Belts is set out in PPG 2. Minerals can be worked only where they are found, and opencast coal extraction need not be incompatible with Green Belt objectives provided that high environmental standards are maintained and that the site is well restored' (para 17).

MPG 6 Guidelines for Aggregates Provisions in England and Wales

'... The issue of mineral working also arises within Green Belt areas and the Government's policy is set out in PPG 2 'Green Belts'. The extraction of minerals need not be incompatible with Green Belt objectives provided that high environmental standards are maintained and the site is well restored' (para 23).

MPG 10 Provision of Raw Material for the Cement Industry

'... Proposals for mineral working also arise within Green Belts. The Government's policy is set out in Planning Policy Guidance Note 2: Green Belts. This states that the extraction of minerals need not be incompatible with Green Belt objectives provided that high environmental standards for working and landscaping are maintained and that the site is well restored to an appropriate use' (para 45).

RPG 1 Strategic Guidance for Tyne and Wear

'... The Tyne and Wear Green Belt serves to check urban sprawl, to safeguard countryside, and to prevent neighbouring towns merging. In addition it protects agricultural land, provides opportunities for sport and recreation. To be a continuing success the Green Belt needs to have stable boundaries that are altered only in exceptional circumstances. UDPs should establish a secure Green Belt which takes proper account of the likely scale of development needs well into the 21st century.

The policies governing the control of development in Green Belts are set out in PPG 2 and UDPs should conform to that guidance.

Green Belts must be permanent and their protection maintained as far as can be seen ahead. The broad extent and purpose of the approved Green Belt remains valid and should be maintained. The District Council should plan to make full use of land within the existing built up area, especially through bringing back into use neglected or derelict land. Where development cannot be provided for within the built up area it should be located in areas not covered by Green Belt. If an alternation is proposed the Secretary of State will wish to be satisfied that the local planning authority has considered opportunities for development within the urban areas contained by and outside the Green Belt.

When preparing their UDP, North Tyneside Metropolitan Borough Council should consider an extension of the Metropolitan Green Belt in North Tyneside, compatible with the guidance in PPG 2 and having regard to the provision of a full range and choice of sites for development within the Borough' (paras 32-35).

RPG 2 Strategic Guidance for West Yorkshire

'... The Green Belt in West Yorkshire protects open land between the urban areas, within the core of the conurbation, and around its outer edges. It regulates the growth of urban areas, prevents the coalescence of settlements, preserves the open land that extends into the urban areas for recreational or amenity use and provides for easy access to open country. It has contributed to the maintenance of the unusually open and often attractive character of the conurbation. It will also assist int he process of urban regeneration. Green Belts are permanent features and their protection must be maintained. The policies governing the control of development in Green Belts are set out in PPG 2 and Unitary Development Plans should have regard to that guidance.

The general area of the Green Belt within West Yorkshire was reviewed and approved int he County Structure Plan in 1980. in some areas detailed boundaries have been determined but there are many areas where boundaries have yet to be finalised. A full scale review of the Green Belt is not warranted for West Yorkshire but the preparation of Unitary Development Plans provides the opportunity to give precision to the Green Belt where boundaries have not yet been clearly defined and, exceptionally, to review the existing boundaries where economic regeneration may be constrained by a lack of suitable industrial sites. The exercise must establish boundaries which are secure having taken account of the likely scale and pattern of development needs well into the next century. If an alteration to the Green Belt boundary is proposed, the Secretary of State will wish to be satisfied that the local planning authority has fully considered opportunities for development elsewhere, preferably within the urban areas, or that the area affected by the boundary change is no longer capable of making a significant contribution to the objectives of the Green Belt. Where land is not needed to meet potential long term needs, it should be protected in the meantime by strong development control policies' (paras 19-20).

RPG 3 Strategic Guidance for London

'... National policies on Green Belts are restated in Planning Policy Guidance: Green Belts (PPG 2). In relation to London, the Green Belt has four main purposes:

- to check the unrestricted sprawl of the built up areas;
- to safeguard the surrounding countryside from further encroachment;
- to prevent London from merging with neighbouring towns;
- to assist in urban regeneration.

The Green Belt also plays a positive role in providing access to open countryside for London's population for recreation and other pursuits.

The permanence of the Green Belt must be maintained as far as can be seen ahead. The Secretary of State will only be prepared to endorse any change in the boundaries of the established Green Belt in exceptional circumstances in accordance with the principles states in PPG 2. The general extent of the approved Green Belt is shown in Map 1 and is set out in detail in earlier development plans. UDPs should show approved boundaries precisely. Where exceptionally boundaries need to be revised, proposed changes should be clearly identified and justified, and the written statement should explain the exceptional circumstances behind any proposed change.

Although Green Belt contains areas of attractive landscape, it should be borne in mind that the quality of the landscape is not a material factor in its designation and continued protection. But there is scope for improving the Green Belt and, where appropriate, UDPs should contain land use policies to assist this. The Countryside Commission's "Planning for Countryside in Metropolitan Areas" contains helpful advice on safeguarding and managing the Green Belt for open-air recreation, conserving wildlife and enhancing the landscape' (paras 57-59).

RPG 4 Regional Guidance for Greater Manchester

'... UDPs must conform with Planning Policy Guidance Note 2, "Green Belts". The Councils should seek to incorporate the Greater Manchester Green Belt as defined in Local Plans maintaining consistency between the Green Belt in Greater Manchester and the Green Belt in surrounding areas.

The agricultural land in Greater Manchester provides for a wide variety of farming, from the uplands in the east to the mossland in the west. In their UDPs the Councils should accommodate both continuing farming needs and the diversification of the rural economy.

Within and around the built-up areas there are areas of countryside and other open land including the river valleys, whose amenity, recreational and wildlife value has been recognised through River Valley Plans and other open land initiatives. UDPs should demonstrate the Council's continuing care for the river valleys and for the open land which helps to project an attractive image of the County. The Councils should seek to promote environmental improvement in these areas, including the reclamation of derelict and unused land, the creation and retention of open scape, opportunities for woodlands, site specific and area-based environmental improvements, and recreation facilities.

In consultation with the Ministry of Agriculture, Fisheries and Food, the Countryside Commission, the Nature Conservancy Council, the Forestry Commission, other appropriate bodies and voluntary groups, the Councils should include in UDPs policies to:

(a)   safeguard the best and most versatile agricultural land;
(b)   maintain rural economic activity, including farming and minerals extraction;
(c)   protect areas of scientific and ecological importance, and also those of scenic, recreational, cultural and heritage value;
(d)   provide recreational opportunities and assist nature conservation.

Greater Manchester contributed significantly to national deep-mined and opencast coal production. Brickclay, gritstone, and sand gravel are also produced, though the County is a net importer of these minerals. Greater Manchester;s continuing role in the national and regional production of minerals should take account of the work of the North West Aggregates Working Party, and must be in line with the Secretary of State's Minerals Planning Guidance. The Minerals Local Plan for Greater Manchester will provide the framework for minerals planning within the County. The Councils should continue to co-operate on minerals planning and their UDPs should have regard to the Plan. The UDPs should set out consistent policies which will safeguard mineral resources, identify areas for mineral working, secure high standards for site operation and the disposal of spoil, restoration and aftercare, and minimise the environmental impact of minerals operations.

Much of the waste arising in Greater Manchester is disposed of outside the County. During the period covered by the UDPs the problems of waste disposal - finding suitable sites and disposal methods - are expected to become more severe. Site selection should have regard to the waste Disposal Plans for the area, and recognise the essential inter-relationship between disposal, site licensing, and planning control. UDPs should, where appropriate, identify waste disposal sites or criteria for identifying such sites. In addition they should set out the criteria for assessing the land use and environmental implications of individual proposals' (paras 11-16).

RPG 5 Strategic Guidance for South Yorkshire

'... The Green Belt has contributed significantly to the conservation of South Yorkshire's countryside. It regulates the growth or urban areas, prevents the coalescence of settlements, protects the open land that extends into the urban areas for recreational or amenity purposes, and preserves easy access to open country. It will also assist the process of urban regeneration.

The policies governing the control of development in Green Belts are set out in Planning Policy Guidance Note 2. Green Belts are permanent features and their protection must be maintained. Alterations to Green Belt boundaries should be proposed only when it can be clearly demonstrated that all opportunities for development within the urban areas have been considered.

The general area of the South Yorkshire Green Belt has been established in the approved structure plan. Detailed boundaries have been finalised in several adopted local plans, but the overall picture is incomplete. The preparation of UDPs provides the opportunity to give precision to the Green Belt where boundaries have not yet been clearly defined and, exceptionally, to review the existing boundaries where economic regeneration may be constrained by the lack of suitable industrial sites. Where land is not needed for immediate development but is omitted from the Green Belt to meet potential long term needs, it should be protected in the meantime by strong development control policies (paras 21-23).

RPG 6 Regional Planning Guidance for East Anglia

'... One Green Belt, around Cambridge, has been formally approved, covering an area of about 107 kilometres, though the outer boundary has still to be finally defined. Norfolk County Council have proposed a Green Belt for the Norwich area. The five purposes of Green Belts, as set out in Planning Policy Guidance Note 2, are to check the unrestricted sprawl of large built areas, to safeguard the surrounding countryside from further encroachment, to prevent neighbouring towns from merging into one another, to preserve the special character of historic towns, and to assist urban regeneration. Policies in Structure Plans for Green Belts should take into account the guidance set out in PPG 2 (para 33).

Appendix C: Green Belts in the Case Study Areas

C.1.   The Tables below give brief summary information on the Green Belt situation, in development plans, in the case study areas. The cut-off point for information is July 1992. It is possible that some of the proposals in Draft Unitary Development Plans or District Plans will not appear in the same form in approved plans.

C.2.   As the situation in most cases is not straightforward, some comments are included, where appropriate, to explain what has occurred.

Table C.1: Green Belt Alterations in Development Plans in Case Study Areas: 1984-1992

area	approved changes	previous status of land
Dorset		
Purbeck	Land for 700-1,000 dwellings; adjacent to Sandford and Holton Heath insets, Purbeck District. Approved in principle South East Dorset Structure Plan - First Alteration (1990)	Interim Green Belt
East Dorset	Land for 2,300 dwellings south of Verwood.	Interim Green Belt

Comment: Some 90 per cent of the housing development approved in the 1990 South East Dorset Structure Plan First Alteration is intended to be within the built-up areas of Bournemouth-Poole. Detailed boundaries in local plans were only approved for around one third of the Green Belt by 1992. Town-scale local plans approved for Sandford (Purbeck), and Corfe Mullen, Wimbourne and Ferndown (East Dorset).

179

Hertfordshire

Dacorum	Area of Special Restraint for needs of high technology industry. Hemel Hempstead, 37 ha (District Plan, 1984)	Interim Green Belt and white land
	Housing sites on edge of Hemel Hempstead c. 10 ha (District Plan, 1984)	Interim Green Belt and white land
Broxbourne	Area of Special Restraint for housing; c. 10-12 ha; Local Plan, 1986)	Green Belt
	Land for c. 700 dwellings in area of derelict glasshouses (agreed in Herts County Structure Plan, 1988)	Green Belt

Comment: The 1988 Structure Plan proposed that extra housing sites should be taken from the Green Belt on the southern edge of Hemel Hempstead. In Dacorum the time period of the local plan was extended during the approval process and new housing sites were found in the Interim Green Belt. The District Council are now proposing that urban 'windfall' sites will provide for housing to 2001 (1992 Draft Plan).

Greater London

Enfield	Tidying up of boundary produced two or three extra sites; creation of two village insets (Borough Plan, 1983)	Green Belt

Oxfordshire

City of Oxford	Land for c. 750 dwellings and hi-tech industrial park (southern edge of City of Oxford, Oxon County Structure Plan, Second Alteration, 1987)	Interim Green Belt, as approved by Minister in 1975
Cherwell	White land (3.5 ha) Yarnton (Oxford Fringe Local Plan, 1991)	Interim Green Belt, as approved by Minister in 1975

Comment: Land for housing and hi-tech use was allocated on the southern fringe of the City. Land now transferred from South Oxfordshire District to Oxford City Council. Other Green Belt boundaries in City not approved since original 1962 Inquiry. Attempts to define the boundary in the mid-1980s were defeated by lack of agreement over the definition of land for longer-term needs. No changes to Green Belt in Oxfordshire Structure Plan, Fourth Alteration, 1992.

West Midlands

Walsall	District 'adopted' detailed boundary in 1985 based on Green Belt Local Plan proposals for Metro County Area. Significant housing and employment related development.	Interim Green Belt as as approved by Minister in 1975
Wolverhampton	District follows boundaries as in 1985 Green Belt Local Plan. Little peripheral development.	
South Staffordshire	County Structure Plan Replacement (1991) agrees 5,100 dwellings for 1991-2001. Agrees implies 360 dwellings on 42 acres of land to be taken from Green Belt in previously approved Local Plans (1980 and 1982). Also 80 ha of land for general hi-tech sites for industry adjacent to M42 Motorway; in accord with approved Regional Guidance (PPG 10).	Green Belt as approved in North Eastern Area District Plan 1980, and Southern Area Plan 1982
Cannock	No significant changes.	

Comments: In Walsall and Wolverhampton the West Midlands County Green Belt Subject Plan was not adopted, due to abolition of the Metropolitan County. Green Belt boundaries formally operate as defined on a map approved by the Minister in 1975. This map contains areas of fully approved Green Belt, and generous areas of Interim Green Belt. The local authorities use the Green Belt Subject Plan for development control purposes until superseded by the approval of new Borough-wide plans.

Cheshire

Macclesfield	Cheshire 2001 Replacement Structure Plan (1992) allocates 7,600 dwellings to Macclesfield Borough area 1986-2001. Agreed that this implies change to Green Belt boundaries south of Macclesfield and creation of new Green Belt insets (1992). Also land	Green Belt as approved in 1985 Macclesfield Local Plan

	required for long term needs.	
Chester	Suggested 800 acres of new development around Chester not approved by Minister 1992.	

Yorkshire

Sheffield	Green Belt Subject Plan approved 1983; no formal changes since.	No significant change
Barnsley	Approved in South Yorkshire Structure Plan 1979. A range of changes in seven local plans prepared in 1982-86.	Deletions of Green Belt in Dodworth Local Plan (1985) 13 hectares; Darton Local Plan (1986) 42 hectares; Wimbwell Local Plan (1984) 7 hectares; and Barnsley Urban Area Plan (1986) 41 hectares. (Percentage of Green Belt deleted in Local Plans since 1974 is 0.8 per cent).
Wakefield	Approved in West Yorkshire Structure Plan 1980, and District Local Plan, 1985.	Widely re-cast from County Development Plans. The three local plans added 5,600 acres to the Green Belt defined under previous development plans.
	388 ha of Presumption Against Development land, which may be required to cater for housing needs over next 25-30 years.	Green Belt in most cases.
Leeds	Approved in sequence of seven local plans over period 1983-89, following approval of West Yorkshire Structure Plan of 1980.	Re-cast from old West Riding plans.

Table C.2: Proposals for Extensions to Green Belt in Case Study Areas: 1984-1992

area	proposal	outcome
Dorset	Extension of South East Dorset Green Belt, 15-16 sq kms around Alderholt, north east of Verwood. Proposed in Dorset (excluding SE), Second Alteration to Structure Plan 1991, and Draft Verwood Local Plan 1991	Not yet decided
Hertfordshire	Extensions around Markgate to define because level of growth of settlement. (In Herts Structure Plan First Alteration 1991).	Rejected, difficult to define limits to growth
	Extensions bordering Bedfordshire, to assist urban regeneration in Luton - Dunstable area.	Rejected
	Extensions northward in East Herts to A1-M1 link road.	Rejected, due to insufficient development pressures to make special policy measures necessary
Staffordshire	Proposed Areas of Restraint beyond Green Belt to perform separating function in Tamworth and Lichfield areas.	Rejected, as unnecessary and confusion with West Midlands Green Belt
Walsall	North of Bloxwich, suggested in Staffs Structure Plan.	Approved
Leeds	Extensions to the north east of the City, to define new development boundary in context of dispersal strategy.	Not yet decided

Table C.3:   Proposals for New Green Belts and Extensions to Existing Green Belts
Outside Study Areas: 1984-1992

area	proposal	outcome
Norfolk	Green Belt around Norwich; average depth two-three miles	Draft modifications letter suggests rejection
Hampshire	Green Belt across South Hampshire from New Forest in west, to West Sussex County boundary in east	Draft modifications letter suggests rejection due to retention of growth status in South Hampshire
Cleveland	Hull-Beverley Green Belt, six miles wide around Hull.	Rejected, due to insufficient development pressures to make special policy necessary
Shropshire	Extensions to West Midlands Green Belt.	Draft modifications letter suggests approval

Table C.4:   Land Between the Urban Area and the Green Belt (White Land) in Case
Study Areas

	white land in approved plans	white land in proposals
Dorset		
Purbeck	None	None
East Dorset	None	None
Hertfordshire		
Dacorum	Area of Special Restraint for high tech industry	ASR to be retained
Broxbourne	Area of Special Restraint for housing	ASR to be extended
Greater London		
Enfield	None	None

184

Oxfordshire

Oxford City	'Green Belt' in City is formally Interim Green Belt	Safeguarded Land; over 100 hectares
Cherwell	White land	White land retained, 4 hectares

West Midlands

Walsall	Interim Green Belt	White land in proposed UDP, 68 hectares
Wolverhampton	None	None
South Staffs	Not known	Three sites in proposed District Plan, 40 hectares

Cheshire

Macclesfield	None	Unallocated land in submitted District Plan, 40 hectares
Chester	None	No proposals

South and West Yorkshire

Sheffield	None	None
Barnsley	Barnsley Urban Area Local Plan	White land retained
Wakefield	Areas of Presumption Against Development; 388 hectares	Some changes to PAD areas in draft UDP
Leeds	None	White land proposed in draft UDP, 100 hectares

Note: These refer to the position at the end of 1992.

Appendix D: Development Control Policies in Local Plans

Selected Development Control Policies

D.1   The following are examples of the types of policy used in Green Belts, ordered as for the list in paragraph 6.16. One of the most complete sets of policies currently operating is found in *The Control of Development in the Green Belt*, published by Leeds City Council in 1990.   Policies from Cherwell (Oxfordshire), East Dorset, Broxbourne (Hertfordshire) and South Staffordshire are also used.

General

D.2   '... Within the Green Belt ... permission will not be given for development for purposes other than that required for mineral extraction, agriculture, small-scale facilities for participatory sport and recreation, or other uses appropriate to a rural area; or the use for hospitals or similar institutional purposes of existing large residential buildings situated in extensive grounds, provided a) the buildings are not suitable for continued residential use, and b) the proposed use is not such as to lead to a demand for large extensions or for additional buildings in the grounds'.
(Hertfordshire County Council (1992) Hertfordshire County Structure Plan Review, policy 1 (part)).

House Extensions and Replacement Dwellings

D.3   '... In the area of the Green Belt, new dwellings will normally be permitted in replacement of existing or recently demolished or destroyed dwellings where:
a) they are on the same site as the previous dwelling;
b) the existing dwelling is not of architectural or historic interest and does not contribute to the character or history of the area.
Extensions to existing dwellings will also normally be allowed.   Both replacement dwellings and extensions will only be allowed where:
c) the totalled gross floor area of the new or extended dwelling (externally measured but excluding garages) does not exceed that of its predecessor as it existed at the time of the establishment of the Green Belt in 1980 by more than one half.
An exception may be made to criterion c) where its application would result in a dwelling whose total floor area was less than 140m2'.
(East Dorset District Council (1991) Verwood, Three Legged Cross and St Leonards and St Ives Local Plan, Deposit Plan, para 6.37).

Agricultural Workers' Dwellings

D.4   '... Planning permission will only be granted for the construction of new dwellings beyond the existing or planned built-up limits of settlements when an essential need for agriculture or other existing undertaking can be established and where such development would not prejudice the purpose and character of the Green Belt or conflict with other policies in this plan'.

The justification states '... Essential need will normally be interpreted as proven necessity for on site supervision, the absence of which would seriously threaten the viability and security of the undertakings concerned. When the proposal is related to agriculture or forestry the Council will require it to be substantiated by the MAFF or by an alternative independent, professionally qualified source'
(Cherwell District Council (1989) <u>Central Oxfordshire Local Plan (Cherwell)</u>, Plan for Deposit, policy GB4 and para 2.16).

Redundant Buildings

D.5   '... Planning permission for the change of redundant buildings in the Green Belt to commercial use or for individual residences shall normally be granted only where:
    a) evidence is provided to show that the building is in a generally sound physical condition (ie is not derelict or in a state of substantial structural disrepair);
    b) the building is genuinely redundant, there being sound reasons why it is unsuitable for its original or most recent purpose and evidence that no other appropriate Green Belt use can be found;
    c) in the case of agricultural buildings, the building must be genuinely redundant and shown to be incapable of further agricultural use. Any building still being used for agricultural purposes will not be permitted to change to another use;
    d) the building is of a size and constructional form such as to have conversion potential without substantial rebuilding, addition or extension;
    e) detailed planning and highway considerations can be satisfactorily resolved; and
    f) the LPA have been satisfied that no significant additional use will fall on public utilities or services.

In general, when considering proposals commercial uses which will benefit the local economy, or will promote recreation or tourism, will be permitted in preference to residential use, unless the applicant provides evidence to show that no such commercial uses can be found'.
(Leeds City Council (1990) <u>The Control of Development in the Green Belt</u>, para 5.4 (part)).

Institutions in Extensive Grounds

D.6   '... The Green Belt concept implies no further building except where there is a positive argument for allowing it. Consequently where planning permission is sought for development for an institution in substantial grounds this shall normally only be granted where:

187

a) it can be shown that there is a need for the proposed development to be located in an open, rather than a built up area and so come within the spirit of the exemption from Green Belt policy;
b) it can be shown that the substantial grounds are necessary for the satisfactory functioning of the proposed institutional use;
c) the grounds rather than the buildings are the dominant landscape feature;
d) the proportion of the site covered by buildings and car parking does not exceed 10 per cent; and
e) buildings and car parking are adequately screened'

(Leeds City Council (1990) The Control of Development in the Green Belt, para 5.23).

Employment Uses

D.7   '... There is a general presumption against development for industrial, office, hotel/motel, restaurant or filling station establishments in the Green Belt'.
(South Staffordshire District Council (1980) District Plan Number One - North Eastern Area, Written Statement, policy 6.5.6).

'... The expansion of existing industrial, office, hotel/motel, restaurant or filling station establishments will normally be allowed if the expansion cannot reasonably be located outside the Green Belt and if it can be carried out without detriment to the appearance and character of the countryside or to the amenity of local residents'.
(South Staffordshire District Council 1980) District Plan Number One - North Eastern Area, Written Statement, policy 6.5.7).

'... A proposal for the extension or replacement or buildings in permitted or established commercial use in the Green Belt will only be approved if:
a) it is essential for the proposed development to take place on the site of the existing premises;
b) the proposal would not prejudice the purpose and integrity of the Green Belt or injure its rural appearance and character, or perpetuate and consolidate badly-sited development;
c) the proposal for extensions is minor in scale in relation to the existing building;
d) the proposal is for a replacement building similar to or smaller than the existing building in terms of floorspace and traffic and employment generation;
e) the proposal does not involve encroachment onto land not already in established or permitted commercial use; and
f) the proposal does not conflict with the environmental and transport policies in this plan'
(Cherwell District Council (1989) Central Oxfordshire Local Plan (Cherwell), Deposit Plan, policy GB 13).

Recreation and Sport

D.8 '... Non-intensive outdoor recreation and allotment uses will normally be permitted in the Green Belt where the site proposed:
   a) is enclosed by boundaries which will prevent or substantially deter trespass onto neighbouring farmland, commercial woodland, sites of ecological importance or residential areas;
   b) does not involve the loss of any significant tree cover and is accompanied by an acceptable landscaping scheme;
   c) retains the predominantly open nature of the land and does not involve the construction of large or conspicuous buildings or unscreened car parking areas;
   d) will not damage the amenities of neighbouring residential properties'
(East Dorset District Council (1991) Verwood Local Plan, Deposit Version, para 6.53).

Garden Centres

D.9 '... within the Green Belt the extension or intensification of use of existing garden centres or the establishment of new garden centres will not normally be permitted'
(East Dorset District Council (1991) Verwood Local Plan, Deposit Version, paragraph 6.49).

'... Each proposal for a garden centre will be assessed according to a) the location of the site, b) size of the site, c) nature of the use, d) amount of building, e) traffic generation, f) adequacy of the access, and g) quality of the landscaping ... In the open countryside of the Green Belt ... a garden centre will not be permitted except as a re-use of redundant buildings'
(Dacorum District Council (1992) Dacorum Borough Local Plan Deposit Version, policy 43).

'... on existing nurseries in the Green Belt there will be a strong presumption against granting planning permission for any development which is not genuinely and directly related to the horticultural activity on that site'
(Broxbourne District Council (1984) Broxbourne District Plan, policy RE4).

Equestrian Activities

D.10 '... small scale facilities (including paddocking) will be permitted if well located in relation to the local bridleway network and carefully integrated into the rural landscape. Existing rural buildings should be used if possible. Any new buildings should be compatible in scale and design with the rural environment and ancillary to the equestrian use. Opportunities to extend or add links to the bridleway network and improve riders' safety will be taken'.

The reasoned justification states '... large scale facilities, such as a racecourse or major show jumping arena, would not fit in with the countryside and Green

189

Belt in Dacorum'.
(Dacorum District Council (1992) Dacorum Borough Local Plan - Deposit Version, policy 76).

'... Planning permission for the development of indoor arenas associated with equestrian activities will be allowed only where the following criteria are met:
a) the proposed development can be shown to be required for participants in an outdoor equestrian activity on the site;
b) seating for spectators and other ancillary facilities are limited to those which are reasonable and sufficient for participants in the outdoor equestrian activities;
c) the proposed development does not create a visual intrusion in a rural landscape or lead towards the physical or visual coalescence of settlements; and
d) detailed planning and highway considerations can be satisfactorily resolved'.
(Leeds City Council (1990) op. cit, para 5.17).

Farm Shops

D.11   '... Farm shops will normally be regarded as an incidental use provided that any goods offered for sale have been produced entirely on the farm concerned and the scale of retailing activity does not exceed that normally associated with local shopping (eg about 10-25 sq m)'.
(Leeds City Council (1985) Pudsey Local Plan, policy GB7).

Garden Extensions

D.12   '... There will be a general presumption against garden extensions into the Green Belt except where such extensions:
a) form a logical infilling or rounding off to the individual settlement;
b) would not affect the rural character of the area; and
c) would not involve a significant loss of agricultural land.
In those cases where permission is granted, a condition restricting permitted development rights will be applied'.
(Leeds City Council (1985) Pudsey Local Plan, policy GB 11).

Fragmentation of Farmland

D.13   '...The Borough Council will seek to make Directions under Article 4 of the Town and Country Planning General Development Order 1977-81, withdrawing certain rights of 'permitted development' where this is considered necessary to prevent detrimental change in the character and appearance of the Green Belt'.
(Broxbourne Borough Council (1984) Broxbourne District Plan, policy RE 6).

Hotels and Motels

D.14 '... Within the Green Belt, proposals relating to freestanding new build hotel/motel accommodation will be refused. However, the Borough Council would be prepared to consider small scale proposals for guest accommodation at existing public houses within the Green Belt where it can be demonstrated, to the satisfaction of the Council, that

a) the site has adequate access;

b) the local highway network can accommodate the traffic generated;

c) the proposal provides adequate off street parking;

d) the scheme does not have a detrimental effect on the surrounding area; and

e) the proposal remains in scale with the existing premises.

(Broxbourne Borough Council (1992) <u>Broxbourne Borough Local Plan</u>, Deposit Version, policy LR 14).

Enhancing the Environment

D.15 '... Within the Green Belt where development proposals are acceptable in principle ... the local planning authority will seek comprehensive landscaping improvements, a direct contribution to the achievement of open land objectives and enhanced visual amenity'.

(Hillingdon Borough Council (1990) <u>Central Hillingdon Local Plan</u>, Uxbridge, HBC, policy GB 3)

'... such development as is permitted in the Green Belt should take account, in its scale, nature and location, of the need to conserve the environment and wherever possible enhance it'.

(Barnsley Borough Council (1986) <u>Dodworth Local Plan</u>, policy E 6).

Park and Ride

D.16 '... Within the Green Belt, proposals for Park and Ride sites will not normally be permitted. Where no appropriate site can be provided outside the Green Belt proposals may be acceptable provided that the site

a) is well related to the York Ring Road;

b) does not detract from the open character of the Green Belt;

c) does not prejudice the Green Belt function of those open spaces which extend from the open countryside into urban areas;

d) minimises the visual impact on the Green Belt; and

e) does not create additional development pressure on adjacent land within the Green Belt'.

(North Yorkshire County Council (1991); <u>York Green Belt Local Plan</u>, Deposit Draft, Policy 7).

'... where exhaustive study shows that no viable alternative sites exist, the development of park and ride car parks at appropriate locations in the Green

Belt ... will normally be acceptable, subject to a high standard of design and subsequent landscaping'.
(Cambridge City Council (1992); <u>Cambridge Local Plan</u>, Deposit Draft, policy NE 5).

'... notwithstanding its location in the Green Belt the City Council would support, with appropriate landscaping, the establishment of a parkway station and car parks in addition to Oxford's main station, at the former South Hinksey Sidings'.
(Oxford City Council (1992); <u>Oxford Local Plan Review: 1991-2001</u>, policy TR 29).

Utilities

D.17 '... Development by public utilities, and public works which require planning permission will only be allowed in the Green Belt if it can be shown that there is no acceptable alternative location which would be less harmful to the environment'.
(South Staffordshrie District Council (1980) <u>District Plan Number One - North Eastern Area</u>, Written Statement, policy 6.5.5).

Table D.1: Green Belt Policies in Local Plans: Case Study Areas

		Leeds	Macc'fld	Cherwell	Brox'b	Purbeck	Wake-field	Dacorum (1989)	Dacorum (1992)	Chester	Enfield	East Dorset	South Staffs
extensions, alterations	1	x	x	x	x	x	x	x	x	x		x	x
replacement, rebuilding dwellings	2	x	x	x		x		x	x	x		x	x
extensions to residential curtilages	3	x			x								
agricultural workers	4	x	x		x	x	x		x		x	x	x
redundant buildings (r)	5	x	x	x		x			x	x		x	x
redundant buildings (other uses)	6		x	x					x			x	x
redundant hospital sites	7	x	x										
agricultural buildings	8	x		x			x			x			x
horse, equestrian	9	x	x		x			x	x		x		
institutions in extensive grounds	10	x	(2) x		x	x		x	x		x		x
recreation/leisure	11	x		x	x	x		x	x		x	x	x
tourist/caravan	12	x	x	x				x	x	x	x		x
hotel/motel	13				x				x				
industrial/commercial	14	x	x	x		x	x		x	x			x
low cost housing/local needs	15					x			x				x
glasshouses	16				x						x		

		1	2	3	4	5	6	7	8	9	10	11	12
fragmentation of farmland	17				x								
nursery gardens	18				x								
garden centres	19					x			x		x	x	
allotments	20	x											
waste transfer	21	x											
farm shops	22	x	x										
gypsy sites	23		x	x									
travelling show	24												
airport op. needs	25			x									
community facilities	26			x									
nursing homes	27			x									x
residential caravans	28			x			x						
TOTAL		15	13	13	10	8	4	7	13	6	7	7	12

Sources

Leeds City Council (1990) The Control of Development in the Green Belt.
Macclesfield Borough Council (1992) Local Plan: Draft Written Statement.
Cherwell District Council (1991) Central Oxfordshire Local Plan, Deposit Version.
Broxbourne Borough Council (1983) Broxbourne Local Plan, Approved.
Purbeck District Council (1991) NE Purbeck Local Plan, Deposit Version.
Wakefield District Council (1991) Wakefield Draft UDP.
Dacorum District Council (1984) Dacorum District Plan, Approved.

Dacorum District Council (1992) Borough Plan, Deposit Version.
Chester City Council (1983) Chester Rural Areas Local Plan, Approved
London Borough of Enfield (1991) Unitary Development Plan, Deposit Draft.
East Dorset District Council (1992) Verwood Local Plan, Deposit Version
South Staffordshire District Council (1991) Draft Local Plan.

Table D.2: Green Belt Policies Proposed in Local Plans: Other Areas

		York	Trafford	Thurrock	Stoke on Trent	Sefton	N'castle	Chelt'm	Gateshead	Fylde	Elmbridge	Dudley	Broxtowe	Erewash
extensions, alterations	1		x	x	x	x	x	x		x	x			
replacement, rebuilding dwellings	2		x	x	x	x		x			x	x		x
extensions to residential curtilages	3			x										
agricultural workers	4			x	x	x	x	x		x	x		x	
redundant buildings (a)	5	x	x			x	x	x	x	x	x		x	
redundant buildings (other uses)	6	x	x	x		x	x	x	x	x	x		x	
redundant hospital sites	7	x								x				
agricultural buildings	8			x			x	x						x
horse, equestrian	9		x	x					x	x	x(3)	x		
institutions in extensive grounds	10	x						x			x(3)			
recreation/leisure	11		x	x	x			x		x	x		x	x
tourist/caravan	12					x		x						
hotel/motel	13							x			x			
industrial/commercial	14		x				x	x	x	x				x
low cost housing/local needs	15					x								

195

Land use	No.														
glasshouses	16	x	x		x										
fragmentation of farmland	17				x(3)										
nursery gardens	18							x							
garden centres	19	x			x			x							
allotments	20														
waste transfer	21														
farm shops	22														
gypsy sites	23				x										
travelling show	24														
airport op. needs	25														
community facilities	26														
nursing homes	27														
residential caravans	28										x	x			
TOTAL		6	5	2	19	8	4	13	6	4	8	9	4	7	4

North Yorkshire County Council (1991) York Green Belt Local Plan, Draft. Trafford Borough Council (1992) Trafford UDP - Consultation Draft. Thurrock Borough Council (1992) Thurrock Borough Local Plan, Draft. City of Stoke on Trent (1991) Local Plan, Deposit Draft. Sefton Borough Council (1991) Sefton Unitary Development Plan, Deposit Draft. Newcastle On Tyne City Council (1991) Draft Unitary Development Plan.

Gateshead Borough Council (1992) Gateshead Unitary Development Plan. Fylde Borough Council (1992) Borough Local Plan, Deposit Draft. Elmbridge Borough Council (1991) Elmbridge Borough Council Local Plan, Draft for Deposit. Dudley Borough Council (1991) Unitary Development Plan, Final Proposals. Broxtowe Borough Council (1992) Broxtowe Local Plan, Consultation Draft. Erewash Borough Council (1992) Erewash Borough Local Plan, Written Statement.

Appendix E: Green Belt Development Control - Previous Work

Introduction

E.1   The range of detailed material on the implementation of development control in Green Belts is quite small. The material referred to here uses a cut-off point of 1982. Included are data from a South East Regional Planning Conference monitoring study relating to the London Green Belt, and monitoring data for the West Midlands Green Belt. In the second case extra analysis was provided by the West Midlands Joint Data Team for the project. More detailed work on High Wycombe, carried out by the School of Planning, Oxford Polytechnic, and for Stratford on Avon District in Warwickshire, is also included.

London Green Belt

E.2   The South East Standing Conference has recently published data on planning permissions for the 12 months to March 1991. These are presented at County level, and for most London Boroughs with Green Belt in their areas. Individual authorities have divided permissions into 'acceptable' and 'unacceptable' categories. The Standing Conference warn that not all of the definitions may be consistent between areas. The data given on Table E.1 should therefore be regarded as indicative only.

Some 1,400 hectares of the approvals falling in the acceptable category are golf courses. The 'unacceptable' category includes some housing on redundant hospital sites, which must be regarded as acceptable providing the tests in policy guidance are met.   Apart from a large B1 business approval in Hounslow the areas involved are very small. SERPLAN suggest the area approved for unacceptable uses is less than 0.05 per cent of the London Green Belt. It should be noted that most of this land may already be in non-agricultural use.

West Midlands Green Belt

E.3   The approved Regional Guidance for the West Midlands requires the monitoring of '... the success of Green Belt in restricting the outward growth of the built-up areas and redirecting development to inner city areas'. Monitoring data for the period April 1988 to March 1991 have been published relating to the first of these. The material is for strategic monitoring, and covers developments proposed in the Green Belt which are significant new development, or are changes of use:

- including five or more dwellings (residential);
- 500 sq metres floorspace or more (non-residential); or
- significant leisure developments.

The Green Belt areas are those defined in adopted local plans, defined in Structure Plans, or approved in a Regional map approved by the Department in 1975. Land which it is proposed to delete from the Green Belt is not included.

Table E.1: Development Approvals in the London Green Belt

authority	'unacceptable'* (ha)	'acceptable'** (ha)	area of green (ha) belt
Bedfordshire	3.81	4.22	26,900
Berkshire [1]	0.37	25.10 [2]	23,400
Buckinghamshire [3]	0.10	77.01 [4]	47,700
Essex [5]	72.38 [6]	578.56 [7]	73,500
Hampshire			
Hertfordshire [8]	105.28 [9]	336.27 [10]	82,600
Kent	62.11	21.09	73,100
Oxfordshire [1]	4.87	0.00	34,900
Surrey	4.80	300.40 [11]	118,500
ROSE total	253.72	1,342.65	480,600 [12]
Barnet	0.05	4.84	
Bexley [8]	-	-	
Bromley [8]	-	-	
Croydon	0.00	0.16	
Enfield	2.40 [13]	23.00 [14]	
Harrow	0.19	3.24	
Havering	3.52 [15]	63.98 [16]	
Hillingdon	1.24	0.04	
Hounslow	52.77 [17]	4.70	
Kingston [8]	0.00	0.27	
Redbridge	0.00	0.00	
Richmond	0.00	0.00	
Sutton	0.00	0.00	
Waltham Forest	0.00	0.00	
London total	60.17	100.23	39,000
SOUTH EAST	313.89	1,442.88	576,700

*   Requiring to be justified by very special circumstances in terms of PPG 2
**   Falling within the categories of appropriate development in PPG 2.

1 For the period April 1990 to March 1991
2 Includes one golf course
3 Wycombe, Chiltern and South Bucks
4 Includes two golf courses
5 For the period April 1989 to March 1990
6 Includes 20 hectares housing on redundant
  hospital site & 22 hectares stables and leisure centre
7 Includes 556 hectares golf courses
8 No comparable data available

9 Includes 48 hectares of residential
10 Includes 319 hectares of golf courses
11 Includes 296 hectares golf courses
12 Excluding Hampshire
13 Plus 932 sq metres
14 Plus 712 sq metres
15 Plus 2114 sq metres
   of commercial development
16 Golf courses
17 Includes 27.9 hectares B1 use

Source: SERPLAN (1991)

E.4   Table E.2 shows a large number of applications for housing over the three year period. Geographically the main pressure areas are to the south and south east of the conurbation, in Warwickshire, Hereford and Worcester and Solihull. Other areas with clusters of applications include the M5 in Bromsgrove District, the M54 area north of Wolverhampton, the southern part of Lichfield District and the Warwick District area. The Solihull/M42 clusters relate to possible sites for new industrial development, as do clusters along the M5 and M54. In parts of Hereford and Worcester Green Belt boundaries have yet to be confirmed, and in Solihull Regional Guidance suggests housing will have to go on land presently in the Green Belt (Table E.3). There has been a large growth in leisure related applications, mainly golf courses, and these are also reflected in Table E.2.

Table E.2: Applications for Development in the West Midlands Green Belt

	housing	manuf. & ware-house	busns & office	retail	leis-ure	other	total
1988-89	45	4	5	3	na	15	72
1989-90	75	16	8	4	7	23	133
1990-91	42	16	9	4	28	18	117
1991-92	63	12	19	6	44	33	175
total	225	48	41	17	79	89	397

Table E.3: Distribution of Major Applications in the West Midlands Green Belt *

area	1988-90		1990-91		per cent
	housing	manuf. & ware-house	housing	manuf. & ware-house	
Hereford & Worcester	20	7	25	7	21.8
Warwick	24	11	32	11	28.8
Staffordshire	11	8	12	4	12.9
Solihull	20	16	10	11	21.0
Rest of Metro	19	13	5	5	15.5
Salop	0	0	1	1	-

* Interpreted from maps in Annual Monitors

E.5   The data on decisions in Table E.4 suggest that applications for residential schemes of five dwellings or more (including conversions) have remained at a similar level over the four year period. Approvals exceeded refusals for the first time in 1991-2. Data for leisure applications have only been collected for the last two years, but already show a significant growth in approvals, to 29 for 1991-92. The proportion of approvals is highest for manufacturing/warehousing (70.8 per cent) and business/offices (68.3 per cent) although the absolute numbers involved are very small.

E.6   At this level of aggregation it is difficult to assess how far, if at all, the approvals relate to sites which were formally greenfield land. The results of investigation of the schedules for Staffordshire are shown at Table E.5. The majority of approvals are for leisure, including two golf course developments (226 hectares), a rural amenity centre (country park), and a golf driving range (nine hectares). The housing approvals were all small, and related to the conversion of existing buildings except for one case where low cost housing was provided. It is expected that this pattern would be reflected elsewhere.

Table E.4. Decisions in the West Midlands Green Belt

use	1988-89		1989-90		1990-91		1991-92		per cent approved
	a	r	a	r	a	r	a	r	
housing	3	42	30	45	17	25	34	29	37.3
business/ office	4	1	7	1	5	4	12	7	68.3
manuf/ w'housing	1	3	11	5	14	2	8	4	70.8
retail	-	3	1	3	2	2	4	2	41.2
other mixed	4	11	8	15	6	12	18	15	40.5
leisure	nc	nc	7	-	13	15	29	13	63.6
total	72		133		117		175		

1.   a = approvals; r = refusals; nc = not collected

2.   Relates to applications made in Green Belt defined in adopted local plans, or Green Belt defined in structure plans and/or the 1975 Regional Map.

Table E.5: Major Applications Approved in the Staffordshire Green Belt: 1991-92

Residential

1. Pattingham	16 dwellings (0.65 ha)	housing trust for low cost housing
2. Shenstone	5 dwellings (0.1 ha)	conversion
3. Weeford	12 dwellings (0.8 ha)	conversion
4. Shenstone	5 dwellings (0.1 ha)	barn conversion (granted on appeal)

Industrial/Business

5. Wall	929 sq m	change of use of country house with historic/architectural interest to offices

Leisure

6. Codsall	101 ha	golfing complex
7. Hednesford	0.7 ha	restaurant, hotel and banqueting suite
8. Weeford	2.0 hectares	hotel-related; change of use from farm buildings
9. Lichfield	not stated	leisure; rural amenity centre
10. Lichfield	125 hectares	leisure; 2 x 18 holes golf; details following previous approval
11. Lichfield	9.1 ha	golf driving range
12. Lichfield	1.0 ha	ski slope; stationing of caravans

Source: Monitoring Schedules covering period April 1991 - April 1992

E.7   The High Wycombe material is an analysis of individual records relating to planning applications for new dwellings and for conversions of at least one unit. Thus extensions and other additions to existing dwellings were excluded, but conversions to at least one new unit were included. The period covered was 1974-81.

Table E.6: Applications by Planning Notation - 1974-81: High Wycombe

notation	number of applications	number of dwellings	average size *
green belt	86	371	4.3
white land	201	3181	15.8
residential	403	1684	4.2
other	34	250	7.4

* number of dwelling units

Source: Wood, M. (1982)

E.8   Table E.6 shows the strong pressure on white land around High Wycombe during the period. The average size of applications for one unit or more was 4.3 units in the approved Green Belt, but 15.8 in the white land area. An analysis of residential 'case histories' in the Green Belt showed around one half of the 371 dwellings proposed were in applications of 11-30 units. A number of applications were speculative, but some were purely for valuation purposes.

E.9   Table E.7 suggests an overall approval rate of 32.6 per cent for applications in the Green Belt. However, these only represented 14 per cent of new dwellings applied for, an absolute number of 52 over a seven year period. The majority of approvals were therefore for single dwellings, represented by infill in rural (washed over) settlements, and agricultural workers dwellings. The very large level of approvals in white land was for public sector schemes promoted by the local Councils.

Table E.7: Decisions by Planning Notation: 1974-81 - High Wycombe

notation		approvals		refusals	
		no	per cent	no	per cent
green belt	a	28	32.6	58	67.4
	d	52	14.0	319	86.0
white land	a	99	49.3	102	50.7
	d	2254	70.9	927	30.1
residential	a	240	59.6	163	40.4
	d	1019	60.5	665	39.5
other	a	22	64.7	12	35.3
	d	194	77.6	56	22.4
all	a	389	53.7	335	56.3

a = applications
d = dwellings

Source: Wood, M (1982)

E.10   Table E.8 suggests that all of the appeals for one or more dwellings in the Green Belt were dismissed during the period.

Table E.8: Appeals 1974-81 - High Wycombe

notation		allowed	dismissed	pending
green belt	a	0	9	0
	d	0	28	
white land	a	4	16	1
	d	60	94	
residential/	a	10	17	6
other	d	29	42	

a = applications
d = dwellings

Source: Wood, M (1982)

E.11   The High Wycombe study contains data on the take up of planning permissions in areas covered by Green Belt. This suggests, by the end of the survey period, only half of the dwellings approved in the Green Belt had been constructed, and a small number of approvals had lapsed.

Stratford-On-Avon

E.12 The analysis of applications for new housing covers a period of 29 months from April 1986 to September 1988, and includes approvals by the local authority, and the Inspectorate at appeal, over the period. Inside the Green Belt 22 per cent of dwellings applied for were approved, a rate of just over 50 dwelling units per year (the District house building rate over the period was 750 a year). Applications for over 500 dwellings in the Green Belt were refused during the period. There is a contrast between Green Belt and other countryside areas, with refusals only comprising 59 per cent of the total. Thus approval was given for 676 dwellings in the countryside area beyond the Green Belt during the period.

Table E.9: Planning Decisions on New Dwellings Proposed in the Green Belt: Stratford-on-Avon District 1986-88

	green belt		open countryside	
dwellings	no	per cent	no	per cent
approved	145	22.0	676	40.9
refused	513	78.0	975	59.1

Source: Stratford-on-Avon District Council (1989) Chart 11, p 7.

References

1. West Midlands Planning and Transportation Sub-Committee (1989-91) Planning Trends in the West Midlands County, 1989-91 Annual Monitors, WMPTSC, Solihull.

2. SERPLAN (1991) A Regional Profile of the South East: 1991, London, SERPLAN.

3. Wood, M. (1982) High Wycombe: The Implementation of Strategic Planning Policy in a Restraint Area in the South East, Working Paper 67, School of Planning, Oxford Polytechnic.

4. Stratford-on-Avon District Council (1989) Planning in Action, Planning Policies and Proposals: Progress and Effectiveness, Stratford, SDC.

Appendix F: Development Control Case Studies

Introduction

F.1   This has involved the conduct of detailed case studies in parts of four County areas. Our aim has been to obtain, from the selected local authorities data on:
- the numbers of applications over the last four years by policy area; eg. 'Green Belt, 'inset village and town', 'open countryside beyond the Green Belt';
- the types of new development, and use changes sought; and
- approval and refusal rates by type of proposal.

Information on the numbers, and outcomes, of appeals lodged in each area have been sought from either the Authorities or the Planning Inspectorate.

F.2   Studies have been carried out in the following areas:
- South Staffordshire;
- City of Chester and Macclesfield Districts;
- Wakefield MDC, South Yorkshire; and
- Dacorum, Broxbourne and East Hertfordshire.

F.3   This Appendix gives an account for each case study area separately, in a consistent format. The case study material for Hertfordshire is more broad-brush than that for the other areas.

South Staffordshire District

Summary

- 1300 applications a year
- 30% of the total in the Green Belt
- 85% of applications in insets towns and villages approved
- 70-75% of applications in Green Belt approved - mainly residential alterations, conversions and extensions
- wide range of agricultural diversification and leisure proposals.

Introduction

F.4   The Green Belt in South Staffordshire covers over 80 per cent of the District. The urban and village settlements are inset, that is excluded from the Green Belt, with boundaries tightly drawn around them. In the north western part of the District there is a small area of open countryside not covered by Green Belt policy. Figure F.1 shows the three basic policy areas, 'Green Belt', 'Inset Settlement' and 'Open Countryside'.

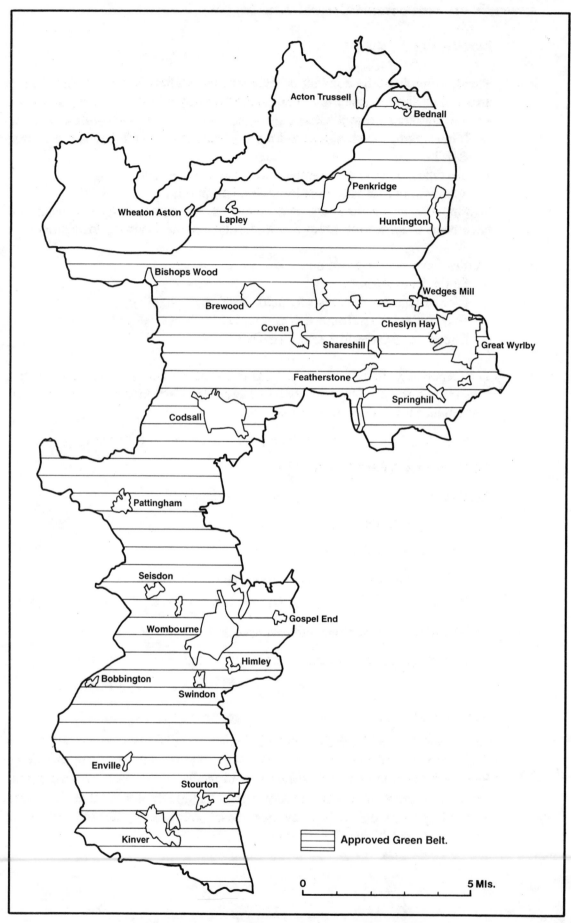

Figure F1 : South Staffordshire District.

F.5   The following sections assess the key findings in terms of:
   • the relative rate of approval in the Green Belt and other policy areas;
   • the mix of land uses applied for in the Green Belt; and
   • the rate of approval by use.

F.6   South Staffordshire has a throughput of 1300-1500 decisions per year, the
        approval rate over the last four years varying from 84 to 88 per cent.

Table F.1: South Staffordshire: Planning Decisions

year	decisions	number approved	per cent approved
1988-89	1501	1321	88.0
1989-90	1521	1278	84.0
1990-91	1307	1150	88.0
1991-92	1302	1099	84.4

Source: DOE Development Control Statistics

F.7   Some 30 per cent of current planning applications in the District are within the
        Green Belt. Only a very small proportion, around three per cent, are in the
        open countryside beyond the Green Belt. The overall rate of approval of
        applications (72-75 per cent) is lower within the Green Belt than for inset
        settlements, on average by 20-25 per cent. The Green Belt approval rate is
        also 10 per cent below the District average.

Table F.2: Applications Made by Policy Area

	per cent			
year	green belt	inset	open countryside	total
1990-91	30.0 (387)	66.7 (861)	3.3 (42)	1290
1991-92	28.1 (377)	68.6 (922)	3.3 (44)	1343

Source: Green Belt Project Survey

Table F.3: Applications Approved by Policy Area

year	green belt	inset	open countryside	total
1990-91	72.4 (280)	92.2 (794)	78.6 (33)	1107
1991-92	75.3 (284)	89.9 (829)	86.4 (38)	1151

Source: Green Belt Project Survey

Land Uses Applied For

F.8   Over two thirds of all Green Belt *applications* are for residential or residentially-related development. They tend, however, to be very small in scale. The largest category of applications are for residential extensions (157 over the two years), followed by permanent dwellings (87), and the proposed conversion of agricultural buildings to dwellings (39). Within the other use categories proposed changes under the heading of agriculture (74 applications over the two years), and leisure (64 applications), were of greater numerical significance than those for industry (44). Table F.4 lists the relevant details.

Table F.4: Land Uses Applied for in the Green Belt

use applied for	1990-91	1991-92
permanent dwelling	44	43
agricultural dwelling	10	9
conversion of agricultural building	20	19
extensions	83	74
internal conversion	14	17
others	45	36
total housing-related	414	
industry	28	16
retail	15	19
leisure	39	25
agriculture	37	37
storage, warehouse	11	7
transport	6	12
others	35	63
total non-housing	350	

Source: Green Belt Project Survey

F.9   The rate of approval of residential, and residentially-related *applications*, is given on Table F.5. This suggests very high levels of approval for relatively numerous small extensions (96 per cent), and an approval rate of around average for the whole Green Belt (77 per cent) for agricultural building conversions. The analysis suggests agricultural conversions are likely to be supplying as many new housing units in the South Staffordshire Green Belt, as permanent dwellings and non-agricultural conversions. Over the two years some 31 applications under the heading 'permanent dwellings' were approved. They included the renewal of a number of existing permissions, and the change of use of listed buildings into residential use. The refusals tended to comprise almost entirely new bungalows in the countryside. The 'conversion of agricultural buildings' category includes applications for the removal of occupancy conditions. Over the two years it is estimated that 20 residential units have been created by conversion, with the other 10 constituting the removal of occupancy conditions. Policy on new agricultural dwellings appears to have been firmly applied, with only around 20 per cent of applications being approved.

Table F.5: Decisions in the Green Belt: Residential and Residentially-Related

	year				
land use	1990-91		1991-92		% *
	a	r	a	r	
permanent dwellings	11	33	18	23	35.6
agricultural dwellings	1	9	3	6	21.1
conversion of agricultural building	17	3	15	6	76.9
extensions	78	5	73	1	96.2
internal conversions	11	3	16	1	87.1
others	29	16	16	20	55.5

a = number approved
r = number refused
* = per cent approval over the two year period

Source: Green Belt Project Survey

F.10   The rate of approvals for non-residential uses varied from retail (59 per cent) to agriculture and forestry related (89 per cent); see Table F.6. The following comments are appropriate for individual uses:

Industry: (36 approvals, 8 refusals) There were very few refusals here. Some of those particularly noted were for vehicle salvage adjacent to a conservation area, a fuel depot, and the re-use of a redundant agricultural building for plant hire and storage.

Retail: (20 approvals, 14 refusals) Examples of changes of use approved here were from residential to restaurant use, and from nursery gardens to garden centres. One of the garden centres was 2.2 hectares in extent, and was accompanied by a Section 106 Agreement.

Leisure: (51 approvals, 13 refusals) This is an important category with some 51 approvals given over the two years. Table 7 lists a number of the recent approvals in the six months to March 1992. They include significant golf and golf-related activities, a site for model aircraft flying and a picnic area.

Table F.6: Leisure Approvals in the Green Belt

model aircraft flying
riding arena
land for paintball games
golf driving range
pitch and putt course
golf course and driving range
canal-related picnic site
floodlights for sports pitches

Source: Green Belt Project Survey

Agriculture: (66 approvals, 8 refusals) These include permissions of two basic types: those for such facilities as barns, slurry lagoons and grain stores falling within the definition of agricultural development in the GDO; and those for stables, equestrian and livery buildings and activities. Between one third and one half of approvals in this category were for horse-related activity.

Warehousing and Storage: (11 approvals, 7 refusals) A number of these applications were refused, including proposals for the storage of various unspecified waste and chemicals.

Table F.7: Decisions in the Green Belt: Non-Residential Uses

	1990-91		1991-92		% *
	a	r	a	r	
industrial	24	4	12	4	81.8
shops, retail	11	4	9	10	58.8
leisure	29	10	22	3	76.6
agriculture	32	5	34	3	89.2
storage, warehouse	6	5	5	2	61.1
transport	5	1	9	3	77.7
others	23	9	52	13	77.3

a = number approved
r = number refused
* = per cent approved over the two year period

Source: Green Belt Project Survey

Transport: Some 14 approvals fell into this category over the two year period. These included such uses as new accesses to farms, some hardstandings, and extensions to public house car parks. A scheme for a large (1.1 ha) secure lorry park was refused.

Others: Approvals here include a number of cemeteries (15.7 hectares in 3 cemeteries in the last 6 months), plant for sewage treatment, overhead power lines, satellite dishes on listed buildings, and a flagpole outside a listed building.

Appeals

F.11   Overall some 19 per cent of appeals were upheld, a figure well below the national average. The number of appeals over the four year period has remained rather similar despite the reduction, in the District, of the number of applications made. In the urban areas, by contrast the rate of appeals upheld is 32 per cent. A higher proportion of appeals were upheld in the most recent year (Tables F.8 and F.9).

Table F.8: Appeals Determined in the Green Belt in South Staffordshire

	1988-89	1989-90	1990-91	1991-92	total
upheld	8	6	8	13	35
dismissed	33	28	40	23	124
withdrawn	8	2	5	6	21
not determined	0	0	1	4	5
total	49	36	54	46	185

Table F.9: Appeals Determined in the Green Belt and Urban Areas 1988-92: Per Cent

	green belt	urban areas
	per cent	
upheld	18.9	31.8
dismissed	67.0	54.1
withdrawn	11.4	11.8
not determined	2.7	2.3
total	100.0 (n=185)	100.0 (n=85)

F.12 In order to complete the picture a full listing is given of all approvals for the year to April 1992. These are the decisions listed on the right hand columns of Table F.5 and F.6. What will be seen from the description which follows, is how small-scale the development being dealt with is.

F.13 The applications approved in the Green Belt in South Staffordshire during 1991-2 were:

New Housing

There were 18 approvals for the building of 105 new houses of which three were for 45, 16, and 17 units each. Two of these sites (45 and 17 units) are departures to conform to Structure Plan housing requirements. The smaller sized development involves the redevelopment of buildings and land previously used for a commercial activity, a religious building; and a gymnasium: a small number are infill development and back garden development in existing 'washed over' settlements. There was one approval for the rebuilding of a house and three approvals for the conversion of listed buildings to form six flats.

Conversion of Agricultural Buildings

There were 15 approvals for the conversion of barns and other farm buildings to houses, creating 28 new units, and one approval for conversion to an office unit. There were three approvals for agricultural workers' dwellings, whilst there were another three approvals for the *removal* of agricultural workers' occupancy conditions.

Residential Extensions

There were 42 approvals for residential extensions and a further 25 approvals for satellite dishes, garden extensions and fencing.

Caravans, Mobile Homes, New Sites

There were four approvals for permanent mobile homes (bound by occupancy conditions) and two for temporary use (time limited to two years). There were two approvals for gypsy sites.

Hotels

There were two approvals for extensions to hotels, one involving 56 additional bedrooms.

Industry

There were nine approvals relating to a variety of industrial uses. These included a car wash, workshops relating to an existing use, and a recycling plant; conversion of a barn to a small industrial unit; a screening plant for minerals; renewal of an existing use certificate for a motor vehicle salvage operation, and a new security fence.

Retail

There were seven approvals in this category involving farm shops, a garden centre, extensions to a private house, a restaurant and a bakery shop.

Leisure

There were 21 approvals for leisure use, with eight involving new golf-related provision covering over 166 hectares of land. Others relate to a sailing club house, a riding area, changing rooms, a model aircraft flying area and floodlighting, and the conversion of a derelict site to a new picnic area.

Minerals

There were two approvals, involving extraction of coal and a new coal conveyor underpass.

Storage

There were four approvals involving the expansion of existing uses for a bottlestore, rescue boat store, nursery and agricultural stores.

Transport

There were 14 approvals for transport-related uses, mainly for new accesses to housing, or nurseries and car parks to public houses.

Educational and Community Buildings

There were 12 approvals in this land use category, with four approvals for cemeteries involving over 30 hectares of land. Other approvals were for school extensions, new living areas for an agricultural college, and new club rooms for a caravan park.

Agriculture

There were 34 approvals for agriculturally-related uses involving new buildings for agriculture, horticulture, riding and stable blocks, grain stores and tractor sheds.

Advertisements

There were 16 approvals for illuminated or non-illuminated signs.

Miscellaneous

There were 18 approvals in this category with nine for septic tanks and other related sewerage and water treatment works, five for overhead power lines; new camera towers for a security area, a flag pole and some telecommunication masts.

City of Chester Council Survey

Summary

- 1550 applications a year

- 15% of the total were within the Green Belt

- 84% were approved in open countryside, and 89% in urban areas

- 82% of applications in the Green Belt were approved - mainly for residential extensions and conversions

- the approval rate for non-residential uses was 5-10% lower in Green Belt than in open countryside

Introduction

F.14 Chester District (population 118,000) area is made up of three policy areas. The first is the City (80,000 population); the second the Chester Green Belt (32 per cent of the District area) separating Chester from Ellesmere Port in the north, and extending five miles south of the City. Third, south of this the larger part of the District, 60 per cent by area, is open countryside. This is covered by a mixture of conservation and rural development policies. Apart from Chester there are no large towns in the District, as Figure F.2 shows.

F.15 The following sections assess the key findings of the development control study covering the period 1988-92 (four years) in terms of:

- the rate of approval of applications in the Green Belt and other policy areas;
- the mix of land uses applied for in the Green Belt; and
- the rate of approval by use.

F.16 Chester City Council has a throughput, on average, of some 1550 applications a year. Table F.10 shows a decline of one third in the number of applications made over the last four years. The approval rate, however, has remained relatively stable at around the 85 per cent level.

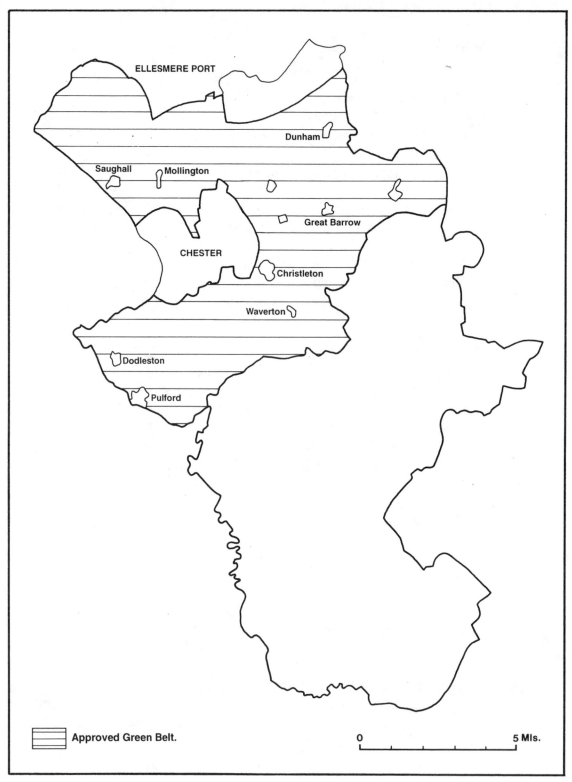

ELLESMERE PORT

Dunham

Saughall

Mollington

Great Barrow

CHESTER

Christleton

Waverton

Dodleston

Pulford

Approved Green Belt.

0   5 Mls.

Figure F2 : City of Chester District.

Table F.10: Planning Decisions

year	decisions	number approved	per cent approved
1988-89	1992	nk	nk
1989-90	1738	nk	82.0
1990-91	1359	nk	86.0
1991-92	1403	nk	87.0

Source: DOE Development Control Statistics

F.17 Some 15 per cent of applications made in the District over the last four years are within the Green Belt. Table F.11 shows a surprisingly large proportion, 42 per cent, are also within the open countryside beyond the Green Belt. The proportions of applications in the various categories have, however, remained fairly constant over the four year period.

Table F.11: Applications by Policy Area

year	green belt	open countryside	urban	total
1988-90	13.6 (482)	42.6 (1505)	43.8 (1546)	3533
1990-92	15.9 (432)	41.4 (1127)	42.7 (1160)	2719
total	14.6	42.1	43.3	

Source: Green Belt Project Survey

F.18 The approval rates by policy area do not differ markedly. The main contrast is between Green Belt (82.5 per cent), and urban areas and insets (89.1 per cent). Table F.12 shows that the rate of approval in open countryside beyond the Green Belt is very close to that for the Green Belt itself.

Table F.12: Applications Approved by Policy Area

year	green belt	open countryside	urban	total
1988-90	80.7 (389)	82.3 (1238)	88.2 (1275)	2902
1990-92	84.3 (364)	85.8 (967)	90.1 (1045)	1376
total	82.5	84.0	89.1	

Source: Green Belt Project Survey

Land Uses Applied For

F.19   Over two thirds of all *applications* in the Green Belt are for residential or residentially-related development. These tend to be small in scale with 166 of the total of 324 applications being for extensions, internal conversions or the conversion of agricultural buildings. Applications for one or more permanent dwellings averaged 35 per year over the period 1988-90, and 25 per year over the period 1990-92. Within the other use categories proposals under the heading of agriculture (73 over the four years), retail (33), and storage, warehousing and transport (27), are of greatest significance.

Table F.13: Land Uses Applied for in the Green Belt

use applied for	1988-90	1990-92
permanent dwellings	71	50
conversion of agricultural building, extensions, internal conversion	166	161
agricultural dwellings	24	14
others	63	49
total housing-related	324	274
industry	13	5
retail	18	13
leisure	6	11
agriculture	35	38
storage, warehouse, and transport	17	10
others	71	82
total non-housing	158	158
n =	482	n = 432

Planning Decisions

F.20   The rate of approval of residential applications in the Green Belt is given in Table F.14. This suggests a high level of approval within the category containing residential extensions (84 per cent), and for agricultural dwellings (79 per cent). The rate of approval of applications for new dwellings, at 49 per cent, is somewhat higher than for South Staffordshire (see paragraph F.9).

218

Table F.14: Decisions in the Green Belt: Residential Uses

applications

| | 1988-90 | | 1990-2 | | % * |
	a	r	a	r	
new dwellings	30	41	29	21	48.8
extensions **	144	20	154	33	84.1
agricultural dwellings	19	5	11	3	79.0
others	54	9	45	4	88.4

a = approved
r = refused
*   per cent approved over the four year period
** includes conversions and internal alterations

Source: Green Belt Project Survey

F.21   The rates of approval in the open countryside were 20 per cent higher for new dwelling applications. However, in the case of new agricultural dwellings approval rates were lower. Table F.15 shows the results for the other categories to be broadly the same.

Table F.15: Decisions in the Open Countryside: Residential Uses

Applications

| | 1988-90 | | 1990-2 | | % * |
	a	r	a	r	
new dwellings	225	95	94	65	67.0
extensions **	642	113	495	42	88.0
agricultural dwellings	19	12	10	5	63.0
others	78	16	93	21	82.2

a = approved
r = refused
*   per cent approved over the four year period
** includes conversions and internal alterations

Source: Green Belt Project Survey

F.22   The average number of new housing units per site approved in the Green Belt over the period 1988-90 was 1.9. The figure of 4.0 for the 1990-92 period is distorted by one large approval of 45 units. If two thirds of the dwelling units approved have actually been constructed, this would constitute an average of 30 per year. This would comprise 5 per cent of the total number of houses built in the District (600 per year) in any one year over the time period. An analysis for units approved in the open countryside (Figure F.16) shows little difference in the numbers of units in sites approved and refused.

Table F.16: New Permanent Dwellings in the Green Belt: Size of Applications Approved or Refused

Green Belt		1988-90	1990-92
approved	applications	30	29
	units	56	115
	average size	1.9	4.0*
refused	applications	41	21
	units	112	85
	average size	2.7	4.0

*One application of 45 units

Open Countryside			
approved	applications	225	94
	units	569	539
	average size	2.5	5.7
refused	applications	95	65
	units	188	184
	average size	2.0	2.8

Source: Green Belt Project Survey

F.23   Decisions on non-residential applications in the Green Belt and open countryside may be compared in Tables F.17 and F.18. Generally approval rates in the Green Belt are around 5-10 per cent lower than in open countryside, this being particularly true of retail and industrial applications. In absolute terms low numbers of applications were made in some categories. For example industry saw 18 applications only in the Green Belt, four of which were refused. In the case of leisure uses only two out of 17 applications were refused. In the open countryside the approval rate for leisure applications, mainly small scale in character, was 100 per cent (Table F.18).

Table F.17: Decisions in the Green Belt: Non-Residential Uses

	1988-90		1990-92		% *
	a	r	a	r	
industrial	11	2	3	2	76.4
retail	14	4	9	4	74.2
leisure	6	0	9	2	88.2
agriculture	29	6	34	4	86.3
storage, warehouse					
and transport	12	5	9	1	77.7
others	65	6	70	12	88.2

a = number approved
r = number refused

* per cent approved over the four year period

Source: Green Belt Project Survey

Table F.18: Decisions in the Open Countryside: Non-Residential

	1988-90		1990-92		% *
	a	r	a	r	
industrial	23	5	8	0	86.1
retail	24	2	29	5	88.3
leisure	6	0	17	0	100.0
agriculture	39	7	49	5	88.0
storage, warehouse					
and transport	11	6	33	3	83.0
others	115	34	129	14	75.0

a = number approved
r = number refused

* per cent approved over the four year period

Source: Green Belt Project Survey

Wakefield Metropolitan District Survey

Summary

-   2600 applications a year

-   10-11% of total were in the Green Belt

-   92% of applications in the District outside the Green Belt were approved

-   77% of applications in the Green Belt were approved -mainly for residential extensions and conversions

-   19% of appeals in Green Belt were allowed

    there was an increase in leisure-related applications over the period

Introduction

F.24 The District covers an area of 130 square miles, with a population of 312,000, and has around 40 different towns and villages. Prominent among these in the northern part of the area are Wakefield, Castleford, Pontefract and Knottingley. Parts of the M1 and M62 Motorways cross the District. The Green Belt (23,445 hectares) covers 70.4 per cent of the District, with the remainder being classified here as within 'development boundaries'. Figure F.3 shows these two basic distinctions.

F.25 The following sections assess the key findings, using computer-generated data from the District Council, in terms of:

-   the relative rate of approval in the Green Belt as opposed to within the development boundaries;
-   the mix of land uses applied for in the Green Belt; and
-   the rate of approval by use.

F.26 Wakefield has a throughput of around 2600 applications per year, the approval rate being fairly steady at around 89 per cent. It is notable that the number of applications dealt with has remained similar over the four years, unlike in other areas further south, where numbers have declined.

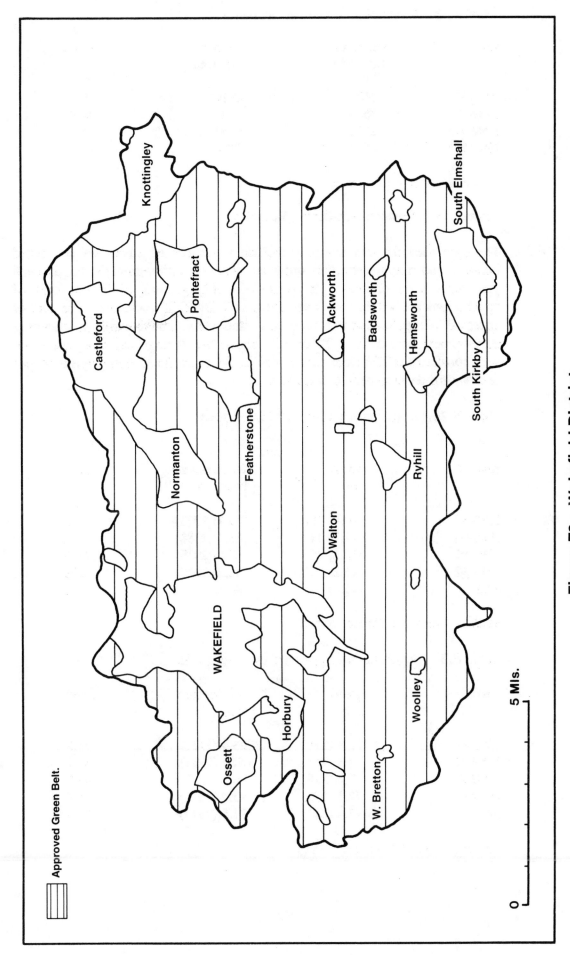

Approved Green Belt.

5 Mls.

0

Figure F3 : Wakefield District.

223

Table F.19 Wakefield: Planning Decisions

year	decisions approved	number approved	per cent
1988-89	2607	2324	89.1
1989-90	2669	2370	88.8
1990-91	2522	2140	84.8
1991-92*	2557	2327	90.0

* estimate based on first three quarters

Source: DOE Development Control Statistics

F.27   The data used for this analysis exclude a number of advertisement, listed building and tree preservation order applications; approximately 100 in each year have been omitted.   In Wakefield only around 10-12 per cent of applications are within the Green Belt, as Table F.20 indicates. The rate of approval of applications is markedly, and consistently, lower than within development boundaries. Table F.21 shows the average approval rate to be very consistent at 75-77 per cent of applications submitted, compared to 90 per cent within development boundaries.

Table F.20: Applications Made by Policy Area

year	per cent green belt	development boundary	total
1988-89	(10.9) 252	(89.1) 2053	2305
1989-90	(11.2) 275	(88.2) 2188	2463
1990-91	(12.2) 281	(87.8) 2015	2303
1991-92	(11.2) 249	(88.2) 1980	2229
total	(11.4)	(88.3)	

Source: Green Belt Project Survey

Table F.21: Applications Approved by Policy Area

year	green belt	development boundary	total
1988-89	75.8 (191)	93.4 (1917)	91.5
1989-90	77.5 (213)	90.5 (1982)	89.2
1990-91	77.6 (218)	88.9 (1797)	87.5
1991-92	77.5 (193)	93.0 (1841)	91.3
total	77.1 (815)	91.5 (7537)	89.9

Source: Green Belt Project Survey

F.28   Just under two thirds of all applications in the Green Belt are related to residential development. Again, a very high proportion of these are small-scale. Table F.22 shows the other use categories applied for. There is a steady throughput of retail applications, most probably relating to garden centres and similar proposals. Applications for agriculture and related uses are also important. The number of applications for leisure uses each year over the four year period.

Table F.22: Land Uses Applied For in the Green Belt

use applied for	1988-90	1990-92	total
housing	351	311	662
manufacturing, offices	23	18	41
warehousing	5	6	11
retail	33	29	62
public services	41	35	76
education	3	9	12
transport	14	9	23
leisure	18	38	56
agriculture	32	37	69
other	43	32	75
total housing-related	351	311	662
total non-housing	174	213	387

Source: Green Belt Project Survey

F.29   The overall rate of approval for applications in Green Belt has altered little over time. The figure for the first two years (76.8 per cent) only increased to 78.2 per cent for the most recent two years. Overall housing applications achieved a slightly lower success rate than the average, as Table F.23 shows. Education and public service were the two most successful categories, followed by leisure at 90 per cent. In the last two years leisure has become the largest non-housing category of approvals, along with public services.

Table F.23: Decisions in the Green Belt

	years					
	1988-90			1990-92		
			%*			%*
	a	r		a	r	
housing	250	99	71.6	231	80	74.3
manufacturing, and offices	21	2	91.3	13	5	72.2
warehousing	2	3	40.0	5	1	83.3
retail	30	3	90.9	24	5	82.8
public service	40	1	97.6	34	1	97.1
education	3	0	100.0	9	0	100.0
transport	12	2	85.7	7	2	77.7
leisure	17	1	94.4	34	4	89.5
agriculture	21	11	65.6	30	7	81.1
others	7	0	100.0	23	9	71.9
total			76.8			78.2

a = approved
r = refused

* per cent approved over the two year period

Source: Green Belt Project Survey

Appeals in the Green Belt

F.30   The Wakefield data give information for appeals dealt with both in the Green
Belt and the remainder of the District each year. Overall, as Table F.24
shows, appeals have averaged 65 a year over the last four years (total 266).
Some 32.3 per cent of these have been in the Green Belt. This suggests
applications refused in Green Belt are three times as likely to go to appeal as
those in the urban areas of the District.

F.31   The proportion of appeals upheld in the Green Belt is half that of the urban
areas, at 18.6 per cent. In total over the four year period studied only four
appeals per year were upheld by Inspectors. Table F.25 suggests there has
been a slight reduction in the number of appeals lodged more recently.
However the proportions allowed and dismissed each year are remarkably
consistent.

Table F.24: Appeals Determined 1988-92

	green belt	%	non green belt	%	total
allowed	16	(18.6)	61	(33.9)	77
dismissed	57	(66.3)	94	(52.3)	151
withdrawn	7	(8.1)	12	(6.6)	19
not determined	6	(7.0)	13	(7.2)	19
total	86	-	180	-	266

Source: Green Belt Project Survey

Table F.25: Appeal Decisions by Year: Green Belt

	1988-89	1989-90	1990-91	1991-92	total
allowed	3	4	6	3	16
dismissed	18	17	12	10	57
withdrawn	2	1	1	3	7
not determined	-	2	1	3	6
total	23	24	20	19	86

Source: Green Belt Project Survey

Macclesfield District Survey

Summary

- 2450 applications a year

- 30% of the total were in the Green Belt

- 82% of applications in inset towns and villages were approved

- 71% of applications in the Green Belt were approved - mainly relating to residential extensions and conversions

- an increase in non-residential applications in the Green Belt

Introduction

F.32   Macclesfield District occupies the north east corner of the County of Cheshire. Important major towns include Macclesfield, Poynton and Wilmslow. The main policy areas within the District shown on Figure F.4 are as follows:

Green Belt	50 per cent of area
Peak District National Park	30 per cent
Urban Areas	10 per cent
Open Countryside	10 per cent

The Green Belt covers the majority of the District outside the National Park. In the southern part of the District the Jodrell Bank Consultation Zone further limits development possibilities outside the urban areas.

F.33   The following sections assess the key findings of the development control study, which covered the four years, April 1988 - March 1992, in terms of:

- the rate of approval of applications in the Green Belt and other policy areas;
- the mix of land uses applied for in the Green Belt; and
- the rate of approval by use.

F.34   Policies in the approved Macclesfield Local Plan (1984), Poynton and Disley (1985), Knutsford (1987) and Wilmslow (1988) Local Plans generally follow PPG 2. Although the County and Districts within Cheshire would prefer more leeway for extensions of pre-existing employment uses in the Green Belt, this has not been approved by the Department. The District contains fifteen 'washed over' villages within the Green Belt. Certain types of infill development are seen as acceptable within 'village core' areas in washed over villages. These are defined by the District Council. These include dwellings for:

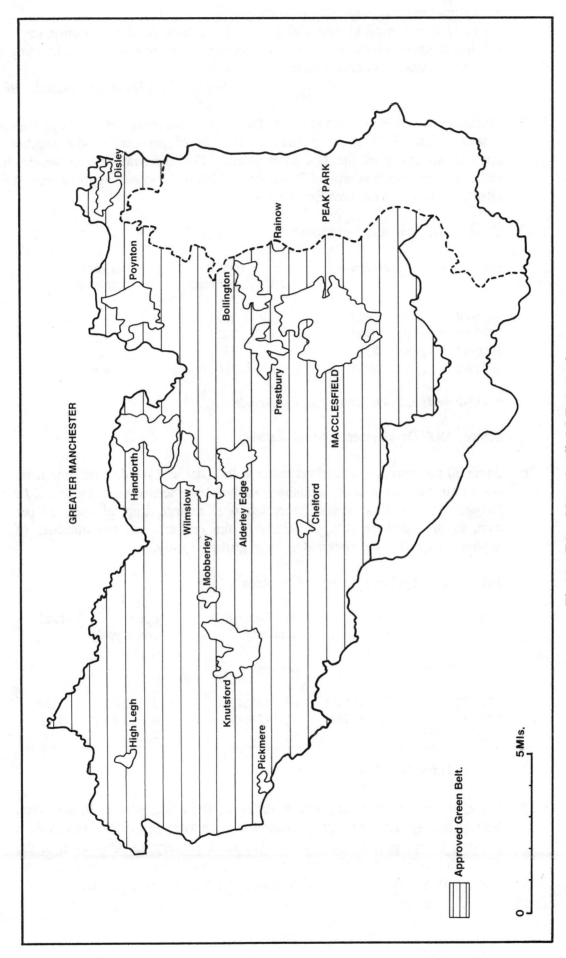

Figure F4 : Macclesfield Borough.

GREATER MANCHESTER

Disley

Poynton

Rainow

PEAK PARK

Bollington

Prestbury

MACCLESFIELD

Handforth

Wilmslow

Mobberley

Alderley Edge

Chelford

High Legh

Knutsford

Pickmere

Approved Green Belt.

5 Mls.

0

229

- agricultural and horticultural workers;
- persons providing an essential service to the local rural community; or
- development which would ensure the long term retention of a building of architectural or historic interest.

(Macclesfield Borough Council, 1984)

F.35 Macclesfield Borough Council has a throughput, on average of 2450 applications a year. Table F.26 shows a decline of over 25 per cent in the number of applications made of the last four years. The approval rate, however, has remained very stable at around 76 per cent. This is the lowest approval rate in the Districts studied in the detailed analysis.

Table F.26: Planning Decisions*

year	decisions	number approved	per cent approved
1988-89	2628	2021	76.9
1989-90	2764	2071	74.9
1990-91	2331	1757	75.4
1991-92	2091	1602	76.6

* withdrawals and non-determinations excluded

Source: DOE Development Control Statistics

F.36 Some 30 per cent of applications made in the District over the last four years are within the Green Belt, including washed over settlements (Table F.27). Between the two time periods there has been a large drop, of some 24 per cent, in the numbers of applications in the urban areas, but numbers of applications within the Green Belt have grown slightly.

Table F.27: Applications by Policy Area

year	green belt	development boundary	open countryside	total
		per cent		
1988-90	27.7 (1440)	68.4 (3561)	3.9 (207)	5208
1990-92	33.3 (1462)	62.0 (2718)	4.7 (206)	4386
total	30.3	65.5	4.2	

Source: Green Belt Project Survey

F.37 The approval rates by policy area do differ, as Table F.28 shows. In the Green Belt the average (70.8 per cent) contrasts with an average approval rate of 81.8 per cent for urban areas and insets. The open countryside area south of the Green Belt falls centrally between the two, with a 75.5 per cent approval rate. The approval rates are remarkably similar for the two time periods.

230

Land Uses Applied For

F.38   Just under two thirds of all applications in the Green belt and washed over villages are for residential or residentially-related development. This tends to be very small in scale, although it is not possible to ascertain detail on new dwelling applications due to the amalgamation of categories in Table F.29. There is a steady throughput of applications of around 20 units a year for dwellings related to agriculture or horticulture. The number of applications relating to agriculture has grown over the last three years, and those relating to industry and offices have remained at similar levels. It is notable, overall, that the number of non-residential applications in the Green Belt has grown by 10 per cent over the two time periods, whereas the number of residentially-related applications has declined by 15 per cent.

Table F.28: Applications Approved by Policy Area: Per Cent

year	green belt	development boundary	open countryside
1988-90	70.6 (1420)	81.6 (2905)	74.9 (155)
1990-92	71.1 (1039)	82.0 (2230)	76.2 (157)
total	70.9	81.8	75.6

Source: Green Belt Project Survey

Table F.29: Land Uses Applied For: Applications

use applied for	1988-89	1989-90	1990-91	1991-92
housing, housing-related*	478	502	424	389
agricultural workers	20	12	24	26
hotel extensions	8	15	10	12
other**	63	57	53	38
total housing-related	569	586	511	465
industrial	22	15	14	22
offices	27	18	18	21
retail	30	57	33	28
leisure	21	18	19	24
transport	28	15	23	27
storage, warehousing	8	14	13	10
community, education	13	16	21	14
agriculture	26	45	63	47
other	31	42	57	42
total non-housing	206	240	261	235

*   includes new permanent dwellings, extensions, internal conversions, and the conversion of agricultural buildings

**   include flats, caravans, communal accommodation, hostels, sheltered accommodation and holiday chalets.

Planning Decisions

F.39   The rate of approval of residential applications in the Green Belt is given in Table F.30.   In comparison to Wakefield the approval rate for house extensions, and new residential use is low. In Macclesfield, the approval rate has grown recently, to 70 per cent, as has the number of applications made. The hotel uses are all extensions.

Table F.30: Decisions in the Green Belt: Residential

| | years | | | | | |
| | 1988-90 | | | 1990-92 | | |
	a	r	%*	a	r	%*
housing, housing related	636	344	64.9	565	248	695
agricultural workers	18	14	56.3	35	15	700
hotel	13	10	56.5	16	6	727
others	81	39	62.3	72	19	791

a = approved
r = refused
* per cent approved over the two year period

Source: Green Belt Project Survey

F.40   Very high proportions of the industrial and agricultural applications were approved over the four years. Retail applications (66 per cent) and storage and warehousing (51 per cent) fared less well, however. Storage uses tend to be particularly intrusive, falling foul of the 'open rural appearance' criterion for Green Belts.   Overall it has become marginally more difficult to obtain permission for non-residential uses in the Green Belt in the last two years, the proportion of applications approved having reduced from 76 per cent to 72.8 per cent (see Table F.31).

Table F.31: Decisions in the Green Belt: Non-Residential

| | years | | | | | |
| | 1988-90 | | | 1990-92 | | |
	a	r	%*	a	r	%
industrial	32	5	86.5	29	7	80.6
offices	33	12	73.3	25	14	64.1
retail	64	33	66.0	40	21	65.6
leisure	33	6	84.6	27	16	62.8
transport	34	9	79.1	35	15	70.0
storage, warehousing	13	9	59.1	10	13	43.5
community, education	26	3	89.7	26	9	74.3
agriculture	61	10	85.9	91	19	82.7
other	50	22	69.4	78	21	78.8
total	346	109	76.0	361	135	72.8

a = approved
r = refused
* per cent approved over the two year period

Source: Green Belt Project Survey

Appeals

F.41 There were a very high level of appeals in Macclesfield, over three times the level of South Staffordshire. A high proportion of the appeals lodged were upheld, the percentages for the Green Belt and the urban areas being little different, as Table F.32 shows. Closer investigation of the numbers upheld suggests that the main categories were:

- house extensions;
- conversions of agricultural buildings for residential use;
- changes of use;
- new dwellings; and
- agricultural workers' dwellings.

These reflect particularly strong local authority policies, particularly in respect of house extensions and farm building conversions.

Table F.32: Appeals Determined 1988-92

	green belt		dev boundary		open countryside	
allowed	95	(34.1)	122	(39.9)	9	(32.1)
dismissed	132	(47.3)	137	(44.8)	15	(53.6)
withdrawn ⁵	44	(15.8)	40	(13.1)	3	(10.7)
not determined	8	(2.9)	7	(2.3)	1	(3.6)
total	279		306		28	

Source: Green Belt Project Survey

Table F.33: Appeals by Land Use Type 1988-92

land use type	upheld	dismissed
new housing	8	31
housing extension	20	32
housing alteration	5	5
replacement dwelling	0	1
housing for agriculture	6	5
conversion of buildings		
agricultural to dwelling	27	24
agricultural to non-residential	0	1
others to dwellings	4	4
agricultural to holiday flats	1	1
nursing home - extension	0	3
hotel - extension	0	4
retail	0	2
garden centre - extensions	0	1
golf - driving range	1	1
golf - club house extension	1	0
other leisure	2	0
office - new	1	1
office - extension	1	0
office - alteration	2	0
transport	0	2
workshop/storage	2	1
change of use	11	6
mobile home and caravans	0	2
agricultural occupancy		
condition - new	1	0
condition - removal	0	1
adverts, signs	4	3
total	95	132

Source: Green Belt Project Survey

The Hertfordshire Case Studies

F.42 This analysis deals with a sub-set of what are termed major applications. The results are not therefore directly comparable with the four previous case studies. A major application for the purposes of these case studies comprises an increase in floorspace of more than 235 sq m, a change in the number of residential units, or a change in the primary land use even if the increase is less than 235 sq m. It will therefore also include a number of small applications in these latter categories by policy area. The data relate to the four years to the end of March 1992.

Dacorum District Survey

Introduction

F.43 Dacorum District has three policy areas; the London Green Belt, the open countryside, and the main urban areas within their defined boundaries. Overall the District processes around 1750 applications per year, with an overall approval rate of 76 to 78 per cent (Table F.34).

Table F.34: Dacorum - Planning Decisions

year	decisions	number approved	per cent
1988-89	2090	1651	78.9
1989-90	2011	1529	76.0
1990-91	1593	1259	79.0
1991-92	1513	1236	82.0

Source: DOE Development Control Statistics

Applications in the Green Belt comprise around one quarter of the total over each of the last three years (Table F.35).

Table F.35: Major Applications Made by Policy Area

year	green belt		development boundary		open countryside		total
	no	%	no	%	no	%	
1988-89	167	40.2	219	52.8	29	7.0	415
1989-90	162	25.8	361	57.4	106	16.9	629
1990-91	123	28.2	199	45.6	114	26.1	436
1991-92	119	25.0	239	50.0	119	25.0	477
total	571	29.2	1018	52.0	368	18.8	1957

Source: Green Belt Project Survey

F.44 The rate of approval of applications within the Green Belt is not significantly different from that in urban areas (Table F.36). The average rate of approval in the Green Belt is 63.6 per cent, in comparison to 65.8 per cent in urban areas. The rate of approval in the open countryside beyond the Green Belt is around five per cent higher each year than that in Green Belt. Approval rates overall are some 10-15 per cent below the District average shown in Table F.38, reflecting the fact that this sub-sample of applications is for larger developments. Larger applications tend to attract a higher refusal rate.

Table F.36: Applications Approved by Policy Area

year	green belt		development boundary		open countryside		total
	no	%	no	%	no	%	
1988-89	104	62.2	144	65.8	nk	nk	nk
1989-90	98	60.5	211	58.4	72	67.9	60.6
1990-91	78	63.4	130	65.3	82	71.9	66.5
1991-92	81	68.1	176	73.7	79	66.4	70.4
total		63.6		65.8		68.8	

Source: Green Belt Project Survey

F.45 We can see that in the 1990-92 period the number of applications for housing in the Green Belt was far lower, by a factor of over three, than in the first two years. Also the level of industry and office applications has reduced somewhat through time. However leisure applications have held up in terms of numbers.

Table F.37: Land Uses Applied for in the Green Belt

use applied for	1988-90	1990-92
housing	183	55
householder *	59	96
industry, office	33	22
retail	7	12
leisure	24	25
agriculture	5	5
storage, warehousing, transport	2	4
other	16	23
total	329	242

* these include, in addition to extensions and conversions, alterations to listed buildings, demolition of listed buildings, minor change of use, and advertisements

Source: Green Belt Project Survey

237

Table F.38: Areas Involved in Approvals/Refusals*

	green belt		development boundary		open countryside	
	a	r	a	r	a	r
1988-89	38.0	10.7	35.3	7.5	5.8	1.7
1989-90	122.0	57.7	80.5	13.3	27.4	17.5
1990-91	124.8	27.5	24.5	10.2	54.1	4.6
1991-92	98.3	8.8	22.2	8.5	135.0	8.6

a = approved
r = refused
* hectares in planning unit

Source: Green Belt Project Survey

Broxbourne District Survey

F.46   Broxbourne District lies astride the M25 and adjacent to the A1(M), and includes the towns of Waltham Abbey, Cheshunt and Hoddesdon.   The throughput of planning applications, at around 1000 per year, is half of that in Dacorum. The rate of approval of applications for the District as a whole is slightly lower (71 to 75 per cent) than for the other case study areas (Table F.39).

Table F.39: Broxbourne - Planning Decisions

year	decisions	number approved	per cent
1988-89	1262	895	70.9
1989-90	1073	783	73.0
1990-91	951	713	75.0
1991-92	na	na	na

Source: DOE development control statistics

F.47   Broxbourne has only two policy areas: land within development boundaries, and land in Green Belt. Around 30 per cent of major applications made are in the Green Belt, and this proportion has remained consistent over the four year period (Table F.40).

Table F.40: Major Applications Made by Policy Area

year	green belt		development boundary		total
	no	%	no	%	
1988-89	79	30.2	183	69.8	262
1989-90	43	21.3	159	78.7	202
1990-91	57	29.5	136	70.5	193
1991-92	40	-	na	-	na

Source: Green Belt Project Survey

F.48 The rate of approval of applications in Green Belt has varied from 48 per cent to 58 per cent over the last four years, although the overall numbers involved are small (Table F.41).

Table F.41: Applications Approved by Policy Area

year	green belt		development boundary		total
	no	%	no	%	
1988-89	38	48.1	102	55.7	53.4
1989-90	25	58.1	102	64.2	62.9
1990-91	29	50.9	89	65.4	61.1
1991-92	22	55.0	na	na	

Source: Green Belt Project Survey

F.49 The number of applications in Green Belt dropped by around one third in the last two years of the study period (Table F.42). Applications for leisure uses were the only ones to increase over the period. The level of business and retail-related applications reduced over the period.

Table F.42: Land Uses Applied for in the Green Belt

use applied for	1988-90	1990-92
housing	57	47
householder *	10	8
industry, office	13	6
retail	4	4
leisure	10	12
agriculture	6	3
warehousing/ transport	10	0
other, incl. education; communication	9	17
total	122	88

* see note in Table F.36.

Source: Green Belt Project Survey

F.50   In terms of the area involved in applications (Table F.42) it can be seen that approvals in the Green Belt normally comprise 20-30 hectares a year. The large figure (141 hectares) in 1989-90 relates to the approval of a new golf course.

Table F.43: Areas Involved in Approvals/Refusals: Broxbourne*

	green belt		development boundary	
	a	r	a	r
1988-89	25.8	24.8	23.3	3.8
1989-90	140.8	34.2	43.4	4.4
1990-91	29.4	48.6	24.0	4.1
1991-92	14.5	93.2	na	na
total	210.5	200.8	90.7	12.3

* hectares

Source: Green Belt Project Survey

East Hertfordshire District Survey

F.51   East Hertfordshire is the largest District in Hertfordshire and includes the towns of Ware, Hertford, Bishops Stortford and Sawbridgeworth. Green Belt policies cover the southern part of the District only, and have recently been extended around Bishops Stortford. A proposal to extent Green Belt coverage northward within the District was rejected by the Secretary of State during 1992. The throughput of applications, at around 2200 per year, is one of the highest for shire districts in the UK and resembles that of Macclesfield (see paras F.32-F.41).

Table F.44: East Hertfordshire - Planning Decisions

year	decisions	number approved	per cent
1988-89	2529	1988	78.6
1989-90	2209	1613	73.0
1990-91	1833	1393	76.0
1991-92	1746	1366	77.7

Source: DOE Development Control Statistics

F.52   The District has three policy areas; urban (development boundary), Green Belt, and the countryside beyond the Green Belt. Although the latter area is far larger than that subject to Green Belt policy the level of applications made over the four years of the study period is rather similar. The Green Belt is clearly under greater development pressure, but there has been a rapid drop in the number of major applications made in the last four years (Table F.45).

Table F.45: Major Applications Made by Policy Area

year	green belt		development boundary		open countryside		total
	no	%	no	%	no	%	
1988-89	204	28.3	348	48.2	170	23.5	722
1989-90	177	22.9	365	47.2	230	29.9	772
1990-91	163	25.6	244	38.4	229	36.0	636
1991-92	134	23.9	239	42.7	187	33.4	560
total	678	25.2	1196	44.1	816	30.7	2690

Source: Green Belt Project Survey

F.53   The rate of approvals in 1988-9 was higher in the Green Belt than the countryside beyond, but during the last three years the position has been reversed. The overall approval rates in the Green Belt are similar to those for Dacorum (see Table F.36). Approval rates in the Green Belt have been five per cent lower than in the wider countryside over the period (65 per cent as against 70 per cent) (Table F.46).

Table F.46: Applications Approved by Policy Area

year	green belt		development boundary		open countryside		total
	n	%	n	%	n	%	
1988-89	133	65.2	255	73.3	105	61.8	493
1989-90	112	63.3	259	71.0	162	70.4	533
1990-91	101	62.0	187	76.6	159	69.4	447
1991-92	92	68.7	176	73.6	149	79.7	417

Source: Green Belt Project Survey

F.54 The 'planning unit' areas involved in Green Belt approvals have been large, but have been dominated by leisure (golf course) uses (see Table F.47).

Table F.47: Areas Involved in Approvals/Refusals

	green belt		development boundary		open countryside	
	a	r	a	r	a	r
1988-89	378.7	37.9	57.0	7.8	21.1	25.6
1989-90	93.9	33.6	85.5	16.5	44.6	23.6
1990-91	122.1	171.2	64.5	11.1	136.0	63.0
1991-92	436.2	82.6	22.5	8.5	263.4	108.0
total	1030.9	325.3	229.5	43.9	465.1	220.2

a = approved
r = refused

Source: Green Belt Project Survey

Appendix G: Briefing Paper on Urban Fringe Issues

[This paper was circulated to the participants to aid discussion at the one-day seminar on urban fringe issues held in Oxford in September 1992].

Introduction

G.1   There appears wide agreement on the basic and longstanding purposes of Green Belts. There is, however, greater concern over the future of land uses, and land use policy, within Green Belts and the urban fringe. This theme is reflected in recently published reports by the London Planning Advisory Committee, the Urban Fringe Special Advisory Group and the Royal Institution of Chartered Surveyors (see Appendix B, pp 149-151). Despite mention of urban fringe issues in the pre-election Government statement 'Action for the Countryside', and in PPG 7, there is little detail in policy. In Scotland, by contrast, the idea of 'The Countryside Around Towns' has received more comprehensive analysis. This has fed through to a well-researched set of Green Belt-wide environmental policies in areas such as Strathclyde.

G.2   Over the last ten years two million additional acres of countryside have become subject to the relatively strict controls that Green Belt policies imply. In such areas, in addition to development control policies, there are issues of countryside management and environmental improvement. Within the last year PPG 12 has stated that policies in plans should now reflect the practical measures needed to improve natural features in the countryside. The aim of this briefing paper is to discuss four broad issues:

- the main economic and social processes at work affecting the urban fringe;

- policy priorities in the urban fringe;

- relationships between urban fringe and Green Belt policy, and

- Green Belt management and the implementation of policies.

Economic and Social Processes

G.3   A number of basic policy notions have traditionally been used in planning the countryside near towns. Firstly, the *urban fringe*, seen as the penumbra of the city, is an area of fragmented land ownerships and intruded farmland, near to the urban fence. In this definition the urban fringe is an area lesser in extent than the Green Belts (see PPG 7, para 3.13). Attention is focused on problems of urban intrusion, trespass and vandalism and, in some areas, on the need for wider environmental improvement. Secondly, the *Green Belt*; an extensive tract of green land to be permanently retained in an open rural appearance.

243

Land uses are to be restricted to those 'appropriate to a rural area', such as agriculture and forestry. Thirdly, *leisure and recreation* activity will be limited to that fitting the townsperson's arcadian view of the countryside. Informal recreation, with few recreational buildings designed to be fitted into the rural scene, is the prescription put forward in guidance. Underpinning this set of presumptions was, until relatively recently, the idea of retaining every hectare possible of *agricultural land* for productive needs.

G.4   Economic forces, and resulting social changes, have placed these cornerstones of policy under pressure. Looking forward, the following issues appear of major concern:

i)   *increasingly dispersed patterns of living;* the decentralization of people from cities to wider functional economic regions has continued. This is aided by the ease of car ownership and travel, allowing an increased separation of home and work. In the medium term a higher quality of life in spacious 'green' surroundings can be achieved. How far such a pattern is efficient or effective in the long term, in planning or transport terms, is an unanswered question (Breheny, 1992; Newby, 1990).

ii)   *agricultural problems;* farmers' incomes have declined rapidly over the past 5-10 years. The impacts of CAP reform and the McSharry proposals are unclear. We may see greater amounts of land set aside, with farmers in the urban fringe particularly opting for this solution. Most scenarios suggest there will be a poor economic base, from within agriculture, for maintaining the urban fringe landscape that people want. Diversification has strictly limited potential, although it would seem important to facilitate such development where it can have wider, economic and landscape benefits (McLaughlin, 1992; Ilbery, 1988).

iii)   *leisure demands;* these are conventionally seen as increasing. However most growth appears restricted to space extensive sports such as golf and watersports, together with some of the motorised sports which are seen by some as more intrusive (Broom, 1992). Data on informal recreation show little growth in participation over the past five years, but the recent Countryside Commission study on transport in the countryside suggests the British 'love affair with the car' will, in future, extend to leisure use of the countryside. The urban fringe and Green Belts appear valuable locations for recreation if this could lessen the length of leisure journeys by car, reduce 'travel for its own sake', and promote greater use of public transport (Countryside Commission, 1992, CCP 382).

iv)   *environmental degradation;* this includes a wide range of derelict and degraded land falling out of extractive and other use, and the general neglect of countryside management. Despite new environmental legislation there is little evidence that the area of derelict and degraded

244

land is reducing, or that widespread landscape improvement work has taken place. Mineral extraction and opencasting will continue to be a problem for the urban fringe. Pressing demands for new landfill sites, incinerators and re-cycling plants are also occurring (Land Capability Consultants, 1991; Environmental Resources Limited and Oxford Polytechnic, 1992).

v)   *local and rural defensiveness;* basically the Green Belt policy instrument has been adopted by local groups, often newly arrived in the outer city, to promote a no growth - no change philosophy. For example local village, Green Belt-wide, and national groups systematically patrol such environments making representations on development plans and planning applications. Their concern is to resist new development, although there is evidence they are seeking, at the same time, high levels of local services (Marsden, 1992). Their views now swamp those of farmers, and others related to rural industries, who have traditionally held a more pro-development stance. Green Belt has thus become a symbol of a life of urban convenience, lived in surroundings with rural visual attributes (Newby, 1988).

Questions

1.   What is the urban fringe? Is it a relatively narrow area with specific problems near to cities, or is it something more extensive?

2.   What are the likely effects on the fringe of changing fortunes in agriculture?

3.   Are leisure demands increasing, and changing? If so, in what ways?

4.   What effect does Green Belt policy have on the economic and environmental problems in urban fringe areas?

Policy Priorities

G.5   Our interviews, together with the review of relevant major literature, suggest widespread agreement over land use objectives (Elson, 1991, Green Belts for Wales). At the same time there was more doubt about methods, resources and priorities. We can expect to see a more multi-activity countryside near towns. Emphasis will be on the interactions between different uses of open land, and the management of conflicts. The other main themes which emerged are:

•   continued support for agriculture, particularly on better quality land;

•   a wider role for sport and recreation, with greater attention to access issues;

245

- the need to enhance safeguards for nature conservation interests; and

- a wish to restore damaged landscapes and derelict land.

G.6   Overall we are seeing a reduction in the primacy of agriculture in the fringe, in terms of the protection of land. But the importance of agriculture as the most effective 'manager' of an attractive rural environment may, in future, be enhanced. The principle of support for agriculture will therefore need to be maintained, but for different reasons. Agriculture and its related activities may become more diverse, assuming certain industrial or tertiary employment characteristics. This may conflict with the strictest ideas of keeping land open. The definition of what are 'appropriate activities' in the urban fringe countryside may therefore need to change.

G.7   The principle that all land should have a positive use is a longstanding one. This implies greater investment by the extractive industries, or institutional users in returning land to some useful purpose after development. The identification of special 'action areas' within the urban fringe (for example in river valleys, or areas subject to extraction) is one way of focusing attention on such problems. This, could imply varying policy priorities in parts of the urban fringe (UFSAG, 1992).

G.8   Support for greater access for sport and recreation would rest on a number of principles. First, the idea that the urban fringe is of high accessibility, and has the potential for much more intensive use in an energy efficient way. Second, that such use would give identity to the urban fringe; and third, that such uses would intercept journeys which would otherwise go to the deeper countryside, or National Parks. Fourth, a wide cross section of social groups could potentially be attracted to urban fringe environments. The urban fringe may also support space extensive leisure activities which cannot easily be accommodated in towns (Elson, 1993).

G.9   The adoption of sustainability principles would imply the stronger protection of semi-natural areas within the planning process, and the identification and positive management of areas with particularly high wildlife value. There would need to be greater emphasis on the need for local level management of conflicting interests; between nature conservation and recreation, and recreation and agriculture, for example. Community Forests could reduce pollution, and provide a landscape matrix for a wider mix of activities. Policies designed to reduce leisure travel, by getting people out of their cars, would increase impacts on the natural environmental and thus the costs of countryside management. The need to support traffic management in the interests of reducing emissions would lead to the siting of Park and Ride schemes or light rail termini in urban fringes. Application of the proximity principle for waste management could lead to the significant use of land for such purposes in the urban fringe.

G.10   In summary there are sufficient indicators to suggest future policies for the
        urban fringe should:

  •   provide for a more multi-activity countryside near towns in an
            environmentally sustainable way;

  •   provide opportunities for greater access for sport and recreation;

  •   safeguard important areas for nature conservation;

  •   safeguard important sites for sport, recreation and tourism; and

  •   provide for an effective system of countryside management and
            enhancement.

This suggests precepts of 'need', 'economy' and 'sustainability' are at least as
relevant in the 1990s as ideas of 'openness', 'rurality', and the creation of a
'clear-cut boundary' between built up areas and the countryside, currently
deployed.

Questions

1.   What should be the principles for land use policy in the urban fringe
        countryside?

2.   Can a broader sustainability rationale be developed?

3.   Should the urban fringe be divided into sub-areas, where different
        priorities would obtain?

4.   To what extent does Green Belt policy obstruct the newly emerging
        priorities for urban fringe areas?

Urban Fringe and Green Belt Policy

G.11   The definition of Green Belts does not, of itself, actively promote new uses or
        countryside management. Current planning guidance, however, refers to wider
        themes and objectives in both areas of Green Belt and the urban fringe.
        Although the justifications for Green Belt are largely urban, PPG 2 refers to
        a positive role for Green Belts in providing access to open countryside.
        Circular 14/84 encourages the environmental improvement of areas suffering
        neglect and damage. PPG 7 defines the urban fringe as areas where 'land use
        conflicts and environmental problems arise', at the same time noting that urban
        fringe is not regarded as a designation. In such areas, it suggests, a positive
        approach to planning and management should be pursued, securing
        environmental improvement, and the beneficial use of land. PPG 17 asks local
        authorities to encourage the provision of recreation facilities in the urban

fringe, and to regard recreation as a buffer land use. There is also support for afforestation schemes, the enhancement of the Rights of Way network, and nature conservation. Indeed the White Paper 'This Common Inheritance' sees Green Belt as a policy with a broadly conservation theme.

G.12   The urban fringe has the potential to perform a number of functions for sport and recreation. It is well placed to act as:

- a *supply* area, with high accessibility to main population centres; one in five informal recreation trips to the countryside have a round trip distance often of ten miles or less;

- because of its proximity to people, an area offering the potential to break away from the dominance of car borne leisure towards *greater access* by foot, cycle and public transport;

- a *safety valve* area, acting to accommodate uses such as playing fields, golf courses or football stadia displaced from urban areas;

- an *intercepter* area, where new provision may reduce pressures in more 'fragile' countryside areas; and

- an *opportunity* area, where environmental improvement and creation of new landscapes can lead to sport and recreation after-uses.

G.13   In 1991 the Government stated it was considering extending the objectives of Green Belts, to include those of:

- enhancing and improving the natural beauty of the countryside, and

- increasing opportunities for quiet enjoyment of the countryside.

The Countryside Commissions' paper 'Planning for a Greener Countryside' suggests these would be objectives of Green Belt, only *after* Green Belts had been defined on the basis of the five purposes in PPG 2. If natural beauty (landscape quality) were to become a criterion for definition this would introduce a different rationale for the weighing of Green Belt and development needs. The Edinburgh Green Belt has landscape objectives, which have led to a range of different arguments surrounding the need to find new land for housing in Lothian. The application of landscape criteria could also lead to arguments for the major extension of Green Belts into the deeper countryside, thus weakening the special nature of the policy.

G.14   A number of local authorities already have provision for outdoor recreation as an objective of Green Belt in their development plans. The definition of Green Belts using this rationale could emphasise the protection of recreational resources, by restricting development possibilities in and around areas of existing heavy leisure use. Another interpretation would give greater emphasis to green wedges, as ways of providing accessible recreation land near towns, and giving greater identity to urban neighbourhoods. The issue of strategic sized areas of detached greenspace in the urban fabric could also be brought into the policy. Notions of a hierarchy including Metropolitan Open Land (or its equivalent), green wedges and Green Belt could make sense of a pattern of open land linking the inner areas of towns and cities to the open country.

G.15   Although golf course demands have declined from the 700 new courses predicted by the Royal and Ancient Golf Club in the mid-1980s, local authorities are still handling a steady throughput of proposals. The County of Surrey, for example, already has 79 golf courses. At December 1991 twenty six more had planning permission, and 20 more schemes awaited determination. New schemes approved and proposed include 12 driving ranges (Surrey County Council, 1992). The main pressures that have resulted have posed the following questions:

- what level of associated facilities should be allowed? Many applicants are seeking restaurant, hotel and country club-style facilities in association with golf. These are argued to have some link in practice with the basic golfing activity. In other proposals where housing, out of town shopping, or some other use is the primary cash generator for the scheme, the golf may only be of 'cosmetic' relevance.

- how far should golf driving ranges, which have a more intensive urban appearance, but are often seen as a complementary activity, be acceptable?

- how far, and in what circumstances, may golf courses be accommodated in Areas of Outstanding Natural Beauty and in historical parkland? (Countryside Commission, 1992, CCP 365).

G.16   In some cases Green Belt policy is being challenged by economic pressures, or urban fringe initiatives. Two prominent examples are farm diversification, and Community Forests. Ilberys' work in the West Midlands suggests that Green Belt policy may restrict diversification (Ilbery, 1988). This is particularly unfortunate as Green Belts are well located for urban markets. Wider questions of how far small-scale industrial, office or tourist development could be allowed on farms, if overall improvements to the landscape would result, remain. Knowledge of how far the development control regime within Green Belts is more strict than in the deeper countryside is sparse, and will only emerge from our development control case studies. If differences do exist then farmers are, in effect, being asked to pay an extra price for Green Belt policy. The question of whether, in principle, a difference between development control in the two areas should exist is not addressed explicitly in policy guidance.

G.17 In July 1989 the Countryside and Forestry Commissions launched a programme to create 12 community forests. These are based on the concept that new multi-purpose woodlands in the countryside around towns will benefit the community at large by enhancing the landscape, providing new environments for recreation and wildlife, attracting development and helping to mitigate the greenhouse effect. The Forest areas are 20-40,000 hectares each, although it is expected that less than half of the land in the areas will eventually be planted (Countryside Commission, 1989 (CCP 270); 1991 (CCP 240)). Forest project teams have been charged with preparing Forest Plans. Grant aid will be available to landowners and farmers for planting, including a special £950 per hectare community woodlands supplement. The first three schemes, Thames Chase (Essex), South Tyneside and the Forest of Mercia (Staffordshire) are all in Green Belt locations.

G.18 Community Forests, when implemented, will represent a positive and permanent use for areas of Green Belt. The original concept saw wide ranging provisions for sport and recreation, including built facilities, suggested. Some of these were not compatible with pre-existing Green Belt policy. There may be a case for widening the mix of acceptable uses in forests, where noise can be more easily absorbed, and buildings can be hidden that would otherwise intrude in the landscape. Suggestions that the proceeds from leisure development, for example for the redevelopment of operational farm buildings, should be used for tree planting, have not been accepted by the Department in the case of Hertfordshire (Pitt, 1991). The draft Forest Plans for Mercia and Thames Chase take care to make it clear they intend to operate within Green Belt policy as currently framed (South Yorkshire Community Forest (1992); Staffordshire County Council (1992)). How the greening of Green Belts, outwith Community Forests, is to be promoted is also a question for policy.

G.19 The need to restore damaged and degraded land in the Green Belt has been promoted as a key policy objective, notably by the Urban Fringe Special Advisory Group and LPAC. This matter retains its salience, not least because developers focus on such land when seeking planning permission. The statements about dereliction in the PPG are perhaps not fully convincing in this regard. LPAC's study of 900 hectares of damaged land near London led to calls for a new urban fringe improvement grant, either within or outside the Department's DLG system. The Urban Fringe SAG suggest, among a range of policies, the definition of UFSPA (Urban Fringe Special Policy Areas) in development plans. These might have special development control regimes, and would provide ' a context for striking a balance between the purely protective aspects of ... Green Belt ... and the positive management improvements that are essential to tackle urban fringe problems'. In exceptional cases, where the costs of improvement exceed the scope of conventional funding, it is suggested that development, not normally permitted in the Green Belt, should be allowed to go ahead. Such exceptional areas would be shown in development plans (Urban Fringe Special Advisory Group, 1992). The Green Belt Company, now in existence in Strathclyde, has the intention of making use of 'enabling development' in a broadly similar way.

Questions

1.   How far, and in what ways, should recreation and landscape objectives be incorporated into Green Belt policy?

2.   What should be the relationship between Green Belt policy and Community Forests?

3.   Should any new principles govern development control in Green Belts?

Implementation and Management

G.20   There is some competition to promote environmental improvement, and countryside management in Green Belts. Green Belts tend not to be treated as a whole for management purposes, the attention given to environmental matters depending on local authority priorities and policies in different areas. Perhaps half of the London Green Belt is covered by Area Management schemes of some type, but the Countryside Commission aim of complete coverage for the London and other Green Belts remains, as yet, unrealised.

G.21   *Community Forests* are an ambitious scheme for packaging a desirable environmental agenda for the urban fringe. They may represent good value for money, the cash spent on planting and management being less than the costs of present agricultural subsidies in the same area (Bishop, 1992). A number of issues remain, however:

•   the schemes are very ambitious; they will require large implementation teams, and greater public resources to create impetus;

•   if early action on the ground does not fit the ideals in the Forest Plans there could be a temptation to re-open the 'enabling development' argument; and

•   although six of the first twelve schemes are in Green Belt, they only cover at best 200,000 hectares, around 15 per cent of approved Green Belts.

G.22   The *Groundwork Foundation* is also in the business of local environmental management. Though a network of nearly 40 local trusts, some 18 of which cover parts of Green Belt, their role is to act as a catalyst, concerting public, private and voluntary sector sources of finance and expertise towards the resolution of environmental problems. The Trusts often bridge urban, urban fringe and countryside areas. Core funding is provided by £9 million per annum from the Government, and other grants are available through the EC. Income is generated from the private sector for schemes such as the New Countryside Initiative, which aims to assist edge of town farmers, and improve relations across the town-country divide. Partners include Business in the

Community, ADAS, MAFF and the Countryside Commission. The Groundwork Foundation is increasingly a conduit for Government funds for environmental improvements, and appears to almost have achieved the status of a new quasi-Government body. The number of trusts is set to grow, with Government support.

G.23 *Countryside management* has traditionally been organised by setting up a section or department within a local authority. However, broader partnership arrangements have a track record of attracting greater financial and other resources. Three types of arrangement have been used: area-based countryside management projects; environmental trusts (mainly Groundwork), and Community Forests. These imply some separate form of organisation, with control over funds being, to a lesser or greater extent, independent of the local authorities. In addition Countryside Commission Section 9 grants are based on the Commission's priorities, and derelict land grants relate to yet another set of criteria in Derelict Land Clearance Areas. Some local authorities we have interviewed have seen all of these mechanisms deployed in their areas, yet how far they have been a success is unclear. For example Thames Chase Community Forest is, in effect, re-working some of the same farms as those which appeared as in need of landscape improvement in the 1977-80 Havering Green Belt Management Experiment.

G.24 Area management is now seen, in retrospect, as only tackling small-scale issues (Kirby, 1990). Groundwork takes a more diffuse form, extending well beyond Green Belts into urban areas, although involving the private sector. In some areas there appear to be overlaps, and Groundwork does not appear to have local political accountability. Local authority priorities are often conditioned by outside funds. Bidding for Community Forests, for example, was intense as they provide a vehicle for additional central Government funds to be channelled to local areas. Both Community Forests and Green Belt Companies have, as yet, an insufficient track record on which to make judgements. It may be concluded that despite considerable efforts by the Countryside Commission, local authorities and others, ways still need to be found to instill greater co-ordination, political impetus and financial funding into green belt management.

Questions

1. What should be the aims and objectives of Green Belt Management?

2. What organisational forms should greening programmes and environmental improvement take?

3. Should the funding of environmental improvements by enabling development be allowed in special circumstances in Green Belts?

School of Planning
Oxford Brookes University
September 1992

Appendix H: Study of Appeals

H.1   This Appendix discusses appeal outcomes, and the factors taken into account in arriving at decisions over the April 1991-April 1992 period. Some 1,201 appeals were identified by the Planning Inspectorate where Green Belt was seen as an important factor in the decision taken. The appeals were dominated by residentially - related schemes, some 46 per cent of those studied relating to these uses (Table H.1). Around 10 per cent of the appeals involved the re-use of redundant buildings for residential or commercial uses. The proportion of appeals relating to leisure, sport, recreation and equestrian activities totalled five per cent. The proposals most frequently upheld at appeal related to the re-use of redundant buildings for commercial uses, office use, and the use of land by gypsies and travellers.

Table H.1: Proportion of Appeals Upheld by Main Use Applied For

use	number	per cent of total	per cent upheld
residential - extensions	245	20.4	34.3
residential - single units	229	19.1	7.9
residential - 2 to 9 units	65	5.4	9.2
residential - 10+ units	19	1.6	5.3
agricultural occupancy	47	3.9	19.1
redundant buildings to residential	88	7.3	28.4
caravans, mobile homes	81	6.7	17.3
gypsies, travellers	29	2.4	44.8
nursing homes	27	2.3	29.6
hotels, pubs, conference	26	2.2	30.7
office	40	3.3	45.0
industrial	22	1.8	36.4
redundant buildings to commercial	37	3.1	45.9
retail	10	0.8	20.0
garden centres, nurseries	22	1.8	22.7
sport and recreation	29	2.4	34.5
equestrian, animal husbandry	31	2.6	35.5
agriculture-related (other)	25	2.2	36.0
transport, vehicles	61	5.1	6.6
storage	33	2.7	15.2
minerals, waste disposal	35	2.9	14.3
total	1201	100.0	22.6

Note: Uses are further defined below. For example the "hotels, pubs, conference" category consists largely of extensions.

Source: Green Belt Project Survey

Residential Extensions

H.2   A total of 245 cases were examined in this category. Some 90 per cent were Section 78 appeals. The rate of approval of Section 78 and enforcement appeals was 34 per cent. Most cases related to one or two storey extensions to dwellings. Others related to 'granny annexes', conservatories, extensions of residential curtilages and domestic tennis courts.

H.3   Local authorities normally permit limited extensions to existing dwellings located in Green Belts. In some cases such policies are set out in development plans, commonly referring to floor area increases of 30 to 50 per cent of that of the original building as appropriate limits. Schemes tended to be approved by Inspectors where it was judged:

• the character and scale of the existing building was respected;

• the appearance of the building would be improved;

• the increased bulk would not be apparent or intrusive;

• overall the building will remain small;

• the development would not add to the erosion of the Green Belt; or

• the extension would solve an overriding deficiency in the dwelling (eg lack of a bathroom).

Additional criteria, where appeals were dismissed, included the adverse cumulative effect of a number of extensions on the house, and the view that personal circumstances are not normally enough to outweigh policy. The effective operation of this aspect of Green Belt policy is particularly important as extensions form the largest single source of appeals. If not carefully controlled their urbanizing effect could be considerable.

Residential Single Units

H.4   Single units were also a large part of the sample. Some 229 cases were examined, only 7.9 per cent (18) of which were upheld. This reflects the strict control that exists over isolated and sporadic housing in the Green Belt. It was found that only limited amounts of infill, and replacement dwellings, can be permissible. The infill issue is particularly relevant to washed over Green Belt villages, hamlets or other development. Often such infill is proposed on existing residential gardens. Many development plans have policies allowing infill which will not harm the objectives of Green Belt policy.

H.5   The appeal outcomes suggested that dismissals tend to occur where the applicant cannot prove that the dwelling constitutes defined infilling or replacement. Debate often occurs as to what constitutes a 'settlement' for the purpose of infilling. Replacement dwellings must not radically increase the bulk of the dwelling on the site. Personal circumstances are only likely to lead to an appeal being upheld where the harm to the Green Belt is already judged to be in equal balance with proven advantages. Even if a single new house is unobtrusively sited the proposal is most likely to be dismissed as it basically contradicts policy. A relaxation of controls over single dwellings could have the effect of creating sprawl in the countryside. The appeal system is therefore supporting this primary purpose of Green Belts effectively.

Residential Schemes - Two to Nine Units

H.6   Only six of the sixty five cases in this category (9.2 per cent) were upheld. Those upheld were generally argued as infill, replacements and re-use. A seven unit scheme upheld utilised a disused industrial building. An eight unit scheme upheld included some development of open land, but this was regarded as rounding-off by the Inspector.

H.7   Dismissal was most clear-cut where development proposed would have constituted sporadic development in the open countryside. Replacing inappropriate existing uses with housing development was also not seen as justified. A similar situation existed where developers argued that derelict and disused sites should be used for new housing. This aspect of policy was therefore also firmly applied.

Residential Schemes - Ten or More Units

H.8   Residential development of this scale is not an appropriate use in the Green Belt. Only nineteen appeals fell in this category over the one year period, and only one of these was upheld. The approval was for sixteen units in a District in Essex. The Inspector found that the site did not perform any specific Green Belt purpose. Due to its position, and nearby land releases, it had become an isolated piece of open land unrelated to the Green Belt. A local plan inquiry inspector had favoured removal of the site from the Green Belt. The site thus appeared destined for release, the local authority originally turning down the scheme on loss of open space, not Green Belt, grounds.

H.9   Analysis of the dismissals here showed that:

   •   extraneous planning 'benefits', offered by the developer, are not sufficient to outweigh Green Belt policy;

   •   low cost housing schemes do not, *per se*, outweigh Green Belt policy; they must accord with PPG 3, and be in settlements reasonably far away from the urban fringe;

   •   enabling development will only be allowed where there is no harm to the Green Belt, listed buildings or the rural scene;

- it is not satisfactory to replace one inappropriate use (eg storage) with another (eg residential); and

- it is not appropriate to allow housing development on run-down and derelict green belt sites.

The marginality of this category, both in total numbers and appeals upheld, demonstrates the effectiveness of Green Belt in discouraging speculative development proposals.

Agricultural Dwellings and Agricultural Occupancy

H.10   Some 47 cases were found in this category. The rate of appeals upheld was low, at 19 per cent, reflecting a strict application of the criteria in Circular 24/73 and PPG 7 (Annex E). Equestrian-related use is not generally regarded as agriculture. Horticultural needs are regarded as agricultural, but dwellings can be more difficult to substantiate without animals to care for. The basic criteria laid down in guidance for the assessment of such uses were fully reflected in the appeals studied. These were:

- the financial test, where the holding must be viable to the extent that the predicted income would sustain one agricultural worker;

- the functional test, where a genuine operational need should be established such that supervision requirements cannot be meet from off the site; and

- any harm to the environment should be insignificant.

Dismissals demonstrate that it is the needs of the enterprise, not those of the owner or occupier, that are important. If viability is not proved a time limited permission for a caravan may result (see para H.14). The needs for security, on its own, is not likely to lead to an appeal being upheld. Agricultural occupancy conditions were only removed where it is proven, by long-term advertisement in the specialist farming press, that no long term-need exists for such accommodation in the area.

Residential Re-Use of Redundant Buildings

H.11   Paragraph 16 of PPG 2 encourages the re-use of redundant buildings for individual residences, among other uses. Recent case law, notably the Pehrsson case, has widened the policy to include existing non-agricultural buildings, although the redundancy criterion remains. Some 88 cases were found under this heading. Only just over one quarter of appeals (28 per cent) were upheld, perhaps a low figure given the policy wording of PPG 2. Forty two of the cases were proposals for barn conversions, and seven cases were non-agricultural buildings such as coach houses. Most of the cases related to single dwelling proposals, with around one quarter being for two or more dwelling units.

256

H.12 The re-use of buildings for residential purposes appears appropriate if the character and appearance of the conversion is judged to be in a form in keeping with the character of the area. Buildings must be genuinely redundant, but need not be listed to secure favourable consideration. Conversions are more likely to succeed where major rebuilding and extension work is not involved, and where the pre-existing building makes a contribution to the local rural scene. Where appeals were not upheld the following factors were relevant:

- detailed problems with conversion, such as alterations to window openings, and the creation of new 'domestic' curtilages;

- spurious redundancy;

- effects on the amenity of neighbouring properties; and

- more generally, the loss of an agricultural appearance to the premises and their rural attractiveness.

Caravans and Mobile Homes

H.13 This category relates to the general residential use of mobile homes and caravans, caravan towing sites, the storage of caravans, and the agricultural use of mobile homes and caravans. Just over 50 per cent of the 81 appeal cases identified related to enforcement proceedings. Enforcement action most often relates to the unauthorised stationing of a single caravan for general residential purposes or, more rarely, for a farm worker.

H.14 General residential use is inappropriate within the Green Belt, the same criteria being applied to mobile homes and caravans as permanent dwellings (see para H.4). Requests for time-limited permissions for residential use are usually resisted. Similarly the storage of caravans is not regarded as appropriate in Green Belts. It is not regarded by Inspectors as an activity which requires a rural location. The visual intrusion likely to be caused is also often referred to. Caravan sites are not generally regarded as appropriate in Green Belts, although proposals for siting towing caravans have been approved where sites are visually unobtrusive and are likely to have no impact on surrounding amenities. Agricultural use can be allowed in certain circumstances, as PPG 7 states (see para H.10). Where the financial test is not conclusive, a caravan may be allowed on a temporary basis to allow the viability of the farm unit to be proven. Dismissals occurred most often, therefore, where no agricultural need (the functional test) had been proven, and where visual intrusiveness would be a problem. Overall this category showed a very low level of appeals upheld, only 17 per cent. These decisions have contributed to the effectiveness of policies to avoid scattered development.

Sites for Gypsies and Travellers

H.15 Gypsy caravan sites are not listed as an appropriate Green Belt use in paragraph 13 of PPG 2. Circular 28/77 however states that sites for gypsies may be acceptable in the Green Belt where a need is proven. They should, in these circumstances, be given special consideration by local planning authorities.. Recent Department proposals to reform the Caravan Sites Act 1968 however have suggested this privileged position may be removed. Some 29 cases were examined in the appeal scan, ten of which were enforcement cases. Forty-five per cent of the appeals were upheld, reflecting that gypsy sites may be acceptable where need is proven. Generally larger sites (six to twenty units) were dismissed, in a number of cases after recovery by the Secretary of State for decision.

H.16 Appeals tend to be allowed where it is shown that the appellant is a gypsy under the terms of the Caravan Sites Act. Case law allows this definition to include those who only travel seasonally, but require a permanent base for childrens' schooling and other purposes. Need is normally assessed by examining local provision, as required to be provided by authorities under the Act. If a district is 'designated' under Section 12 of the 1968 Act this implies a satisfactory provision of sites exists. Whether need is actually met, however, is often a source of debate. A local connection is normally required to secure approval, provision being allowed for locally-connected gypsies who wish to settle on a permanent private site of their own. The cases approved generally had minimal impact on the environment of the Green Belt, or there were compelling need arguments, such as a severe shortage of sites locally.

Nursing Homes

H.17 Twenty seven appeals relating to nursing home use in Green Belts were examined. Most related to the extension of existing nursing homes, although some involved the re-use of existing large residential properties or the construction of new facilities. Some 30 per cent of appeals were upheld, virtually all of these relating to relatively small extensions to existing buildings which were regarded as not harming the visual amenities of Green Belts. It is often argued by appellants that nursing homes fall into the definition of institutions in extensive grounds. This is generally accepted by Inspectors. Major discussion however surrounds the question of what constitute extensive grounds, and whether such grounds are sufficiently large to fall within paragraph 13 of PPG 2. Where nursing homes are judged to be in grounds of insufficient size they are not considered appropriate in Green Belt policy terms. This issue is a fruitful cause for delay and some confusion. In our scan grounds of 1.74, 1.16 and 0.56 hectares were not considered to fall within the definition, whereas grounds of 2.7 hectares in one case were seen as appropriate. Other issues were also considered, apart from size. For example the contribution of the site generally to the openness of the Green Belt was considered important. Applications for 'close care' apartments, or retirement homes, in the grounds of existing nursing homes were not upheld at appeal as they were seen as development affecting the open nature of the site.

Hotels, Public Houses and Conference centres

H.18 These are not regarded as appropriate uses in Green Belts. The scan included 26 appeals, the level of those upheld being one third (31 per cent). The six proposals for new-build hotels were all dismissed by the Secretary of State. Where appeals related to small-scale extensions to existing hotels they were most likely to be upheld. These were usually argued as comprising very special circumstances.

H.19 The issue most often raised by appellants was need, whether for a specific market (for example a low cost motorists' hotel, or a quality hotel) or for extra beds *per se*. These arguments, even if accepted as substantiated by the Inspector, were not seen as sufficient to override Green Belt policy. Hotels were not regarded as a recreation use appropriate to Green Belts. Government exhortations to promote tourism development were also not seen as outweighing Green Belt policy. The view that hotel development would aid urban regeneration in a nearby urban area was also not accepted. Inspectors often suggested that needs could be met on non-Green Belt sites. Overall the scan demonstrated a strict view of tourism-related development in Green Belts.

Offices

H.20 Some 40 cases were found in this category; the rate of appeals upheld being 45 per cent. One quarter of the appeals were enforcement cases. Office development is not seen as an appropriate Green Belt use, except as a possible re-use of existing buildings (see para H.22). Basically approvals related to three categories of case:

- where the re-use of an existing site was involved, and this created a measure of improvement to the site;

- where extensions were seen as small-scale and not affecting the open character of the Green Belt; and

- in rare cases, where the Secretary of State upholds a large-scale proposal (three of these were found).

All of the above categories were argued as very special circumstances that would not harm the Green Belt. Where redevelopment of an existing employment site is involved the issues can be particularly difficult. If a proposal involves intensification of the use and activity on the site (or in the area) this is normally sufficient for refusal. Inspectors frequently argue in refusals that businesses can locate in urban areas, and on land allocated for B1 purposes.

Industrial Development

H.21 These comprised a small category with only 22 cases being found. The proportion of appeals upheld was 36 per cent. Industrial development is not an appropriate Green Belt use, and very special circumstances must be established for any development of this sort to be acceptable. The erection of new buildings for convenience, or the erection of speculative buildings, was invariably not allowed. From the scan the appeals upheld relate to minor matters such as improved access, small scale intensification, or the satisfaction of a genuine operational need. In one or two cases schemes to replace poor quality existing buildings were allowed to go ahead where no demonstrable harm to the Green Belt accrued.

Commercial Re-Use of Redundant Buildings

H.22 Some 37 cases were included in the scan. Forty-six per cent of appeals were upheld reflecting Government advice encouraging the re-use of buildings in PPG 2 and PPG 7. This category comprises the re-use of mainly agricultural buildings for activities not directly related to the husbandry of the land, such as craft workshops, offices and light industry. It is acknowledged in guidance that conversion for commercial purposes may often be less damaging to the rural character of buildings than residential conversions.

H.23 The re-use of redundant buildings can be an acceptable use in the Green Belt subject to certain stipulations. The appeals covered in the scan showed the following factors to be of prime importance:

• the buildings must be genuinely redundant;

• the buildings must be worthy of conversion; and

• the specific proposal must not involve excessive rebuilding and extension.

Dismissals tend to occur where the new use is likely to have an impact on the surroundings by noise or intrusion (for example vehicle repairs), or is visually intrusive. Some inspectors took from PPG 2 the view that buildings required to be 'substantial and attractive' for conversion to be possible, whereas others did not accord this phrase the same weight reflecting the Mathews v SSE and Bracknell Forest Borough Council judgement of 1990, and the introduction of PPG 7, during the period covered by the scan.

Retail

H.24 Only ten retail cases were found. These related to regional shopping centres at one level, down to an individual shop unit as a re-use of an existing building. Retail development is clearly not an acceptable Green Belt use, reflected in the fact that only two of the schemes were approved. One scheme approved was a regional shopping centre in Kent, accepted by the Secretary of State as a very special circumstance; the other was a change of use of an existing building from retail to hot food take away use.

Garden Centres and Nurseries

H.25   Garden centres are seen as commercial retail outlets and therefore not an appropriate use in the Green Belt. A nursery, in that it relates to the cultivation of the land, is seen as appropriate, together with any outlet to sell the produce from that holding. Any outlet involving the importation of produce to the holding for subsequent sale in significant quantities is not seen as appropriate. These precepts of policy are reflected in the 22 appeals in the scan, 23 per cent of which were upheld. Schemes for new garden centres on open Green Belt land are invariably dismissed, as are the additions of such uses as coffee shops, ski equipment sales outlets or landscape contracting/gardening premises. New garden centres are seen as capable of, and suited to, accommodation within urban areas. The appeals upheld were for small scale changes to existing nurseries or garden centres already located in Green Belt. In all cases the changes involved were minimal.

Leisure, Sport and Recreation

H.26   These uses can be appropriate in Green Belts as long as they relate to outdoor sport and recreation. Only buildings which are strictly necessary for the outdoor sport to take place are normally approved. Spectator accommodation which is substantial in scale is not accepted. The scan revealed a wide range of uses being applied for within the 29 cases, some 35 per cent of which were upheld.

H.27   The schemes involving buildings tended to be dismissed, especially where the uses were 'desirable' rather than necessary (for example a cafe at a fish hatchery). A number of golf course appeals were upheld, but all of the golf driving range schemes were rejected. Driving ranges were seen as visually intrusive, as well as creating extra traffic on small country roads. Proposals for combat games were treated on the individual merits of the site although they were regarded as an outdoor recreation activity and thus in principle acceptable. Pitches for sport were clearly seen as appropriate, in conjunction with floodlighting in one case. Whippet racing was seen as appropriate in one case in Dartford.

Equestrian uses

H.28   Twenty cases involving equestrian use were examined. These varied from the erection of small stable blocks in fields for private use, to a major equestrian centre with stabling for 100 horses and a 7,250 sq m eventing arena. Nine of the twenty cases were upheld reflecting the position that equestrian use is appropriate in principle in Green Belt under the category of outdoor sport. Buildings will often be allowed, subject to strong environmental safeguards, and as long as they do not harm the open rural character of the Green Belt.

In practice this means that small private schemes tend to be found acceptable more often than larger commercial schemes. This distinction is already found in some local plan policies. In other local plans local authority policies seek to restrict equestrian uses in parts of Green Belts. These have been upheld at appeal.

Agriculture

H.29   There were 20 appeals investigated here. These involved eight enforcement cases. These latter related to unauthorised activities in existing farm buildings, for example the breeding of maggots or the creation of a retail outlet. The appeals upheld included a number of cases of applications for access roads.

Transport and Vehicles

H.30   This comprises a large category, with 61 cases being examined. The proportion of appeals upheld was one of the lowest for any category, at seven per cent. Well over half of the cases, some 37, were enforcement cases, reflecting the often intrusive nature of transport uses. Table 3.6 shows this to be the most significant area of enforcement activity in Green Belts.

H.31   Transport uses and the parking/stationing of vehicles are clearly not appropriate Green Belt uses. Very special circumstances must therefore be demonstrated for an appeal to be upheld. Such circumstances are rarely sufficient to outweigh the harm expected to be caused to the Green Belt. Typical proposals in this category include filling stations, garages, service areas, vehicle repairs and storage, and HGV operations of various kinds. The only Section 78 case upheld related to a small-scale expansion of an existing transport business which was judged to cause no visual harm, thus comprising a very special circumstance. However it was generally not considered appropriate to extend existing commercial activities (eg garages) which are seen as an inappropriate Green Belt use. Generally car sales and repairs were not seen as appropriate uses for redundant rural buildings. The storage of vehicles on open land was seen as particularly harmful to the interests of Green Belt policy.

Storage

H.32   Some 33 cases were found under this heading. Only five appeals were upheld, comprising 15 per cent of the total. This reflects the inappropriate nature of storage uses in the Green Belt. Considerable enforcement action exists in this area, as Table 3.6 shows. A large number of proposals involved the storage of non-agricultural materials on open farmland. These were clearly seen as damaging to visual amenities. Storage within existing buildings fared no better, being seen as commercial activity unrelated to agriculture. The schemes approved were for storage ancillary to agriculture, small-scale schemes adjudged to have no impact on Green Belt amenities, or schemes to which a time limit could be attached.

262

Minerals and Waste Disposal

H.33 This section comprised some 35 schemes, over half of which were enforcement proceedings. Most of the cases involved unauthorised tipping of refuse, hardcore, soil, and other materials on farmland. This comprised a third of all schemes. None of these appeals were upheld. A number of the sites involved for waste were in the three to twenty hectares range, capable of having considerable impacts on the landscape. Five of the 25 schemes looked at in detail in this category were Secretary of State decisions. Green Belt policy operates firmly with respect to waste only 15 per cent of the cases, mainly the smaller ones and those on sites with a history of waste disposal, being upheld.

Secretary of State Decisions

H.34 Table H.2 shows that nearly eight per cent (38) of the appeals were decided by the Secretary of State. The main areas of intervention were in large residential schemes of ten or more units, hotels and retail uses, and minerals and waste disposal. This clearly reflects the potential impact of such schemes on Green Belt amenities.

Table H.2: Secretary of State Decisions by Appeal Land Use Category

use	Secretary of State decisions	total in category
residential - extensions	0	25
residential - single units	0	25
residential - 2 to 9 units	0	24
residential - 10+ units	5	19
agricultural occupancy	0	25
redundant buildings to residential	0	25
caravans, mobile homes	1	25
gypsies, travellers	4	25
nursing homes	1	25
hotels, pubs, conference	6	24
office	3	25
industrial	1	22
redundant buildings to commercial	0	25
retail	5	10
garden centres, nurseries	3	22
sport and recreation	1	25
equestrian, animal husbandry	1	25
agriculture related	0	20
transport, vehicles	2	25
storage	0	25
minerals, waste disposal	5	25
total	38	491

Source: Green Belt Project Survey

Appendix I: Local Authorities, Agencies and Individuals Consulted During the Research

Conservation and Development Interests

Countryside Commission
Scottish Natural Heritage
Scottish Office Environment Department
DOE Directorate of Rural Affairs
National Farmers Union
Confederation of British Industry
Sand and Gravel Association
Royal Institution of Chartered Surveyors
London Planning Advisory Committee
Country Landowners Association
Council for the Protection of Rural England
SERPLAN
English Nature
House Builders Federation
J Sainsbury
Groundwork Foundation
English Tourist Board
Sports Council
London Green Belt Council
Rural Development Commission

Local Authorities

Dorset County Council
East Dorset District Council
Purbeck District Council
Hertfordshire County Council
Dacorum District Council
Broxbourne District Council
Enfield Borough Council
Tonbridge and Malling District Council
Walsall Borough Council
Wolverhampton Borough Council
Staffordshire County Council
South Staffordshire District Council
Cannock District Council
Cheshire County Council
Macclesfield Borough Council
York City Council
Chester City Council
Oxford City Council
Oxfordshire County Council
Cherwell District Council

Wakefield City Council
Leeds City Council
Barnsley Borough Council
Sheffield City Council

Strathclyde Regional Council
Eastwood District Council
Motherwell District Council
Lothian Regional Council
Edinburgh City Council
Midlothian District Council

Urban Fringe Seminar

Kevin Bishop	Department of City & Regional Planning, University of Wales College of Cardiff
Alan Cave	Chestertons Chartered Surveyors, Birmingham
Giles Dolphin	Principal Planner, London Planning Advisory Committee (also Urban Fringe Special Advisory Group)
Jed Griffiths	Chief Strategic Planner, East Sussex County Council (also Urban Fringe Special Advisory Group)
Carolyn Harrison	Department of Geography, University College London
Keith Howcroft	Planning Department, Oldham Metropolitan Borough Council
Peter Jackson	Head of Strategic Plans, Hertfordshire County Council
Mike Kirby	Director, Operations, Countryside Commission
Brian McLaughlin	Head of Land Use, National Farmers Union
Jim Park	Deputy Director of Planning, Strathclyde Regional Council
Tim Shaw	Department of Town and Country Planning, University of Newcastle Upon Tyne (also Member of RSA Study Group)
Elizabeth Wilson	School of Planning, Oxford Brookes University

Transport and Vehicle Emissions Seminar

Carmen Hass-Klau	Environmental and Transport Planning
Lynne Devereux	MEPLAN
Gordon Stokes	Transport Studies Unit, Oxford University
Peter Headicar	School of Planning, Oxford Brookes University (also Royal Town Planning Institute)
Russell Kilvington	Steer Davies Gleave
Jeffrey Lee	Cheshire County Council
Chris Cousins	Oxfordshire County Council
Howard Jackson	Nottinghamshire County Council
Reg Harman	SERPLAN
Keith Gardiner	London Planning Advisory Committee
Ken Robertson	Countryside Commission

Printed in the UK for HMSO   Dd0296677   7/93